Books are to be returned on or before
the last date below.

Bu

D1313453

Also by Owen E. Hughes
Public Management and Administration, 3rd edition

Business, Government and Globalization

Owen E. Hughes
and
Deirdre O'Neill

First published 2008 by
PALGRAVE MACMILLAN
Houndmills, Basingstoke, Hampshire RG21 6XS and
175 Fifth Avenue, New York, N.Y. 10010
Companies and representatives throughout the world

PALGRAVE MACMILLAN is the global academic imprint of the Palgrave
Macmillan division of St. Martin's Press, LLC and of Palgrave Macmillan Ltd.
Macmillan® is a registered trademark in the United States, United Kingdom
and other countries. Palgrave is a registered trademark in the European
Union and other countries.

ISBN-13: 978–0–333–69319–3 hardback
ISBN-10: 0–333–69319–1 hardback
ISBN-13: 978–0–333–69320–9 paperback
ISBN-10: 0–333–69320–5 paperback

This book is printed on paper suitable for recycling and made from fully
managed and sustained forest sources. Logging, pulping and manufacturing
processes are expected to conform to the environmental regulations of the
country of origin.

A catalogue record for this book is available from the British Library.

A catalog record for this book is available from the Library of Congress.

10 9 8 7 6 5 4 3 2 1
17 16 15 14 13 12 11 10 09 08

Printed and bound in China

Contents

List of Boxes, Figures and Tables

Boxes

Figure

Table

Acknowledgements

The authors and publishers would like to thank the following who have kindly given permission for the use of copyright material:

IMD for a table in Box 6.1; Palgrave Macmillan for a table in Box 6.1; OECD for the chart in Box 6.3; Oxford University Press for Figure 4.1, and the WTO for Box 7.1 and Box 7.3.

Preface

The relationship between business and government is often one of some tension. Within the nation-state, particularly in market societies, government needs business to provide economic activity for its citizens, including the generation of its revenue from taxation. Business also needs government for infrastructure, including that required for markets to work with a reasonable level of efficiency and public support. In spite of this essential co-dependence, business and government often have quite different ways of looking at the world and each other's role in it.

This book is an attempt to look at the business–government relationship as a matter of theory and principle, internationally, rather than as a particular set of relations that take place within an individual country. It aims to examine the business–government relationship through the lens of globalization, that widely used word if somewhat elusive concept.

In a world that is becoming more international there are a number of policy areas where the business–government relationship is itself becoming internationalized. Governments may still be able to make trade policy, but only within limits that are set by their membership of international organizations such as the World Trade Organization in agreements that have been willingly entered into. Competition or anti-trust policy is still made by national governments but with the explicit or implicit agreement of regulators in other countries. Environmental policy is innately a policy area that crosses borders and, for instance, governments of all persuasions are trying to make agreements to reduce greenhouse gas emissions.

Business, too, is increasingly responsive to the changed international environment. Even if it operates completely within a domestic market, some awareness and understanding of the international environment is necessary. The smallest domestic firm can be affected by trade agreements; international standards affect product design everywhere. Some firms are so international that their home base is often obscured or irrelevant to their operations. International firms can decide to locate in one country or another depending on their perception of political risk. The relationship between government and business is very limited if confined to a single nation-state.

A new pragmatism has emerged in more recent years as the highly ideological debate over the role of government – particularly the economic role – has become more muted. Inside the nation-state in Western democratic nations there is now a greater degree of consensus as to those kinds of things governments should or should not do. There may be arguments at the edges or arguments about levels – social spending is too high or too low, for instance – but these are at the margins. Governments in many parts of the world face similar issues with regard to their interaction with business and practice has harmonized to some extent in such policy areas as regulation, the environment, and competition policy. In these areas and others there is a reasonable consensus as to what constitutes good public policy. With pragmatism has come substantial policy convergence, in which competition policy in the European Union, for instance, largely follows principles and precedents established in the United States, and cooperation where national regulators work together.

There is also greater consensus between nations as to those things that governments or businesses should do, or should not do, and substantial cooperation between nations about matters involving business. This does not mean dominance of a single world view or the imposition of an agreed set of policies on unwilling nations. While international cooperation is increasing, national governments remain firmly in charge of their nation-states and have substantial scope in how they prepare for participation in the global economy. They do, however, make binding agreements, engage in diplomatic and other political behaviours that increasingly impinge on domestic public policy. A globalizing world changes the relationship between business and government in many ways looked at here; there are opportunities for governments and businesses alike to be able to find an effective partnership rather than a mutually antagonistic one.

There are a number of people to thank. Owen Hughes wishes to thank Cathy Woodward and their daughters Caitlin, Sophie and Lucy; Deirdre O'Neill wishes to thank Paul Mentor and their children James, Arabella and Juliet. We both wish to thank our colleagues at the Australia and New Zealand School of Government and the Faculty of Business and Economics at Monash University for their support and encouragement, Sarah Lawson, for providing invaluable assistance in the final stages of the book and those at Palgrave Macmillan, particularly our publisher Steven Kennedy, for their usual patience and professionalism.

OWEN E. HUGHES
DEIRDRE O'NEILL
Melbourne 2008

Chapter 1

Business, Government and Globalization

Introduction

It may be an obvious truism that business and government are the most important institutions within market economies. Business involves itself in an economic market; governments carry out their activities in response to the demands of a political market. Business and government are not separate; their spheres of activity necessarily overlap, and the relationship between these great forces is crucial to the societies in which they interact.

Despite what is often an uneasy relationship, business and government are dependent on each other. Governments need business to provide employment for their citizens, to provide taxation revenue, to provide the goods and services demanded by societies; in short to provide the prosperity demanded by the citizenry, which is essential too for political survival and social well-being. Business also needs government, no matter how much business groups may speak of the desirability for government to get out of the way of business. Business needs government to provide a system of law for the enforcement of contracts, infrastructure, education, regulation and the like. Markets may arise without government – trade and barter existed long before formal government organization – but they are likely to remain underdeveloped without the institutions provided by government. The earliest formal business organizations – chartered companies – were sponsored and created by governments through the political system and it is still the case that business must operate within the legal framework set up by governments. An anarchical business world might be able to exist – some form of market has existed in all societies – but it is unlikely to be one that thrives.

In recent decades, the most important factor impinging on the business–government relationship has been the internationalization

1

of business; what was once seen as domestic business has become essentially international business. Governments have had to respond to what could be seen as a challenge to their authority and in many parts of the world they face quite similar problems with regard to their interaction with business. Policy areas and policy responses by different governments tend to converge even if they do not necessarily become identical; there are fewer issues that are purely domestic. Even an issue normally regarded as domestic, such as taxation, has its international dimensions. Responding to transfer pricing, where a multinational company can avoid taxation by manipulating the price its subsidiary in one country charges its counterpart in another country, requires cooperation between different national taxation authorities. There has also been some convergence of business taxation across nations as national governments, fearful that businesses will leave or not invest, lower their rates to similar levels to those of other countries. Environmental regulation, once considered to be domestic public policy, is now much more international with agreements such as the Kyoto Protocol on greenhouse gas emissions affecting government and business within a single country. In the same policy area, the activities of worldwide non-governmental organizations (NGOs), such as Greenpeace, often target particular businesses and indirectly their national hosts.

Most of the policy areas in succeeding chapters illustrate the international character of much of the business–government relationship. Trade, the environment, protectionism, competition policy have aspects that are international, even global; theories of regulation find application in a variety of national and international settings.

The increase in internationalism, or globalism, has led theorists to postulate that 'globalization' is upon us all. The extent of globalization or whether or not 'globalization' is as accurate a description as 'internationalization' are questions on notice for later discussion (Chapter 10). For now, though, it is clear that it is more and more difficult to separate the local from the national, the national from the international, and the international from the global, in the relationship between business and government.

Business, government and globalization, then, are ever-present in debates over the future directions of societies. The first two of these have been around for a long time, but could be argued to be constantly reinventing themselves and adapting to changes in the societal environment. And, even if the precise meaning of globalization is not altogether clear – as will be discussed – the current era is one of greatly enhanced international contact and economic integration. It does appear that the relationships between business, government and globalization are of much increased importance and that this importance is not likely to diminish in the foreseeable future.

Business

Business and government are substantially different from each other, even at the most fundamental level. They operate from differing perspectives on their role. It can be argued that business relies on choice, persuading consumers to buy its products; governments rely on force and compulsion. From another viewpoint, business relies on base individual motives where government results from people working together; in a democracy, government is presumed to be the collective will of the society. Through business, individual desires for goods and services can be created and supplied; through government, there is provision of collective goods and services for the shared needs of the community.

A good working definition is that business is 'any organization that is engaged in making a product or providing a service for a profit' (Lawrence, Weber and Post, 2005, p. 4). Business can refer to a single firm; business can also be a wider societal actor, as in a group of businesses in the same or different industries – the business interest.

The etymology of the word 'business' is curious. *The New Shorter Oxford* finds two main meanings with 16 finer definitions. The first main meaning is that of 'the state of being busy', which hardly explains much. The second main meaning is 'the object of concern or activity' with the definitions of 'a profession, a trade' dating from the late fifteenth century, and the more common usages today – 'trade; commercial transactions or engagements' – dating from the early eighteenth century; and a business in the sense of a firm – 'a commercial house, a firm' – dating from as recently as the late nineteenth century. Businesses engage in the market for goods and services, in trade, in transactions, in activities that are voluntary at base. A business cannot force a potential client to buy its wares, it can only attempt to persuade. For the most part, markets and the businesses that serve them supply *private* goods or services, where consumption devolves to whoever paid for them and others can be excluded. A person who buys a motor vehicle can exclude others from using it; the car has an owner.

Government

Government is at base about the legitimate use of force, the exercise of authority, the word deriving from the Latin *gubernare* meaning steer, direct or rule. A government is the institution that has the authority to make laws and rules. Being able to use force, even if this is not often invoked, is a difference in kind from the private sector.

The public sector is defined by Hicks as 'engaged in providing services (and in some cases goods) whose scope and variety are determined not by the direct wishes of the consumers, but by the decision of government bodies, that is, in a democracy, by the representatives of the citizens' (1958, p. 1). The public sector is the result of public, political decision-making, rather than involving market processes. Governments are command-based – they can force people to comply – where markets are voluntary. Governments provide public goods and public services and businesses do not, although governments have often supplied private goods as well.

Even if governments have the legitimate usage of force at their disposal, it would be more correct to say that only in the final analysis and in rare instances are the police or the army needed to be used as enforcers of government will. Most people in societies, particularly democracies, obey willingly. Many societies would be unworkable if they were only based on force. Through participation in the choosing of governments and in limiting their powers, citizens more often regard government as their own creation. Even the delegation to the legal system of each individual's ability to exercise force is of general benefit.

Globalization and internationalization

The term 'globalization' is frequently used to describe a trend following from the obvious increase in linkages, in economies and societies being apparently closer than ever before. There are many arguments about what globalization is, whether or not it is already here, or whether or not it is even able to be defined (Bisley, 2007).

One view of globalization, as set out by Keohane and Nye (2001), is that it is essentially an end-state, the logical extension of interdependence and globalism. *Interdependence* refers to mutual dependence and, in world politics, 'refers to situations characterized by reciprocal effects among countries or among actors in different countries' (Keohane and Nye, 2001, p. 7). Countries may depend on each other, but are clearly still independent. For example, the Detroit-Windsor area is a major hub of the motor vehicle industry, despite the fact that the former city is in the US and the latter is in Canada. Canada and the US are each other's major trading partners, but they remain interdependent and regional rather than global.

Globalism is a kind of interdependence referring to multiple relationships not single linkages, to multi-continental distances not regional. Like interdependence, globalism can increase or decrease. It is a *process*. Keohane and Nye refer to four different dimensions of globalism – economic globalism which is the 'long-distance flows of goods, services, and capital, and the information and perceptions that accompany market exchange'; military globalism, 'long-distance networks of interdependence in which force, and the threat and promise of force, are employed'; environmental globalism, 'the long distance transport of materials in the atmosphere or oceans or of biological substances such as pathogens or genetic materials that affect human health and well-being'; and social and cultural globalism which involves 'movements of ideas, information, and images, and of people – who of course carry ideas and information with them' (Keohane and Nye, 2001, pp. 231–2). Globalism has existed for a long time, but early globalism was 'thin', meaning that although there was some interaction between different parts of the world it was not substantial. There was some economic linkage between Asia and Europe in medieval times – silks and spices were traded over the Great Silk Road – but it was a limited form of interchange and an example of 'thin globalization' (Keohane and Nye, 2001, p. 233).

In this meaning of the word, *globalization* refers to an increase in globalism, or 'the process by which globalism becomes increasingly thick' and the 'degree of thickening of globalism is giving rise to increased density of networks, increased institutional velocity, and increased transnational participation' (Keohane and Nye, 2000, pp. 7–9). In this view, globalization can be seen as an end-point, a state of finality, where the process of increased globalism has effectively ended. A second view of globalization is that rather than an end-state, it is a *process*. Globalization in this sense is synonymous with 'globalism' as defined by Keohane and Nye. Seeing globalization as a process is more akin to the normal meaning of 'globalization' in discussion in the community as a whole. Held *et al.* define globalization as 'a process (or set of processes) which embodies a transformation in the spatial organization of social relations and transactions – assessed in terms of their extensity, intensity, velocity and impact – generating transcontinental or interregional flows and networks of activity, interaction, and the exercise of power' (1999, p. 16). This is very much a process view.

Bisley argues that globalization is 'a set of related social, political and economic consequences of a series of transformations in the social world, though the causal character of the transformations is uneven and often very unclear' (2007, p. 30). This correctly points to globalization being wider than economic change, but is, in essence, a process view not dissimilar to that of Held *et al.* (1999).

The end-state definition and the process definition are very different from each other. Here, however, the distinction does not need to be drawn too far, as the discussion is about the relationship between business and government in an age of globalization and either or both definitions are adequate for this purpose. It will be argued later (Chapter 10) that while there is an undoubted increase in globalism and that this may well have accelerated in recent decades, the end-point or end-state of globalization, under the first meaning, has not yet arrived. The process of globalization, in the second meaning, is clearly ongoing. Much of the increased activity and action is between nations or bodies representing nations and, therefore, 'internationalization' is, arguably, a better term for now.

A single economic model

The end of the Cold War and the collapse of communist regimes means there is one dominant ideology throughout the world, one relying on free markets and an open trading system. This system is global, as it includes all countries with the possible exceptions of North Korea and Cuba.

It follows that capitalism has no serious ideological competitor now in the economic sense, although international concerns over terrorism do illustrate another kind of threat to the capitalist system. As long as countries like East Germany or the Soviet Union existed, even if in practice they were at some remove from idealized communist or socialist societies, there could be arguments that there was more than one competing economic system. Even China, once the archetype of one variant of communism, started in 1978 to become part of the world economic system and has since become more and more of a society operating on free-market principles even as it is still governed by the Communist Party.

There are substantial divisions that remain between nations, even, as some argue, a 'clash of civilizations' (Huntington, 1996), particularly in the religious sense with threats of long-lasting conflict between Christianity and Islam. But what there is not is a conflict over economic organization of the same kind as that between capitalism and socialism and countries professing to be from one or the other credo. Class-based economic conflict arguably started with the 1848 revolutions in Europe and the *Communist Manifesto* by Karl Marx and Friedrich Engels of the same year and persisted for more than a century. In 1989, the fall of the Berlin Wall symbolized the end of the communist regimes of Eastern Europe, although some, notably Hungary, had started earlier. The Soviet Union did not intervene and later went through its own abandonment of communism. And after this, there appeared to be no serious competitor to capitalism and the world trading system.

The seeming triumph of capitalism in defeating communism was followed, in 1992, by Fukuyama who argued that there was an 'end of history', an end of ideological conflict as societies were either liberal democracies with market systems or aspired to those things. He argued that liberal democracy had 'conquered rival ideologies like hereditary monarchy, fascism, and most recently communism', that liberal democracy may constitute the 'end point of man's ideological evolution', the 'final form of human government', and this meant the end of history (1992, p. xi). He argued that the *ideal* of liberal democracy could not be improved. Liberal democracies were not without problems, but 'there is now no ideology with pretensions to universality that is in a position to challenge liberal democracy, and no universal principle of legitimacy other than the sovereignty of the people' (Fukuyama, 1992, p. 45).

Fukuyama's view now seems to have been very time-specific and not borne out by subsequent events. In the economic sense, the market system prevails around the world, although Venezuela and a few other Latin American countries are trying a different path. But conflict over economic systems is no longer as central to debate as it once was. Conflict has not ceased, but is more about cultural, ethnic, religious difference and separatism rather than economic. The liberal ideal has by no means won.

In looking at the long conflict between the theories of capitalism and socialism, Stiglitz argued (2001, p. 341):

> For almost a hundred years, two theories had competed for the hearts and minds of people struggling to break free of poverty – one focusing on markets, and the other on government. The failure of the socialist economies appeared to demonstrate that the second model was not viable. But another conclusion sometimes drawn, that markets by themselves would provide the answer, also has not been justified by economic theory or by historical experience.

If markets do not provide the answer by themselves, it follows that there is a real and substantial role for governments in ameliorating market forces, in making firms actually compete, and in maintaining public support, even as positive features of markets – allocation without governmental fiat, individual opportunity and entrepreneurship – are kept largely intact. As Mintzberg argued following the fall of communist regimes in Eastern Europe, 'capitalism did not triumph at all; balance did', adding that 'we in the West have been living in balanced societies with strong private sectors, strong public sectors, and great strength in between' (1996, p. 75).

A consistent argument here is that while markets are powerful, they exist and thrive due to benefits they receive from government. A market system needs laws to enforce contracts. A market system needs laws to protect property, and to protect persons from physical harm. Markets need governments and even if there are legitimate arguments about whether or not a particular activity belongs in the public sector or the private sector, a pure free-market society is as illusory as a pure socialist society was. Government is needed to do many things, not least to allow a market to run well. Individuals will set up markets by themselves, in the sense that individual trade is an innate characteristic. But without the full panoply of regulation and laws, such markets are not likely to be optimal.

In the 1980s and 1990s, there were arguments made that governments needed to disappear and leave the scene to corporations. Writers such as Ohmae (1990, 1995) would declare that government, national governments, had no role in the global economy. What role there is has been greatly reduced and the less it does the better. The efficient, enterprising, innovative parts of society are companies. Ohmae's view was not one that attracted a lot of supporters and is found much less often in more recent years. With societal crises, especially after 2000, there were increased demands on government. Only government could act in many areas; it was not about to wither away. Its direct economic role, notably in running its own enterprises, did decline but there were many other areas – security, defence, social regulation – where it was bigger and more intrusive than ever and with general public support.

The biggest problem with the minimal-government point of view is that it relegates politics and political action to a minor role and there is no evidence that the affected citizenry in the advanced societies will accept this. Economic outcomes are the resultant of market forces as well as political forces and it could be argued that any society dominated by one or the other is unlikely to be particularly successful. Societies where the forces of the market and those of government and politics are in reasonable balance, such as in Europe, North America, Oceania and parts of Asia, are historically those which perform best. There may be some contesting of the precise shares of political and market forces, but the basic parameters remain largely settled.

Approaches to business and government

There are differing ways of looking at the relationship between business and government. The most common accounts of business–government relations have tended to see interactions as taking place firmly within the nation-state, or are comparative accounts as between nation-states. The argument here is that while nation-states are undoubtedly important, the relationship between business and government can be looked at from an international perspective of principle and theory and common approaches to shared policy problems.

An example of the domestic kind of business-and-government study is that of Weidenbaum (2004) which focuses on domestic business and government; the institutions and policies looked at are those of the United States, including the US Constitution and its guarantees of economic freedom. This perspective is understandable given the size and importance of the US economy. The wealth of detail about interactions between government and business in that country is well explained by Weidenbaum but it is always possible that the particular instance is not generalizable to other countries.

Wilks (1999, pp. 156–9) refers to six models of economic policy and the distinctions between them may be used for examining interactions between government and business. The first perspective is that of *pluralism and liberal democracy* where government, political and bureaucratic, mediates over the demands that derive from the society and deals with them by attempting to balance the various interests and does so democratically. The second is what Wilks terms *neo-pluralism: vested interests and policy networks*, where public policy-making is segmented and the agencies or groups with an interest in the field 'cooperate, recognize their dependence on one another, and strike bargains that are at least minimally acceptable to all core actors'. The third is *corporatism*, which is a system where three key parties – peak business groups, organized labour and government – negotiate and come to agreements at that level which are then imposed on the society at large. The fourth perspective is that of *regulatory capture and the power of business*. In this view, business becomes pre-eminent and controls political life. As will be discussed later, regulatory agencies may be captured by the businesses they are meant to be controlling and thereby become ineffective. Wilks argues that business 'may acquire excessive political power. It may distort policies, exploit vulnerable groups within society, and may pursue support and subsidy rather than efficiency and competitiveness'. Fifthly, there is the perspective of *bureaucratic power: the administrative state*, where the bureaucracy is regarded as being in effective control of government. To Wilks, 'they dominate policy making by developing legislative options and by the use of discretion in implementing policy', and they can 'utilise secrecy, information, permanence, patronage and bureaucratic networks to influence politicians towards their desired policy goals'. Finally, to Wilks, there is the *new institutionalism and historical continuity*. In this view, existing policies and institutions are interconnected and represent the culmination of past compromises and negotiations. Politics and policy-making do not start anew but work with and through existing institutions which structure ideas and behaviour. The new institutionalism explicitly recognizes the possibility of change and conscious institutional design.

The perspectives set out by Wilks are all useful but are generally confined to actions and interactions within a nation-state. This is a rather limited perspective given the importance of international factors for the business–government relationship.

A second approach to business–government relations is one that is expressly comparative. There have been comparisons of industrial policy focused on Asia (Wade, 1990) which suggest that a more interventionist approach by government can improve the competitiveness of business and, consequently, the nation. It is also possible to argue that there are differences in approach in different countries but these can be examined comparatively, by looking at business–government relations in particular countries (Wilson, 2002).

Another interesting approach is that of Lodge (1990) who argues that the business–government relationship of states can be divided into two classes; individualistic states, such as the United States, and communitarian states, exemplified by Japan. Individualistic states are those where government is seen as not being the answer to societal problems and its powers should be minimized. In such societies, there is an individualistic and adversarial government–business relationship. In these societies, business tries to limit the impact of government policies and actively lobbies to reduce the influence of government. National governments 'whose function is as much as anything to protect the individual, tend to be more fragmented and decentralised and accompanied by loosely organised business groups with which it has distant, if not adversarial, relations' (Lodge, 1990, pp. 3–4). The states where individualism was dominant were the English-speaking developed countries – the US, UK, Canada, Australia and New Zealand.

Outside these few the idea that business and government are necessarily locked in conflict is regarded as unfamiliar. In a communitarian state, to Lodge (1990, p. 4):

> government is prestigious and authoritative. Its function is to define community needs over the long term and short term and see they

are met. Government is a vision setter, it defines and ensures the rights and duties of community membership. Government plays a central role in creating or imposing consensus, even by coercion. Communitarian societies may be either hierarchical or egalitarian.

Lodge argued for Western states, particularly the US, to learn from the communitarian countries. He argued that for the global firm, 'an obvious need emerges to manage governmental relations in a far more sophisticated way than in the old days when government was regarded as merely an obstacle to be hurdled' (Lodge, 1990, p. 13). How well a business handles its relations with government can assist its competitive position.

In an analytical sense, there may be something in the distinctions made by Lodge between individualistic and communitarian societies but these are less appropriate than they once were. The problem with such views is that they still take place firmly within the nation-state. Even if nations are being compared, there is behind them a realist notion of the role of the nation. In this, governments may pursue their own economic policies without constraint and businesses, even if multinational, also fall within the power of the nation-state. With all of these the frame of reference is still firmly that of the nation-state, but since the early 1990s, the debate has moved on.

It is argued here that the business-and-government relationship should be looked at from an international perspective. If a business transaction is carried out completely on one side of a border, it is not international; if a part of the transaction crosses the line it becomes international. It could be argued that the innate content of the transaction has not changed and that business is business wherever it is carried out. But the key point is that when a transaction crosses a border and becomes – by definition – international, governments are inevitably involved. There are problems of air pollution or security or global warming that are not able to be considered by any one nation. Held argues that some of the most fundamental problems 'are not issues which can any longer be solved by states or a people acting alone', rather, we are all in 'a world of "overlapping communities of fate,"' where the fate of different peoples is interconnected, set either by powerful states or by processes – from financial markets to the environment – which are global in their scope and ramifications' (Held *et al.*, 1999, p. 445).

Despite this, national governments do retain substantial power within the area of their jurisdiction and are unlikely to give this up. In addition, governments have standing in the legal sense in dealing with other nations through the various forms of diplomacy in ways that business does not have.

One important lesson is the more limited room for manoeuvre national governments now have. Domestic economic policy must be made in such a way as to satisfy international markets, particularly currency markets. Government actions incur an immediate response from foreign exchange markets which limits the range of conceivable policies. Particular groups may also demand political favours because of their importance for trade. These points together mean that, as the domestic economy becomes more integrated into the international economy, domestic politics is much more constrained than it once was. Governments find their powers are even more limited because there are more events beyond their immediate control.

It is not possible to completely separate domestic concerns from comparative or international, indeed they are often present in the same policy issue. A seemingly domestic environmental issue, such as water quality, can be influenced by international standards and even by the cross-border flow of pollutants. An international issue such as global warming has direct domestic implications on industry, on living standards and the responses of foreign governments can affect domestic policy.

Inwardness and outwardness

Approaching the relationship between business and government as something that only takes place within the nation-state misses considerable parts of the interaction. Businesses often have to deal with many governments. National governments have to deal with domestic and international companies, other governments as well as interest groups, domestic and international, that interpolate themselves into the policy process. Business–government relations are much more complicated than they once were.

Seeing the business–government relationship as being largely about international business or the competition between nations also misses an important dimension. Within a society there are those who are comfortable with being part of an international or global community and those who are not. In other words, the propensity to be international in outlook or not is often a dividing line within societies. For instance, even as the United States has most often favoured free trade and open markets, there are many within that society who actively oppose these ideas. On many international issues there is a lively debate within societies and differing points of view, rather than a national consensus.

For instance, within economics and for most policy-makers in the developed world, free trade is a desirable end in itself and one that promotes the overall public good. But this view is not shared by many within societies, who often have, as will be discussed later, a view that industry protection or promotion must be better for the nation and its workers. Such views cross traditional political lines; many on the left and the right would agree, as do similar groups in other societies. Policy-makers then must be mindful of simultaneous domestic and international impacts – both political and economic – from what they decide to do.

Different views over the increased importance of international business cross the older, ideological dividing lines. Within societies the debate over business and government tends to be between those who wish to be more actively part of the world economy and those who oppose this. Norris refers to this as between 'nationalists' and 'cosmopolitans'. She argues (2000, p. 159):

> *Nationalists* can be understood as those who identify strongly with their nation-state, who have little confidence in multilateral and international institutions, and who favour policies of national economic protectionism over the free trade of goods and services. In contrast, *cosmopolitans* can be understood as those who identify more broadly with their continent or with the world as a whole, and who have greater faith in the institutions of global governance. The nationalism-cosmopolitan dimension can be expected to crosscut traditional ideological cleavages, although there may be some overlap.

This is a useful distinction. The relationship between government and business and conflicts over their roles are now far less often about the traditional differences between capital and labour or over redistribution through a social welfare system, and much more about views and attitudes to internationalization or globalization. It is becoming common for the workers and businesses in an industry sector to jointly press for government action to, say, restrict imports of competitors' products, rather than for there to be traditional conflicts between the two over wages and conditions. Or, depending on the issue at stake, there can be traditional ideological conflicts one day, followed the next day by cooperation. Far left and far right seem to find common cause over such matters as the apparent decline in national sovereignty.

In the specific area of trade, Bhagwati argues the need to distinguish a *cosmopolitan* view from a *nationalist* one (1988, pp. 33–5). The cosmopolitan view is that freer trade is good for the entire world and that governmental attempts to artificially improve one nation's comparative advantage should be ruled out. The nationalist view is that trade needs to be managed for the national benefit. The GATT and WTO are essentially cosmopolitan institutions but it is also the case that individual nations are more likely to act in trade for nationalist reasons with the cosmopolitan effects only incidental.

On a relatively straightforward – if enduring – issue, such as free trade versus protectionism, debate may focus on the views of particular nations. More important than this perspective is the divide within countries. It is undoubted that there are cosmopolitan individuals with similar views to similar people in other countries, and both may be quite divergent from views held by others within their own societies.

These ideas are summarized in Box 1.1.

Mutual dependence

There is a new pragmatism emerging as to the relative roles of business and government; the distinctions between them should not be overdrawn. The two institutions are effectively co-dependent; they are often co-producers, even as they have important differences. Business needs government in order to thrive, indeed, the modern market system has been argued to be an artefact of government in that it is government which provides the laws that regulate markets and market behaviour. Wilson argues that the modern corporation 'is, in historical terms, a comparatively modern creation of the state' (1990, p. 4). And, further, 'no matter how much modern businessmen may presume to the contrary, the company was a political creation' (Micklethwait and Wooldridge, 2003, p. 60).

Box 1.1   Cosmopolitan and nationalist approaches to trade – key differences

Cosmopolitan approach to trade	*Nationalist approach to trade*
Faith in global governance institutions	Little confidence in multilateral and international institutions
Free trade benefits the world as a whole	Favours economic protectionism
Rules out attempts to improve one nation's comparative advantage	Trade to be managed to improve national advantage

Trade and commerce might exist without government institutions, but are not likely to be optimal. Small-scale markets and small-scale trade obviously existed before governments arose and still arise as black markets in societies where there has been an attempt to ban markets altogether, in for instance, Pol Pot's Cambodia. But markets do not thrive in such circumstances. It is through actions of government in upholding contracts through the law and establishing property rights that markets are more likely to work well.

There is now a better understanding of the role of government with respect to markets. There is also a much-diminished ideological debate over the economic role of government. Once it was easy to assume that left-wing parties would favour expanding the role of government and consequently diminish the role of business. Right-wing parties, in government, would behave in the reverse way. For example, in the UK from the 1940s, the Labour Party would attempt to nationalize the 'commanding heights' of the economy, and the Conservatives to denationalize when they were in government. In the 1980s, in the UK there were deeply felt ideological debates as to the line between business and government as the Thatcher government privatized many of the public enterprises. This kind of debate has greatly diminished. The Labour Party in office is no longer 'anti-business', the Conservatives show no real desire to push back the frontiers of the state. As in the United States, political debate in the early years of the twenty-first century seems more about social or cultural issues – religion, immigration – and far less about wealth creation or distribution. The second George Bush as President, while a profound conservative, greatly increased government spending.

Much economic development has occurred in spite of any notion that government is best kept minimal. As McCraw notes (1997c, p. 523):

> Leaving aside command economies, we also know that the market lies at the heart of all successes of the Japanese and Korean sort. Yet in every case of late industrialization (and in several of early, such as Germany), it has not quite been a Smithian market process. For most such countries it has been a guided market. It's been shaped. It's been planned. And in some places it has worked far better than the most optimistic planners in those countries would have dared to predict.

Wolf argues that deciding between government provision and market provision is the 'cardinal policy issue facing modern economic systems'; however, the choice 'should not be dichotomized ... as a choice between relatively perfect governments ... and imperfect or inadequate markets ... or between relatively perfect markets and imperfect or inadequate governments', as the actual choice is 'among imperfect markets, imperfect governments, and various combinations of the two' (1994, p. 7). There is no axiomatic role for government and similarly no axiomatic role for business. Rather they should be in reasonable balance, as Mintzberg (1996, p. 82) argues:

> Business is not all good; government is not all bad. Each has its place in a balanced society alongside cooperative and non-owned organizations. I do not wish to buy my cars from government any more than I wish to receive my policing services from General Motors.

More important in many ways than what governments and business do is the institutional framework within which the interaction takes place.

Governments assist business by providing infrastructure such as roads and bridges. They provide education to varying levels depending on the national system. Even Adam Smith, the eighteenth-century philosopher credited with founding economics, advocated government assistance for the provision of education.

An educated workforce is capable of greater productivity than an uneducated one and some of the cost of this falls to the state. Governments provide funding for basic and applied research that often benefits business. The legal system enables the state enforcement of private contracts and rules governing labour markets. Many of these can be gathered together as consisting of the institutional environment provided by government.

Conclusion

The business–government relationship is important but can no longer be seen as referring to one government and its relationship with the businesses located within its borders. There are many issues that cross national borders; there are many companies that operate within different governmental jurisdictions.

With there being effectively only one economic theory prevailing across most of the world, it follows that governments and businesses find similar issues and approaches to those issues wherever they are located. Regulation is often cross-national and the politics of business and government is as well. Issues such as Brent Spar, where the Shell oil company was eventually persuaded not to sink an old oil-drilling platform in the ocean due to pressure from environmentalists, cannot be seen as confined to the nation-state where this took place. It became an issue affecting Shell's reputation and political standing in many countries, so much so that Shell changed its plans and agreed to dismantle the oil rig. This event is by no means isolated; what would have once been a domestic media story can run in many countries. The actions of individual governments also have implications for other governments. However, it is arguable as to whether or not this is evidence of globalization. Increased globalism there certainly is, as well as increased interdependence, but still despite the constraints involved in getting international action, what we see are governments acting in their own jurisdictions or together with others on matters such as global warming. The interaction of business and government needs to be seen in its international context rather than as a narrow phenomenon that takes place only within nation-states.

Chapter 2

The Role of Business

Introduction

Business is obviously an important economic, political and societal actor. Businesses large and small employ many of the workforce and their views and attitudes about the economy and society are both influential and sought after by government. Business is accountable to its owners and shareholders, but increasingly societies and governments are demanding a wider accountability, even if quite how this is to work in practice is far from settled. Business rarely speaks with one voice as business interests are disparate and diffuse. Small business often has completely different views to big business on particular issues. Even for a single issue such as the policy response over tariffs for a single commodity, for example, steel or sugar, there is likely to be a wide range of business views. Some favour trade liberalization – importers and downstream users in these cases – while other business interests – domestic producers – might seek government protection.

Business may share with government a certain unpopularity in the general community, notably in Europe, but even in the United States where business is more celebrated, a series of corporate scandals in the early 2000s – Enron, Worldcom – led to greater regulation through the Sarbanes-Oxley Act. And populist anti-business sentiment in the 1890s led to the Sherman Antitrust Act. Even as everyone shares in the products of business, the sector as a whole is often regarded with some suspicion. Even many of those who work for business are less than enamoured with its practices. And yet business image and reputation are important assets in terms of keeping customers buying products, in attracting workers and a basis of support from the community. Business needs to be seen as part of the society, not separate from it, and how it acts in the wider sense is important alongside the more traditional accountability to its owners.

The origins of business

Trade between individuals and cultures dates from the earliest of societies, having begun in prehistoric times. It is not possible to precisely determine when individual trade started. Trade in stone tools and weapons existed in Neolithic times; navigation at the eastern end of the Mediterranean had become established by 3000 BC, when the Phoenicians had a virtual monopoly on seaborne trade (Cameron and Neal, 2003, pp. 32–3). Certainly, 'in the long sweep of history, business is both nearly as old as human beings and almost brand new' (Means, 2001, p. 3). Exchange has existed for a very long time, what we now call 'business' is much more recent and heavily dependent on definition.

Moore and Lewis (1999) argue that the first multinationals date from Assyrian times around 2000 BC, with the first truly entrepreneurial economy that of the Greeks from 800–400 BC. Such historical views are more about trade, rather than business as it would now be recognizable, but clearly the very idea of commerce has been around a long time. Marco Polo's travels in Asia and return to Venice from 1271 to 1295 are an early example of an extended business trip.

In medieval times, family enterprises were the most common form of organization and for good reason; in the absence of a reliable system to enforce contracts, trust was found in familial links. The merchants of the Hanseatic League, operating in the Baltic and North Seas from the twelfth century, were individual merchants and families rather than formal companies. And in the fifteenth and sixteenth centuries the Fugger family operated a business empire across several countries, starting in Venice; indeed, banking began in Italy, with the word 'bank' deriving from '*banco*' in Italian.

The precursors to the modern corporation were the monopoly trading companies set up in Europe in the early colonial period. In the early sixteenth century the Spanish crown had granted trading rights with its American colonies to particular traders. Later in the same century the English established the Muscovy Company in 1555 with a monopolistic trading charter to trade with Russia, and the Turkey Company in 1583. The Hudson's Bay Company and other American companies were set up in the following century. Unlike the direct monarchical control of the Spanish empire, much of the Dutch and English overseas trading empires were really trading companies until well into the nineteenth century rather than true empires, and with local power structures little changed in most instances. The East India Company was formed as a royal monopoly in 1600 and gradually became the effective ruler of India. It lost its monopoly in 1813 and was disbanded in 1858, but prior to that maintained its own army and navy, conducting war on its own behalf and only by extension acting for the English crown.

The Dutch in 1602 set up the Vereenigde Oost-Indische Compagnie (or Dutch East India Company), known more commonly by its acronym VOC. This had the innovatory feature of being a joint-stock company; the company could be larger than otherwise possible as the risks were shared between shareholders as were the profits. The VOC's charter 'explicitly told investors that they had limited liability' and Dutch investors were 'the first to trade their shares at a regular stock exchange' (Micklethwait and Wooldridge, 2003, p. 28). The bourse (1608) and the Exchange Bank of Amsterdam (1609) added to the institutions required for modern business structures and were located close to each other in the city of Amsterdam. As Padfield argues (2000, p. 76):

> The Exchange Bank was the solid anchor of Dutch commerce, the bourse its extravagant antithesis whose transactions primed and regulated the capital flows, and in so doing set the price indices for all other European trading centres. This was indeed the hub of world commerce. In the bourse, the city hall and the taverns and coffee shops in the immediate vicinity could be found all the legal and technical skills connected with shipping, insurance, classification, commission agency and markets the world over.

There were other financial innovations derived from Amsterdam, including the mortgage, the promissory note, and the bill of exchange, which enabled the 'quick transfer of funds between banks without the burden of physically shipping gold and silver coins, which were the only legal tender in early eighteenth-century Europe' (Botticelli, 1997, p. 56). The Dutch became true masters at trade, most importantly of the institutions to facilitate trade, with the English only becoming serious rivals much later in the seventeenth century. The foundation of the Bank of England as a private bank in 1694 was another important step and led to a financial system where London began to rival Amsterdam in the trading of stocks and bonds.

The trading companies were important pioneers of international trade but gradually lost their power. They were commercially successful, indeed 'so much so they paved the way for their own demise' (Botticelli, 1997, p. 59). Competitors arose and trading conditions became such that smaller firms began to compete with the trading companies. Gradually the British government moved away from keeping access to trade to favoured individuals or groups and towards a reduction in exclusive trading; 'the government would provide a legislative and power-political framework of support for trade, but individual merchants and firms would work out their own destiny' (Kennedy, 1983, p. 47).

In this early period, trade followed the gun and sometimes preceded it. The undoubtedly rapacious practices of the early imperialistic companies perpetrated injustices on what more recently have been called Third World countries, with practices used in the age of imperialism that would not have been contemplated in the home countries. The connection between business and government, between trade and war, is much less obvious now than it was, but current suspicion as to the motives of multinational corporations is in part due to their history.

Company and corporation

Trade, exchange and commerce can take place between individuals, but the national and international economies rely most of all on companies. A company can be merely an organization engaged in business; more specifically, 'the limited liability company is a distinct legal entity ... endowed by the government with certain collective rights and obligations' (Micklethwait and Wooldridge, 2003, p. 4). There are three key ways of conceptualizing 'company': as a legal entity; as a production function, that is, an entity to capitalize on the division of labour; and, finally, as a governance structure.

A legal entity

The three forms of business proprietorship are a single proprietor, a partnership, or a corporation, with the differences between them mainly those of legal status. A single proprietor or family firm is the simplest but is constrained in terms of spreading risk or operating for a long period of time; a partnership is similarly restricted. It is really only with the rise of the company or corporation that business starts to resemble its present-day structure.

A company does have a legal meaning, one that was quite revolutionary in its development. A corporation, as the word itself suggests, is the embodiment of an entity other than a person. This means it has legal status or standing of its own, separate from the individuals within it. The entity is able to borrow money and pay interest, to employ people or operate its accounts in ways that are separate from its owners or managers in their personal capacity. A corporation is 'legally, an artificial legal "person", created under the laws of a particular state or nation. Socially and organizationally, it is a complex system of people, technology, and resources generally devoted to carrying out a central economic mission as it interacts with the surrounding social and political environment' (Post and Crittenden, 1996, p. 678).

The main impetus to the company or corporation becoming the most important organizational form came with the idea of limited liability. A company could be an 'artificial person, with the same ability to do business as a real person; that it could issue tradable shares to any number of investors; and that those investors could have limited liability, so they could lose only the money they had committed to the firm' (Micklethwait and Wooldridge, 2003, p. 5). This was a revolutionary idea. If an investor was only liable for that particular venture, then the risks of losing other assets, even their own home, would be removed. This would encourage investment in general, as unlimited liability discouraged wealthy investors. Prior to the adoption of limited liability, individual investors were liable for the full debts of a company they had invested in, as opposed to the amount that they risked in that particular venture. Limited liability was introduced in the UK in 1855 and led to investment in potentially risky ventures such as the railways that would not have occurred so readily without it.

A production function

Under one set of definitions, a corporation can be regarded as a production function. As Lodge (1990, p. 23) asserts, it is:

... a collection of people and material brought together to complete a process: it gathers resources, designs and produces goods or services, and distributes them to the communities that it serves. To do this, it must develop skills among its employees, provide motivation to them and exert organizational control over them. It should do this as efficiently as possible, maximising benefits and minimising costs.

The production function view derives from the concept of division of labour, made famous by Adam Smith (1976 [1776]), although there were antecedents as far back as Ancient Greece. After observing the operations of a pin factory, Smith argued that if one worker did all the functions in producing a pin he could make say 20 a day, but if several workers each performed a limited operation some 48,000 could be produced in a day. This great increase in the quantity of work produced was 'in consequence of the division of labour' (Smith, 1976, pp. 8–11). By specializing, the overall output is enhanced many times over. It therefore makes sense for a factory to be set up as a place where the various specialists in particular parts of the job can work together. This could be as a cooperative or where an owner or entrepreneur can set up the factory and then hire workers for the specialist tasks. Although individuals could and did own factories personally, as the scale of operations grew ever larger, it made sense for the capital to be raised and the risks diversified through a company structure.

At the beginning of the twentieth century, the division-of-labour idea reached a high point with the idea of Scientific Management, usually credited to Frederick Taylor (1911). There were two main points to Taylor's theory: standardizing work, which meant finding the 'one best way of working', and 'controlling so extensively and intensively as to provide for the maintenance of all these standards' (Kakar, 1970, p. 3). Scientific Management involved (i) time-and-motion studies to decide a standard for working; (ii) a wage-incentive system that was a modification of the piecework method already in existence, and (iii) changing the functional organization. Taylor did not invent time-and-motion studies, but did carry them out more thoroughly than his predecessors. There was a series of famous experiments with shovel size, bringing the work closer to the worker, reducing the number of movements, all carried out with the ever-present stopwatch. Taylor advocated paying workers by a modified piecework method, so that someone who produced above the measured standard for a day's work would be paid more for the entire output, while performance beneath the standard would attract the normal rate (Kanigel, 1997, pp. 210–11). Above all, the Taylor system was an extension of the division of labour. It added the dimension of carefully measuring how the individual components in a production chain could be improved in order to make the whole more efficient. The factory assembly line was the main area of society following Taylor's ideas. There is no proof of direct connection between Taylor and Henry Ford but it is inarguable that the automobile assembly line is a direct descendant of Taylor's ideas. Starting in 1913 and through meticulous study of the steps involved and their cost, Ford was able to drop the price of the Model T over its twenty years of production to a third of the original price, despite increasing wages to an industry-high level.

What is missing from the production function view, derived from the division of labour, is any mention of hierarchy or the circumstances in which a firm is set up that distinguishes it from a market. Nike, for instance and famously, owns no factories making sports shoes, rather it contracts with factories to carry out the work from its designs. And design can also be contracted out. This is another kind of division of labour further removed from the individual artisan; in some circumstances it can be entirely rational to divide the tasks into ones that are carried out in-house and others which are purchased. It would be possible for a skilled worker or group of workers to be contractors or to operate in a market rather than have a firm at all.

A governance structure

Instead of seeing the firm as a production function, it is 'more usefully regarded as a governance structure' (Williamson, 1985, p. 13). It is not immediately obvious as to why companies would form. There are substantial transaction costs in running activities in-house rather than by contract or purchasing from other providers. Some fifty years earlier, Coase (in a 1938 article reprinted in 1988) argued that organization within a firm meant that market transactions were to be replaced by an entrepreneur who directed production. However, organizing internally instead of through markets creates transaction costs; therefore, a firm would exist only if the transaction costs of organizing internally were less than the costs of operating through a market. What a firm does in a production sense is less important, then, than how it is organized and how it internalizes activities within a governance structure.

Early companies were family enterprises, or trading companies; they were not recognizable as modern business enterprises until the great era of railway-building, notably in Britain and the US. Chandler argues that the railways were the first modern business enterprises as they were 'the first to require a large number of salaried managers; the first to have a central office operated by middle managers and commanded by top managers who reported to a board of directors'. More importantly, in looking at firms as being essentially a governance structure, railways were the first 'to build a large internal organizational structure with carefully defined lines of responsibility, authority, and communication between the central office, departmental headquarters, and field units; and they were the first to develop financial and statistical flows to control and evaluate the work of the many managers' (Chandler, 1977, p. 120).

It may be sufficient in some circumstances to see a firm as being organized to achieve an outcome and that the different parts of it mesh together with a single-minded focus on results. In large firms this is unlikely to occur. As Fear (1997a, p. 564) argues:

> The concept of a firm affects how the company is coordinated as a whole. Any industrial business firm has to coordinate – account for – at least four distinct areas: production, finance, sales, and personnel. None of these areas can be said to have internally consistent objectives and the goals of one may contradict those of another ... Engineers may want a production process that cannot be financed or manufacture a product that marketing managers will not sell. People may not want to work for a company. Management may want to reinvest but shareholders may want higher dividends. By its very nature, then, a business firm is a contested terrain that can be 'rationalized, economized, maximized, optimized' in any number of directions.

There is no single output or outcome that is optimal, rather there are essentially political decisions that lead the firm in one direction or another.

A firm may or not be organized as a production function through the division of labour. It will need to be organized as a governance structure and the calculation does need to be made constantly as to whether or not specific activities should be carried out in-house or contracted with other parties.

International business

Many businesses operate only domestically, often only locally; others operate across national borders. Some, relatively few, can transcend borders so much that their corporate home is not obvious or is technically in a tax haven like the Cayman Islands. Sometimes called transnationals or multinationals – there appears to be no essential difference in meaning – international companies are praised by some for bringing technology and consumer goods to wider audiences and vilified by others for their role in fostering international trade, environmental degradation and corruption of officials in developing countries. Border-crossing, multinational firms are controversial.

A multinational enterprise usually has its headquarters in one country and its operations in others. For a company to move operations or to sell into other countries may be simply to find customers wherever there is demand. After all, the transactions are essentially the same as in the domestic economy and demand may exist somewhere else, either inside or outside one country. A company facing substantial competition at home may be able to build up its strength by selling overseas and use its increased scale and scope to cut costs. On the other hand, selling into or setting up in another country is not without risk.

The separation of domestic business from multinational business could be argued to be rather artificial. The innate content of the transaction has not changed and it could be said that business is business wherever it is carried out. As a standard text argues, 'Simply put, domestic business involves transactions occurring within the boundaries of a single nation (or sovereign state), while international business transactions cross national boundaries' (Mahoney *et al.*, 1998, p. 9). The key point is that when a transaction crosses a border and becomes – by definition – international, more than one government is involved.

There is a long history of companies operating across borders, indeed the first companies given royal licences in Britain, as noted earlier, had this specific purpose. However, the controversy surrounding the operations of multinational corporations really only started in the 1950s, when it appeared that some companies were intervening in politics and foreign policy. Some US corporations such as United Fruit in Latin America were regarded as highly exploitative and neocolonial at this time.

Three arguments are often made about the power of multinational corporations (MNCs) in terms of governance: first, the power of MNCs to shape outcomes has increased in relation to governments; second, MNCs prefer to see regulatory authority shift away from national governments and toward supranational institutions, and third, that, 'as part of the MNC agenda, supranational regimes facilitate the lowering of regulatory standards across jurisdictions, particularly in the areas of labor, environment, health and safety (the race-to-the bottom hypothesis)' (Levy and Prakash, 2003, p. 132).

Multinational companies are said to be highly mobile; willing to set up or move from particular countries and driving a form of competition between nations to attract and hold them. They are presumed to have an agenda to reduce the power of domestic governments and to induce adherence to the capitalist world-trading system, as well as forcing a lowest-common-denominator regulatory standard. Multinational companies are often much larger in terms of revenue or value-added than many of the governments with which they deal. This kind of power asymmetry could lead to smaller national governments being in thrall to multinationals.

On the other hand, it could be argued that allowing foreign firms to compete with domestic firms is better for consumers than having large firms that are dominant in a domestic economy (Legrain, 2002). Monopolies or near-monopolies are more readily found within a nation-state, especially if protected by government regulation. When opened to international competition, prices do tend to fall.

Multinational companies may be actively involved in political lobbying and at times their size and role are ones of apparent power compared to governments. Governments are often in competition with each other to attract the investment of such companies, which are invariably tough negotiators. But the argument about a 'race to the bottom' where standards are reduced to attract and retain multinational companies is not supported by evidence. Foreign investment is overwhelmingly in countries with high standards rather than flowing to countries with low environmental and labour standards. A government, however minor, still maintains its sovereignty but its actual power is circumscribed by its need to keep favour with the companies. Companies were and still are often accused of participating in bribery and corruption and home-country attempts to modify behaviour have been tried. The US passed the Foreign Corrupt Practices Act in 1977 to prohibit corrupt payments to foreign officials. While there may have been some salutary effects on business practice, there were few prosecutions as the burden of proof made it difficult to establish contraventions, and the Act was weakened some ten years later.

When examined in more detail, evidence for the above propositions cannot be found, indeed, Levy and Prakash argue, 'MNCs in international governance are neither omnipotent ogres nor gentle giants pursuing the common interest; rather, they bargain with states, NGOs, and other actors over the form and structure of particular international agreements and regimes' (2003, p. 147). They also argue that firms may be powerful actors, but do not impose regimes and their behaviours are inconsistent with 'simple hypotheses such as the decline of the regulatory state or the race-to-the-bottom' (p. 147).

In general, the arguments about multinational companies taking over are made much less often than they were in the 1970s. National governments are much stronger than they appeared to be and the home governments of corporations do not support their companies by sending in the military as they once did. In a number of formal ways national governments constrain the effective power of corporations. Even though there is no single authority for international conduct, 'negotiations among governments, firms and NGOs are leading to the establishment of regimes – rules, norms, codes of conduct, and standards – that constrain, facilitate, and shape MNCs' market behaviour' (Levy and Prakash, 2003, p. 132). Multinational companies are in a political game of their own, in that their reputation nationally and internationally becomes a decided asset in dealing with governments and even consumers.

Governance and accountability

Business has several stakeholders: shareholders, communities, employees, customers, governments. It is a rare business that can make its decisions without consideration of opinion from the outside and indeed, its acceptance in society, even its very legitimacy can depend on what various stakeholders think of the business. Businesses must interact with government, and governments of all persuasions actively seek business input for many of their decisions. Of course, not all that business wants is granted but it is fair to say that business does hold a relatively privileged position within society.

Both government and business are subject to varieties of governance. Since the late 1990s, there has been increased public concern about the ethical and moral behaviour of businesses and their employees. However, in some countries, corruption is still a real problem affecting both markets and governments. Companies need to change their conception of accountability to reflect wider notions than merely that of accountability to shareholders. Corporate social responsibility is accepted by more companies as a normal operating requirement rather than as a new and unwelcome form of accountability imposed from the outside.

Principal/agent theory

This theory was developed for the private sector to explain the divergence often found between the goals of managers (agents) in private firms and those of shareholders (principals). According to Vickers and Yarrow, the general agency problem can be characterized (1988, p. 7) as:

> A situation in which a principal (or group of principals) seeks to establish incentives for an agent (or group of agents), who takes decisions that affect the principal, to act in ways that contribute maximally to the principal's objectives. The difficulties in establishing such an incentive structure arise from two factors: (a) the objectives of principals and agents will typically diverge, and (b) the information available to principals and agents will generally be different (for example, the former might not be able to observe some of the decisions of the latter).

How the interests of agents and principals diverge and are to be dealt with has given rise to an extensive literature dealing with issues of accountability and their effects on organizations. Shareholders want maximum profits, while managers, their agents, might want long-term growth, and higher salaries for themselves. Firms may not necessarily maximize profits for the benefit of the shareholders because the separation of ownership from control reduces shareholder power. There must be some profit, although perhaps not to the extent of profit and dividend maximization.

Principal/agent theory attempts to find incentive schemes for agents to act in the interests of principals. The activities of agents are monitored by shareholders, by the possibility of takeovers or bankruptcy while the presence of a non-executive board may help in 'attenuating the discretion of management' (Vickers and Yarrow, 1988, p. 13). In addition, to ensure their behaviour complies with the wishes of the principals, agents should have contracts that specify their obligations and rights. In the private sector the theory of principal and agent does not supply a complete model or answer to the general problem of accountability, but accountability relationships are at least well known, as are some remedies, such as providing clear contractual obligations.

Corporate social responsibility

Companies are increasingly pressured to show that they are corporate citizens whose activities benefit the society as a whole. They need to be able to show, through 'triple bottom line' and other accounting and accountability mechanisms that they are serving a wider purpose than merely assisting their shareholders. Into this domain comes the term 'corporate social responsibility' (see Box 2.1). Corporate social responsibility means that 'a corporation should be held accountable for any of its actions that affect people, their communities, and their environment' (Lawrence et al., 2005, p. 46). In other words, a corporation has wider responsibilities; it has more stakeholders than its shareholders (Bonnafous-Boucher and Pesqueux, 2005).

There is an ongoing argument between Anglo-Saxon views of capitalism that argue the only responsibility of the corporation is to the shareholders, shareholder capitalism, as opposed to stakeholder capitalism as is more usually found in continental Europe or in Asia. In the shareholder model, the sole aim of the corporation is to maximize shareholder value and from this derives economic efficiency that benefits consumers, shareholders and the society as a whole.

Box 2.1   The European Alliance on Corporate Social Responsibility

The European Alliance on Corporate Social Responsibility (CSR) was launched in 2006, as part of the European Commission's *Second Communication on Corporate Social Responsibility*. A network of businesses, membership-based business associations and business advocacy groups, the Alliance aims to implement strategies that will realize the European Commission's vision of Europe as a model of excellence in CSR.

The Alliance has number of priorities, which encompass: fostering innovation in sustainable technologies, assisting business with strategies to address the social and environmental implications of their activities, enhancing dialogue between businesses and stakeholders, and encouraging greater responsiveness to issues of equity and diversity.

Some 160 companies and 70 organizations support the Alliance, including: Air France-KLM, BMW AG, Bosch Siemens Haugeräte GmbH, Citigroup, DaimlerChrysler, Epson, IBM, Johnson & Johnson, KPMG, Nokia, e Italiane, Sony, Business and Society Belgium, Croatian Employers' Association (HUP), Confederation of Danish Industries (DI), Mouvement des Entreprises de France (MEDEF), Confederation of British Industry (CBI), Green Business Network Norway and Confédération des Employeurs Espagnols.

Source: CSR Europe.

According to Lawrence *et al.* (2005, p. 53):

Business managers and economists argue that the business of business is business. Businesses are told to concentrate on producing goods and services and selling them at the lowest competitive price. When these economic tasks are done, the most efficient firms survive. Even though corporate social responsibility is well-intended, such social activities lower business's efficiency, thereby depriving society of higher levels of economic production needed to maintain everyone's standard of living.

In the stakeholder model, there are other actors involved than shareholders only – the employees, clients and customers, even the towns or communities in which plants or other major operations are located. While shareholder capitalism is still present, companies are increasingly required to operate on ethical principles and be responsible to multiple stakeholders. As Micklethwait and Wooldridge (1996, p. 201) argue:

> Nowadays, a company's board has to think about a different sort of accountability. Many of the assets they are charged with looking after are intangible ones – notably the firm's reputation. In an environment where more and more consumers in the developed world make commercial decisions on 'non-commercial' grounds, Milton Friedman's maxim that a company's only responsibility is to make money legally looks ever less defensible. A firm that does not break the law but is seen as socially irresponsible has a tough time. By the same token, companies such as Levi Strauss, Johnson & Johnson, Body Shop and Ben and Jerry's have all prospered from their 'ethical' reputations.

It is difficult to quantify the precise accounting value of reputation but companies that are perceived as being ethical and well-run do seem to attract a premium on the share market and in the ongoing requirement to attract talented employees, a company which has a good reputation can be regarded by potential employees as a better place to seek work.

More and more companies are seeing engaging with corporate social responsibility as something they should do. A number of banks have adopted the Equator Principles for managing environmental and social issues associated with lending (see Box 2.2).

Ideas of a broader responsibility to the society, or corporate social responsibility, are a long way removed from the idea that the only responsibility of business is to its shareholders. There does seem to be an increasing realization that businesses can gain benefits in reputation, in the war to attract talent and in their relations with governments and the society as a whole by engagement of this kind.

Business and politics

With so much at stake in terms of how governments can affect the profitability of business by regulation or other action, it is unsur-

Box 2.2   Socially responsible and environmentally friendly finance: the Equator Principles

In 2003, the International Finance Corporation developed a set of guidelines for managing environmental and social issues in project finance lending. The guidelines were termed the 'Equator Principles' and were adopted by ten international commercial banks. By June 2006, 41 banks had adopted the principles. The principles were revised in July 2006, and now apply to project financings with capital costs above US$10 million across all sectors in all countries. The preamble to the revised principles states:

The Equator Principles Financial Institutions (EPFIs) have ... adopted these Principles in order to ensure that the projects we finance are developed in a manner that is socially responsible and reflects sound environmental management practices. By doing so, negative impacts on project-affected ecosystems and communities should be avoided where possible, and if these impacts are unavoidable, they should be reduced, mitigated and/or compensated for appropriately. ... We will not provide loans to projects where the borrower will not or is unable to comply with our respective social and environmental policies and procedures that implement the Equator Principles.[1]

Institutions that had adopted the Equator Principles as at June 2007

ABN AMRO Bank, N.V.	Banco do Brasil
ANZ	Banco Galicia
Banco Brandesco	Banco Italú

prising that business is profoundly interested in politics. It is not altogether common, however, for the business community to sponsor one political party to the exclusion of all others in a democratic system, neither is it common for individual business leaders to become political leaders and those that do are often unsuccessful. The game is more about influence, having input into the political process, rather than overt politicking.

Despite the potential influence of business on government, there are many other groups that seek influence as well. The state should be seen 'as a forum within which competing or conflicting social

Bank of America	JP Morgan Chase
Barclays plc	KBC
BBVA	La Caixa
BES Group	Manulife
BMO Financial Group	MCC
BTMU	Millenium bcp
Caja Navarra	Mizuho Corporate Bank
Calyon	Nedbank Group
CIBC	Nordea
CIFI	Rabobank Group
Citigroup Inc.	Royal Bank of Canada
Crédit Suisse Group	Royal Bank of Scotland
Dexia Group	Scotiabank
Dresdner Bank	SEB
E+Co	SMBC
EKF	Standard Chartered Bank
FMO	TD Bank Financial Group
Fortis	Unibanco
HBOS	Wachovia
HSBC Group	Wells Fargo
HypoVereinsbank	WestLB AG
ING Group	Westpac Banking Corporation
Intesa Sanpaolo	

Note:
1. World Bank Group (July 2006) *The 'Equator Principles': A financial industry benchmark for determining, assessing and managing social and environmental risk in project financing*, p. 1.

Source: World Bank Group, www.equator-principles.com/index.htm.

forces contend as well as an institution with the powers to compel obedience' (Wilson, 1990, p. 5). The private sector as a whole and even individual companies need public support or there will be demands for further governmental action to restrict what they do. The market does generally deliver results for individuals. It also provides some protection against the arbitrary and unchecked power of the state and yet if the market is seen to fail, 'if its benefits are regarded as exclusive rather than as inclusive, if it is seen to nurture the abuse of private power and the spectre of raw greed, then surely there will be a backlash – a return to greater state intervention, management, and control' (Yergin and Stanislaw, 1998, pp. 417–18). And for a business, the possibility or even threat of government intervention means a need to be involved in the political process.

In developed societies there is usually one political party that leans towards business interests and another that leans towards those of workers. Trade unions can involve themselves in political action both at the enterprise level and in the wider society. Employers and employees do not necessarily have the same goals and may differ on where to go in the long run. In reality, the difference is more often than not one of tendency rather than of sharp distinction. Socialist parties may not be as actively opposed to business as they once were, but there are still many in various societies who are suspicious of business and who want business power reduced through the exercise of politics.

Many businesses make representations to government and the political system for favourable treatment. In trade policy, firms lobby for policies to reduce foreign competition and 'the task of policy makers, legislators and civil society is to ensure to the greatest extent possible that such rent-seeking behaviour is controlled and filtered through institutions that limit the risk of capture by the powerful' (Hoekman and Kostecki, 2001, p. 462). However, in trade policy it is hard to point to a general business interest. Some individual businesses – steel, agribusiness, for example – may wish to increase protection but others would oppose this, notably downstream users of products. In such cases, small organized groups tend to gain benefits ahead of larger diffuse interests (Olson, 1982).

Another important constituency is that of groups representing the environmental interest. Challenges to business by groups such as environmentalists in the US in the late 1960s and early 1970s contributed to a massive expansion of business's own political activities. This will be further discussed in Chapter 9.

Conclusion

The fundamentals of business have been around for a very long time, in the sense that individuals, and later companies and corporations, have traded with each other with the aim of making a profit from the transaction. Business is clearly important in society, although its importance and effectiveness within the political system is somewhat diffuse rather than it being a monolithic, single-minded force. Business views on issues vary and business rarely finds itself having a unified political voice. This reduces its effectiveness when it comes to lobbying and influencing political debate. Individual firms or sectors, such as the car industry, are sometimes able to influence government policy to their advantage but overall, the political power of business is somewhat overrated.

There is an extensive debate over multinational business. To some, multinational business is taking over the world; governments are in its thrall (Klein, 2000). However, much of the same argument as for domestic business applies; multinational businesses are not as powerful as they are often portrayed. Rather than businesses exploiting a national population, in particular in developing countries, and forcing governments to do what they wish, more often it is national governments offering more and more incentives to have a multinational business locate within their borders. Rather than a government complaining about too much activity by multinational companies within its borders, more often a government will want more such activity, more investment, more jobs.

Even the weakest government can impose its will on a business through passing laws or regulations – it has jurisdiction. After trying persuasion, a business can only accept this or relocate, incurring costs in doing so. Rather than there being a 'race to the bottom' as companies try to locate in countries where laws are lax, it would be more common to locate in countries where laws and regulations are well structured and enforced, since this provides some measure of certainty that the investment is reasonably secure. And when governments get together, as they increasingly do, to regulate and set standards affecting business, it is clear that in the final analysis, government can prevail.

Chapter 3

The Role of Government

Introduction

The power position of government may be clearer than that of business in that governments have the legitimate use of force at their disposal; in the final analysis, the power of government may be that of the police and the army, even if these are rarely used. Government, backed by these forces, can make laws to compel anyone in the society to do what it wants, including business. Despite these undeniable powers, governments are often ineffective as they often do not know what they want, change their minds frequently and, in areas that intersect with those of business, often seem to find it hard to understand what this other party wants. Governments have their own interests as well as being the arbiter between the views of business groups, or between business groups and consumers, producers or those in the society interested in third-party effects on, for example, the environment. Governments may also run businesses themselves – public enterprises – although this sector has been greatly reduced in many countries.

Particularly in the 1970s and 1980s, the institution of government was often regarded as the single greatest impediment standing in the way of national economic advancement, especially by Chicago School economists such as Stigler (1975) and Friedman (Friedman and Friedman, 1980). It became more widely accepted that government provision of private goods through its own production and distribution channels was more often than not inefficient and ineffective compared to the private sector.

Widespread privatization of public enterprises started in the United Kingdom and New Zealand in the early 1980s and was adopted as policy by many other countries, including in the developing parts of the world, and notably in formerly communist Eastern Europe after 1989. Twenty years later, it could be argued that the reform programme of privatization in many countries was largely complete, but it was also notable that arguments about greatly reducing the role of government were made much less. There seemed to be much less ideological heat about the role of government, either about further reduction or in defending the existing role of government. Business, in general, no longer wants government to go away; rather it wishes for a dialogue, for certainty.

Government as an organization

That government is fundamentally based on the ability to compel those within its jurisdiction was noted earlier. Of course, while governments may be able to use force, they do not often need to do so; most in the society willingly comply with the law. In addition, the citizens are able through the political system to influence the making and implementation of laws that affect them. In legal activities – criminal behaviour is different as the incentive structures provide for the use of force – business does not have any power of compulsion; only government does.

There are, then, two important differences between the private sector and the public sector. The first is that, in a democracy, 'the individuals who are responsible for running public institutions are elected, or are appointed by someone who is elected' and the second is that government is 'endowed with certain rights of compulsion that private institutions do not have', such as forcing the payment of taxes and the right to seize property provided it pays compensation (Stiglitz, 2000, p. 13). All government actions do not derive from force and, even if many do, most in the society accept that their membership of it carries some obligations. The power of government is most often not needed but is still there. And as Stiglitz also argues, 'More generally, all transactions between parties other than the State (other than theft and "accidents") are voluntary' (1989, p. 21).

Ostrom (1989) argued that bureaucracy and markets are opposing forms of organization; bureaucracy relies on force and markets rely on choice. This may well be an interesting dichotomy but the choice between the two may not be so stark. Total bureaucracy and completely free markets should be seen as the ends of a line; a continuum with degrees of market and bureaucracy at different points rather than a binary choice, either the one or the other. Neither extreme has been fully seen and neither extreme is likely to be effective. Earlier communist societies tried to completely control the economy through their bureaucracies, in for instance, East Germany, but a black economy is still likely to exist alongside the regular economy. A total market economy is also unlikely to be seen, given the need for markets to have established laws and mechanisms for enforcing contracts.

Economically developed countries have generally evolved to a mixed economic model, with the private sector playing a major role and government also playing a major role. If a line can be conceptualized with a total free market at one end and total government ownership at the other end, developed countries are somewhere between the two extremes. The United States is usually seen as more free-market than, say, Germany, but the differences are those of emphasis rather than kind.

The rise of the nation-state

The precise point as to when the nation-state system arose is usually regarded as dating from 1648 and the Treaty of Westphalia. This treaty brought the Thirty Years' War to a close and effectively ended the system where the sovereign owned territory personally. The model of Westphalia is (Held, 1993, p. 29):

- The world consists of, and is divided by, sovereign states which recognize no superior authority.
- The processes of law-making, the settlement of disputes and law enforcement are largely in the hands of individual states subject to the logic of 'the competitive struggle for power'.
- Differences among states are often settled by force: the principle of effective power holds sway. Virtually no legal fetters exist to curb the resort to force; international legal standards afford minimal protection.
- Responsibility for cross-border wrongful acts [is] a 'private matter' concerning only those affected; no collective interest in compliance with international law is recognized.
- All states are regarded as equal before the law: legal rules do not take account of asymmetries of power.
- International law is orientated to the establishment of minimal rules of coexistence; the creation of enduring relationships among states and peoples is an aim, but only to the extent that it allows national political objectives to be met.

- The minimization of impediments on state freedom is the 'collective' priority.

Where earlier, empires had ruled, after Westphalia there were separate nation-states. The Holy Roman Empire ceased as an overarching institution over what became separate German states. Borders became fixed as did the idea that the state was the only institution able to monopolize force within those borders. Instead of a sovereign who in some way owned territory personally, the state became an institution above and beyond the sovereign. If the citizens of a state were no longer to be subjects – owned by their monarch – their support for government needed to be based on other factors; a state was legitimated because 'it reflected and/or represented the needs, wishes and interests of its citizens' (Held, 1999, p. 46). Once the divine right of monarchs became discredited, the ownership of a state by a king gradually became less important than the ownership of the nation-state by its people. Government could persist without being seen as directly carrying out the monarch's will. In Britain, limits on the monarch's power began in 1215 with Magna Carta and were more firmly established by the Glorious Revolution of 1688 and the Bill of Rights the following year. Other European countries moved away from absolute monarchy over the next two centuries with the last being the Tsar of Russia as late as the early twentieth century. A nation became seen as an embodiment of the culture, wishes and aspirations of the people within its borders, rather than being the personal property of the ruler.

Governments and markets

There is an ongoing debate as to the kinds of activities government should carry out and the kinds that markets should. The dividing line between them has varied historically and in different societies. Governments have several instruments at their disposal. These include *provision* – where the government provides goods or services through the government budget; *subsidy* – the government assists someone in the private economy to provide government-desired goods or services; *production* – governments produce goods and services for sale in the market; and *regulation* – using the coercive powers of the state to allow or prohibit certain activities in the private economy. The extent of these has varied at different times. In the mercantilist era, regulation was most important; in the welfare state, the dominant instrument is that of provision.

The dividing line between government and market has always been one of debate. In 1776, in the first modern formulation of the role of government, Adam Smith argued there were three 'Duties of the Sovereign' (1976 [1776], pp. 208–9):

> First, the duty of protecting the society from the violence and invasion of other independent societies; secondly, the duty of protecting, as far as possible, every member of the society from the injustice or oppression of every other member of it, or the duty of establishing an exact administration of justice; and thirdly, the duty of erecting and maintaining certain public works and certain public institutions, which it can never be for the interest of any individual, or small number of individuals, to erect and maintain; because the profit could never repay the expense to any individual or small number of individuals, though it may frequently do much more than repay it to a great society.

The first duty, that of national defence, is the classic public good, in that it must be provided by government as there is no way of collecting from each member of the society the amount each is willing to pay. The assessment of risk of invasion or other foreign adventure would vary from person to person and there are 'free-rider' problems in that those who are unwilling to pay, or are less convinced that there is a real threat, are unlikely to pay their share of the cost. Only government can overcome this problem through its powers of compulsion.

Smith's second duty establishes a system of justice – internal defence – to defend members of the society from others who may be violent or otherwise oppressive. This includes the enforcement of contracts; without this a viable private sector is unlikely to arise. Smith's first and second duties are still generally seen as providing good arguments for the need for government.

The third duty is more controversial. The intention was to account for the construction of economic infrastructure – a bridge, canal or a road – that cannot be paid for by the direct users. Although it might be feasible to charge users, the cost and likely return are unattractive for a potential investor, but there could be great benefits to the entire society. The extension of government into many activities could be justified by this 'duty' as it could include much of what later became termed infrastructure. Education to at least a basic standard was also advocated by Smith, indeed, this could be included as infrastructure necessary for economic development.

In the mercantilist era, really to the end of the eighteenth century, government was not particularly large but was very intrusive in terms of economic regulation. This meant the political part of society was to dominate the economic. Following this time, the nineteenth century in Britain saw the dominance of *laissez-faire* economics, where government stayed out of economic life as far as possible. It was argued that market processes would, by themselves, lead to better overall outcomes than those which could be achieved by government. The basis for this theory is the reverse of mercantilism. For the proponents of *laissez-faire* government, politics and government institutions were less important than the drive to self-betterment through the economic system; government should be simply the facilitator for the market and should step in reluctantly and only as a last resort.

Marx and others regarded the social conditions arising from this kind of economic system as highly problematic. It has been argued that the extent of *laissez-faire* in the nineteenth century in Britain was not as severe as often portrayed, and indeed, that it was something of a myth (Cameron and Neal, 2003). Eventually, and with the extension of the franchise, new regulations were passed of a social kind to improve the lot of ordinary workers. These led to the beginnings of the welfare state in the late nineteenth century.

Notably in Europe, and later and to a lesser extent in the United States, social regulations were passed, interfering in markets to be sure, but popular with the broader community. Pensions began in Germany under the arch-conservative Bismarck. There were other interventions in housing, in minimum working age, health and safety. The economic system was still largely that of markets but government action was needed to assist those unable to thrive in a strict market system – pensions for the aged, assistance to children, widows and so on. Such programmes were electorally popular and were perhaps related to the extension of the franchise. In the United Kingdom and Europe, but not the United States, there was also a related programme of industry nationalization in order that the commanding heights of the economy should be kept in public hands (see Yergin and Stanislaw, 1998). In the period after World War II, most European countries adopted ever more elaborate welfare programmes to safeguard their citizens 'from the cradle to the grave'. They provided generous unemployment benefits, universal health schemes, educational assistance and social aid programmes aimed at the disadvantaged.

However, the welfare state was never uncontroversial. It was an attempt to reassert the political over the economic, and was therefore diametrically opposed to the *laissez-faire* system. There were three problems. Firstly, there was an aggregate problem of financing as the welfare state 'increasingly brought countries face-to-face with the issue of affordability' (Holmes and Shand, 1995, p. 559). Someone had to find the money to pay for welfare programmes, which, in the end, must derive from taxes on the wealth generated by the economic system. Secondly, and related to the first point, a political programme of this kind relies on broad-based political support, which in the later 1970s and 1980s was no longer given as freely as it once was. The Reagan and Thatcher governments did tap some resentment in the community about the size and scope of government and concomitant levels of taxation in the welfare state period. Thirdly, the economic and political theories behind the welfare state became less fashionable. Within the economics profession, the neoclassical school came to enjoy a new ascendancy and provoked a reaction against the welfare state. Neoclassicists advocated a return to a more dynamic economic society based once again on the ideas of Adam Smith.

Since the mid-1970s, there has been a movement away from the larger, implicitly collectivist role of government which was present for most of the last century. Although the extent of change varies between countries, there certainly was a 'turning of the tide' (Friedman and Friedman, 1980). The Friedmans argued that Smith was about right in setting out the allowable activities for government in his 'three duties of the sovereign' mentioned earlier, but added a fourth duty, to 'protect members of the community who cannot be regarded as "responsible" members', adding 'we do not believe in freedom for madmen or children' (1980, p. 53). In other areas than these, the Friedmans argued that the great increase in government that had occurred should be reversed. Government should be minimized; it should get out of the way of business. Within the ranks of governments, among policy advisors, and in

Table 3.1   *Public social expenditure as a percentage of GDP,*
1983–2003

Country	1983	1993	2003
France	22.4	28.1	28.7
Japan	11.5	12.5	17.7
Sweden	30.0	36.2	31.3
Switzerland	14.9	17.4	20.5
United Kingdom	19.4	21.0	20.1
United States	14.1	15.3	23.9
OECD average	17.4	20.4	20.7

Source: Adapted from OECD (2007) *Factbook 2007*. Paris: OECD.

key parts of the bureaucracy, there is now a dominance of this neo-classical economics. It seems that the ideas of neoclassicism are so well established in the economics profession, and in what remains of the bureaucracy, that welfarism seems to belong to an earlier age.

On the other hand, increased costs, ageing populations and growing entitlements have meant that actual expenditures on social programs have increased since the early 1980s.

Table 3.1 shows an increase in public social expenditure in the OECD as a whole. Also (not shown in the table), from 1980 to 1983 the OECD average increase was from 15.9 per cent of GDP to 17.4 per cent. The definition of public social expenditure is quite broad, but even so, the increase shown in Table 3.1 in the United States, at the time when less government was being argued for, is notable. The increase in Japan is also notable, as is the decline in Sweden; perhaps there is some convergence towards the OECD average. Even though the theoretical move was in favour of minimal government, as was political rhetoric, political demands and institutional inertia led to further increases, albeit at a slower rate than in the past.

The role of government has waxed and waned over the past 250 years in Western societies. Change in the role of government, really a conflict of theories about government, remains important today. And yet, the extent of variation has not been all that substantial. McCraw argues that there are four broad categories of potential government intervention in capitalist economies (1997a, p. 317):

1. *laissez-faire*, with minimal intervention;
2. frequent, uncoordinated intervention in a mostly free market;
3. systematic state guidance of private decision-making;
4. thorough state management and decision-making for the whole economy.

He argues that 'the record throughout American history hovers around category 2' (1997a, p. 317). Most other economically advanced societies would be in that category as well, with occasional attempts at category 3. This is probably also the case with other developed societies. The UK did experience a period in the nineteenth and early twentieth centuries when category 1 was tried, and perhaps after 1945 category 3 was followed for a while. But other societies have been less experimental and category 2 – frequent, uncoordinated intervention in a mostly free market – is a better general description of reality.

The method of government involvement has also varied. In the mercantilist era, the main instrument used was government regulation, as budgets were very small and there was little government production. The era of the welfare state relied heavily on government provision of goods and services through higher general taxation and redistribution of resources to the poorer sections of society. Government production was relatively high in some countries, such as the postwar United Kingdom, when it was believed that, through nationalization, there would be benefits from government ownership of major industries such as steel, coal and utilities. While there are adherents to the different ideological perspectives that have historical antecedents, one sign of a new pragmatism is that there seems to be less heat generated by the economic role of government than in recent decades. There is currently little argument in favour of further extending the reach of the public sector, but neither is there much ideological argument anymore in favour of further widespread slashing.

Market failure as the basis for public policy

The market mechanism alone cannot perform all economic functions as there are some desirable goods and services that will not be provided or will, at least, not be provided to a satisfactory level. Theories and models can be developed which state that government action should only occur where markets fail, providing governments would do a better job in those particular circumstances. Some of those goods or services which markets may not provide optimally include: education, law and order, environmental values, national defence, roads and bridges, hospitals and health care, welfare services, public transport and the like. The key areas where market failure can bring government into play are outlined in what follows.

Public goods

Public goods benefit the society regardless of whether or not individual users can be found to pay for them. They are 'non-excludable', that is, if provided to one, they are available to all. There are roads and bridges that benefit a particular community, but for which tolls or some other way of charging individual users are not feasible or too costly. It is not possible for citizens to decide what level of national defence they individually want and then pay precisely that amount in their taxes. There seems to be no way except for government to provide such public goods.

The literature also points to *merit goods*. These are services, such as education and health care, that are socially desirable, but which markets may not provide optimally. The market may provide them in a technical sense – they are excludable – but there are benefits to the whole society from some government involvement. An educated workforce is economically desirable as an educated worker is able to perform more complex tasks; government provision or assistance may improve overall educational outcomes for the benefit of society as a whole. But how education is funded is a general problem.

Health care is another difficult merit-good issue. While the delivery of health services by doctors and hospitals is broadly consistent across developed countries, there are varying mechanisms of financing with some countries seeing health care essentially as a private good (US), others as a public good (UK), and still others as a mix of both (Canada). Even in the US there is some provision for those who cannot pay – most countries do have an involvement of government in at least financing health care.

Externalities

Market transactions often have effects on third parties, or on the environment, that only government action can alleviate. It is possible to buy a car and its fuel through the market, but the externality or 'spillover' effects on air quality or vehicle accidents are not captured by the price paid for the items causing the problem. Environmental effects are usually seen as requiring some kind of government action, as there is no market way of coping with these effects. There are ways of providing solutions to externalities without recourse to government. One is to internalize the externality, to assign property rights and to use the legal system to gain redress for damages. Stiglitz argues (2000, p. 222) there is still a need for government intervention as there are free-rider problems, transaction costs, and problems with litigation including differential access to the law. There are market approaches to government action, such as tradable pollution permits, but these are used within a framework of government regulation.

Natural monopoly

There are some goods which are characterized by declining marginal cost, that is, when supplied to one customer it becomes cheaper to provide them to the next. It is in utilities with networks – telephone, electricity, gas and water – that the problem of natural monopoly is most prevalent. Adding an extra user is likely to be much cheaper than establishing a whole new network. A new entrant to the industry is faced with a large sunk cost before the first consumer is connected. Competition is constrained, as the cost of a new customer for a new entrant must be higher than the rate which could be charged by the incumbent. This is most often the case with public utilities, where, without regulation, monopoly prices can be charged as an effective competitor is not likely to emerge (see Chapter 5).

The beneficial effects of competition are not likely to occur when there is a tendency towards a monopoly supplier. The existence of natural monopoly has been used as a rationale for some form of government involvement, or even ownership, although there are fewer industries or parts of industries now universally regarded as natural monopolies. Government involvement need not mean direct government provision, and there is now a worldwide trend to privatization of such services but with some form of government regulation attached.

Imperfect information

There is a case for poor information, or 'asymmetric information'

(Kay and Vickers, 1990), being considered an example of market failure. Market theory assumes perfect information for buyers and sellers. To the extent that information is not gained, especially by the buyer, markets can be less than optimal. Consumer protection, and packaging information, might be examples where, through government action, information can be provided so that markets function better. Regulations imposed on blatantly unsafe products may be seen as providing information to those unable or unwilling to gather it for themselves (see Chapter 4).

Box 3.1 Privatization in the OECD

The privatization of state-owned enterprises in the United Kingdom following the election of the Conservatives in 1979 marked the beginning of a trend towards privatization across the OECD countries. In 2000, OECD countries raised nearly two thirds of global privatization revenues. Western Europe contributed over two thirds of all OECD proceeds, largely due to privatizations in preparation for the launch of European Monetary Union.

In a number of OECD countries, the total proceeds from privatization between 1990 and 2000 were equivalent to a significant percentage of GDP. In Ireland, privatization raised funds equivalent to over 10 per cent of GDP. In each of Greece, the Czech Republic and Poland, proceeds from privatization equated to 15 per cent of GDP. The Australian government raised an amount equivalent to 20 per cent of GDP, and in Portugal and Hungary, funds accumulated from privatization equated to 25 per cent of GDP.

As the figures in the accompanying table illustrate, the high-point of privatizations over this period came in the late 1990s.

Global amount raised from privatization, US$ million, 1990–2000

Area	1990	1992	1994	1996	1998	2000
OECD	24,724	17,396	50,884	68,250	94,011	65,063
Other	8,494	16,098	17,974	21,493	45,153	35,000
Total	33,218	33,494	68,858	89,743	139,164	100,063

Source: Adapted from OECD (2001) *Financial Market Trends*, No. 79, June 2001. Paris: OECD.

Limitations of market failure

Some market economists, notably Stigler (1975) and the Friedmans (1980), disagree with the notion that market failures provide a justification for government action, as they result in too much government and too much intrusion and regulation (see Chapter 4). On the other hand, there are arguments for additional kinds of market failure. Stiglitz argues that market failures include imperfect competition and unemployment and other macroeconomic disturbances (2000, p. 85). These are not in the standard lists of market failures but they are certainly ways in which markets do not provide optimal outcomes. Markets may be incomplete and competition is not guaranteed unless there are regulations to make competition occur (Chapter 5). As to whether there are additional kinds of market failure, the theory can provide some signposts to government action, but particular aspects may be problematic if used as a complete guide to what governments should or should not do.

In recent decades, government is generally better at delineating the activities it does well and those it does not. In the 1980s and 1990s, there were attempts in some countries to greatly restrict the role of government, through reducing the scale and scope of activity, through privatization, contracting out and the like.

After the late 1990s, demands to cut government were becoming muted, with institutions such as the World Bank and the International Monetary Fund seeing the need to improve government capability through institution-building where once they had argued for minimization of government roles. There has been a greater appreciation of the positive role of government and the public sector.

Government and institutions

There is now greater appreciation of the importance of institutions in the operations of societies (Hall, 1986; North, 1990; Putnam, 1993; Weaver and Rockman, 1993). As has been shown by the multifarious problems the former Eastern bloc nations have found on the transition to a market economy from a socialist planned economy, there are a number of institutions which need to be present and to work reasonably well for markets to thrive. It is not a matter of simply allowing markets to exist; there need to be laws to facilitate market transactions, laws to ensure that competition occurs and institutions to step in if, for instance, contracts are not honoured. North sees institutions as the rules of the game in a society or as 'the humanly devised constraints that shape human interaction' (North, 1990, p. 3). There are three components to these: formal rules, informal rules, and enforcement mechanisms.

Formal rules are the written rules of a society, such as laws governing contracts, regulation in its various forms and criminal law; *informal rules* are the unwritten rules of a society, such as culture, norms of behaviour, codes of conduct, and so on; *enforcement*, as the third component, is especially important in that without it, institutions are often ineffective. Indeed, enforcement 'may be the single most important element in explaining differences in economic performance' (Yeager, 1999, p. 10). It is the institutional framework of a nation that determines the level of transaction costs. Clear, well understood formal rules, informal rules and enforcement mechanisms can reduce transaction costs. The greater role for institutions has led in turn to a greater appreciation of the positive, facilitative role of government. Without government-created and government-maintained institutions, markets or indeed societies will not perform at their optimal level.

The World Bank (1997) argued that 'an effective state is vital for the provision of the goods and services – and the rules and institutions – that allow markets to flourish and people to lead healthier, happier lives'. A well-functioning government and, by extension, a well-functioning public service were now to be regarded as particularly important institutions for the society as a whole. The need for government to provide a suitable institutional framework seemed to be forgotten during the 1980s and early 1990s, when developing countries were urged to simply reduce the size and scope of government. The change of stance in the World Bank and other international organizations was a recognition that markets require good governance and government in order to work effectively. Indeed the key economic role for the government may well be to create an institutional framework that lowers the costs of transacting; 'a well-functioning economy requires a well-functioning government' (Yeager, 1999, p. 41). It is now realized more widely that it is better to have *appropriate* government – a public sector and public service that enhance the overall society – without preconceptions as to size.

Institutions and markets

Several institutions are required for markets to function well and these are provided by government as part of the infrastructure of society. The role and significance of institutions is often downplayed and it is assumed that markets, once allowed to be free, will thrive by themselves. The importance of suitable institutions was shown with the opening of markets in Russia and the former Eastern bloc countries. In most instances, the early years of these countries' transition to a market economy were years of failure, due not usually to markets themselves failing but more often to a failure of the kind of institutional arrangements taken for granted in Western countries. There were political failures, failures of regulation including insufficient planning for what would replace public enterprises, and failures within public services. Free markets function optimally only with suitable institutions, so that the single crucial success factor in development has been the existence of institutions to govern the operations of markets. In more recent years these countries have grown much faster, as shown in Box 3.2, due in no small part, to institutions working better.

There are several perspectives on exactly what institutional arrangements are needed for markets to work. A common view is that there are two fundamentals; 'trade cannot prosper without legal security of property rights and mechanisms to enforce contracts' (Hoekman and Kostecki, 2001, p. 20). McCraw (1997b, pp. 532–3) points to the same two ingredients required for a country to be considered 'capitalist':

> It must have a market economy, and its legal system must protect private property and the sanctity of contracts. The 'value' of a good or service must be determined not by some external notion such as a 'just price', but instead by the simple test of what someone will pay for it. Property must be alienable. Wages must be paid in money. Entrepreneurial opportunity and technological advance must be encouraged ... The essence of capitalism itself is a psychological orientation toward the *future* – the pursuit of wealth and income as much for tomorrow as for today.

North argues, 'obviously, competition, decentralized decision making, and specified contracts of property rights as well as bankruptcy laws are crucial to effective organization' (1990, p.

Box 3.2   Governance and growth

In the early years of transition to a market economy, growth in the Russian Federation and former Eastern bloc countries was unstable, as governments grappled with the complexities of the new economic order. Developments in governance and improved economic stability in recent years have seen the Czech Republic, Hungary, Poland and the Slovak Republic become accepted as members of the European Union. However, none of these countries has as yet joined European Monetary Union.

Annual growth (%), Russian Federation and selected Eastern European countries, 1991–2005

Country	1991	1993	1995	1997	1999	2001	2003	2005
Czech Republic	–11.6	0.1	5.9	–0.7	1.3	2.5	3.6	6.1
Hungary	n/a	-0.6	1.5	4.6	4.2	4.1	4.1	4.2
Poland	–7	3.7	7	7.1	4.5	1.1	3.8	3.2
Russian Federation	n/a	n/a	n/a	1.4	6.4	5.1	7.3	6.4
Slovak Republic	n/a	1.9	5.8	4.6	1.5	3.2	4.2	6.1

Source: Adapted from OECD (2007) *Factbook 2007*. Paris: OECD.

81). He also argues, 'the inability of societies to develop effective, low-cost enforcement of contracts is the most important source of both historical stagnation and contemporary underdevelopment in the Third World' (North, 1990, p. 54). This could be extended to a respect for the rule of law more generally, in that without some confidence in the application of the legal framework there are obvious difficulties in getting or retaining any kind of private investment. What we have then from North is, most importantly, the enforcement of contracts as well as, perhaps less importantly, competition laws and bankruptcy laws. Decentralized decision-making may be more controversial as a strict requirement, but North and other institutionalists argue that decentralization is closer to those affected by governmental and private sector decisions. If all decisions are made centrally, in for instance, an absolute monarchy, the outcomes are not likely to be optimal.

Yeager's main institutional requirements are a stable monetary system, property rights for buyer and seller and a legal system 'that specifies and enforces property rights, establishes contract law, and promotes competition' (1999, p. 83). Institutions can 'lower transaction costs by clearly defining property rights to the goods and services being exchanged so that measurement and enforcement costs are lowered' (p. 157).

Fairly obviously, a foundation of law is required for markets to work at all, at least for legal markets. As Yeager argues, 'transaction costs are dramatically higher without a reliable method for resolving contract disputes' (1999, p. 83). The second point is that of property rights, including establishment of property rights, protection of property rights from criminals and a fair and reasonable judiciary. This may be more contentious. On property rights Yeager (1999, p. 83) argues:

> This task is at the heart of constructing the institutional framework vital to lowering transaction costs and creating a dynamic market economy. Specification of property rights goes beyond the initial phases of privatisation. Rights concerning inventory, lease arrangements, intellectual property, and so on must be specified as clearly as possible.

And yet, markets have existed in some countries without secure property rights. However, while this might be so, it could be argued that markets have not existed *optimally* in the absence of property rights. When markets start without property rights, there is later a clamour to establish such rights. With further development there is a demand for the protection of intellectual property and other intangibles. A firm's real assets are more and more likely to be in the skills of its workforce, its value-added in terms of design and innovation – in intellectual property, in other words – rather than in being a price-taker from what it produces. Institutions that can protect information and property rights attached to information become more important as a result.

These two key features – enforcement of contracts, and property rights – are argued to be the most important institutions for markets. The existence of a legal system for contracts is the single most important element, as without it markets are not likely to get beyond low-level transactions. The development of a legal system is 'at the heart of constructing the institutional framework vital to lowering transaction costs and creating a dynamic market economy' (Yeager, 1999, p. 83). Property rights are desirable and will be demanded once markets become established.

Yet other institutions can enhance the operations of markets. To contracts and property rights, Grindle adds 'independent central banks and tax agencies, stock markets, and regulatory bodies for privatised industries and financial institutions' (2000, pp. 180–1). Additional institutions such as independent central banks, stock markets and economic regulation are obviously useful, but are not as fundamental as a legal system to enforce contracts and property rights for buyer and seller. A country that established a legal system that could operate independently to enforce contracts and to ensure property rights would be one well on the way to being a market society. Other institutions, such as democratic elections, antitrust regulation and so on, are helpful but are not necessarily needed prior to the existence of a market society.

Even for developing countries it is argued that good government is needed for economic development. Countries that are regarded as having weak institutions attract much less foreign direct investment (FDI), a significant factor in economic growth. FDI is overwhelmingly attracted to countries with good institutions as far as market perceptions are concerned, as indicated in Box 3.3. The arguments about greatly reducing government are from an earlier era. This does not mean that scope and scale should not be examined, but rather that the ideological heat has greatly reduced.

Government is now more often seen as having a positive role. Governments need to provide the institutions necessary for markets to work optimally. As Stiglitz argues, 'If markets are to work effectively, there must be well-established and clearly defined property rights; there must be effective competition, which requires antitrust enforcement; and there must be confidence in the markets, which means that contracts must be enforced and that antifraud laws must be effective, reflecting widely accepted codes of behaviour' (2001, pp. 346–7).

Box 3.3   Governance and foreign direct investment

The International Development Association's Resource Allocation Index (IRAI) ranking measures institutional performance of developing countries. In 2005, countries were ranked from 1 to 76, with a ranking of 1 representing the most favourable performance against Country Performance and Institutional Assessment (CPIA) criteria, and a ranking of 76 indicating the weakest performance. Armenia, as the top-ranked country, attracted much more FDI than the Central African Republic in 75th place. This indicates the importance of good governance in securing foreign direct investment (FDI). It is noteworthy that even as FDI is of vital importance in economic development, by far the largest FDI goes to already wealthy OECD countries.

IRAI rankings and FDI inflows, selected countries, 1990–2005

Country	IRAI ranking (out of 76)	FDI inflows ($US million)				
	2005#	1990–2000§*	2002*	2003*	2004*	2005*
Central African Republic	75	1	6	3	–13	6
Armenia	1	57	144	157	217	220
France	OECD	22,611	49,035	42,498	31,371	63,576
United States	OECD	109,513	74,457	53,146	122,377	99,443

§ Annual average

Source: Adapted from World Bank Group (2007) IDA Resource Allocation Index (IRAI), http://go.worldbank.org/MUB7VN2IV0.

* *Source*: Adapted from United Nations Conference on Trade and Development (2006) *World Investment Report 2006*, www.unctad.org/wir, or www.unctad.org/fdistatistics.

Evidently, the role of government in a market society will remain a matter for debate. Where there has been something of a consensus is that governments are not particularly good at running businesses themselves, notably those producing private goods. Similarly, there is consensus that government 'should not privatize national defence' (Stiglitz, 2000, pp. 208–10). The recognition of mutual dependence provides an opportunity for a working relationship that is positive for both government and business. Each needs to realize that together much more can be achieved than if the relationship is necessarily antagonistic.

Protecting industry

Another role for government, discussed at length later (Chapter 8), is in supporting and nurturing domestic industry. Arguments about using the role of the state to strengthen the economy have a long history, notably through the mercantilism of the seventeenth and eighteenth centuries. Indeed, this idea has never really disappeared and still has manifestations today.

In most developed countries, debate over whether or not government should assist business has continued for much of the past two hundred years. In the late nineteenth century, at a time in which Britain seemed totally dominant in manufactures, the German theorist Friedrich List argued, 'in order to allow freedom of trade to operate naturally, the less advanced nations must first be raised by artificial measures to that stage of cultivation to which the English nation has been artificially elevated' (1885, p. 131). Free trade may be a desirable aim in the future but a nation should be allowed to develop its industry before being subjected to the full force of competition.

For List, the nation is something larger and more important than the individuals within it and this point is the fundamental argument with Adam Smith. Using the power of the state to enhance the entire economy is seemingly obvious and is often regarded as common sense by many. It forms what is probably the longest-lasting and least settled argument as to the role of government in business. Should a government assist businesses that are located within its borders? The standard economic answer is that it is not justifiable, but political reality and the views of interest groups are often against this. Governments are often involved in industry, not always to the general benefit.

International governmental organizations

Individual nation-states get together in a bewildering array of international agreements and organizations. These may be seen as effectively decreasing the power of individual governments, but in no way decrease the power of *government* itself. It could even be argued that having governments collaborating with each other increases governmental power, as cross-jurisdictional outcomes can result.

International government has a long history. Numerous international institutions have been set up, some of which have a history of well over a century. The 1856 Declaration of Paris on maritime law abolished privateering and set out rules for neutral shipping and shipped goods in time of war. In 1864, the first Geneva Convention on the treatment of the wounded in war was followed by others on the rights of prisoners and non-combatants. The 1899 and 1907 Hague Peace Conventions tried to set standards for the behaviour of combatants during war and, more ambitiously, to agree on reductions in military expenditure and on ways of resolving disputes without war. This category would include the naval conferences in the early 1920s to restrict the number of ships and their arms, the Kellogg-Briand pact of 1928 signed by 15 countries to renounce war, and the Geneva Disarmament Conference which started in 1932 until it was overtaken by events that led to war.

There have been intergovernmental agreements more directly related to business. In 1865, the International Telegraph Union (now International Telecommunications Union) was set up by agreement of 20 European nations to arrive at standards for the connection of telegraph lines. This was later extended to other telecommunications; the ITU still exists and plays a very important role. It could be argued that its standards, indeed standards generally, constitute globalization by stealth. When the United States set its own standards for digital mobile telephones (cell-phones) that were different from those of the ITU, the incompatibility meant that 'international roaming' did not work in the US while it did almost everywhere else. In 2007, the ITU had 191 members and operated around 3,000 standards, which although non-binding are generally followed as it is in every country's interest to follow the same standard. There are many other standard-setting international agreements and organizations – the Universal Postal Union

(1874), conventions on road signs, vehicle standards, specifications for materials and many others.

In 1919, the League of Nations was set up from the Treaty of Versailles after World War I 'to promote international cooperation and to achieve peace and security'. The League was formed without the participation of the United States, despite it having been sponsored by US President Woodrow Wilson. Its members agreed not to go to war with each other except in resistance to aggression and if authorized by the League.

Due in part to the US retreat into isolationism between the two world wars the League of Nations became a weak and ineffective multilateral institution. However, despite its overall failure, and more especially its failure to prevent World War II, the League did have some successes. It settled some minor disputes; its related International Labour Organization continues, and with more than 60 members over its lifetime, the League did at least establish the principle that nations could work together and that multilateral solutions had their advantages.

Even before World War II was over, high-level multilateral meetings were already taking place to plan the postwar international architecture. At Bretton Woods in New Hampshire in July 1944, delegates from 44 countries (see Box 3.4) designed the international economic system, setting up several multilateral organizations: the International Monetary Fund (IMF) – to oversee the system of fixed exchange rates; the International Bank for Reconstruction and Development, later known as the World Bank – to promote development; the General Agreement on Tariffs and Trade (GATT) – to oversee trade. The latter was to soon become an international trade organization, but agreement on bringing this about was slow in coming and was not achieved until 1994 when the Uruguay Round of trade talks agreed on the creation of the World Trade Organization (WTO).

In June 1945, representatives of 45 nations – originally those in the war against Germany and Japan – met in San Francisco to set up the United Nations; its Charter was signed in October that year. The League of Nations was disbanded the next year with much of its property and function being taken up by the United Nations.

The UN's Charter is wide-ranging – to 'save succeeding generations from the scourge of war' – and speaks of fundamental human rights, human dignity and equal rights, international law, social progress and better standards of life, and, importantly, 'to

Box 3.4   Who was at Bretton Woods?

The following governments sent delegations to the conference at Bretton Woods, July 1944:

Australia	El Salvador	New Zealand
Belgium	Ethiopia	Nicaragua
Bolivia	France	Norway
Brazil	Greece	Panama
Canada	Guatemala	Paraguay
Chile	Haiti	Peru
China	Honduras	Philippines
Colombia	Iceland	Poland
Costa Rica	India	South Africa
Cuba	Iran	USSR
Czechoslovakia	Iraq	United Kingdom
Dominican	Liberia	United States
Republic	Luxembourg	Uruguay
Ecuador	Mexico	Venezuela
Egypt	The Netherlands	Yugoslavia

employ international machinery for the promotion of the economic and social advancement of all peoples' (UN Charter). Nations committed themselves to multilateral solutions to problems rather than conflict; future peace and prosperity would rely on more effective international institutions than those in place in between the wars. And if joined with the Bretton Woods economic institutions, a complete set of international institutions seemed to be in place.

Sixty years later, many of these multilateral institutions have their problems. The United Nations is often regarded as bloated and has clearly lost support in some countries, notably the United States. Wars still occurred despite the UN Charter. Poverty persisted and while peacekeeping operations in many parts of the world did help reduce some conflict on many issues, the UN was rather ineffectual. The UN involves itself more in domestic affairs, such as election monitoring, and even intervention in security issues. In 1991, the UN General Assembly declared itself in favour of humanitarian intervention without the request or consent of the state involved.

The views of the economic institutions formed at Bretton Woods became known as the 'Washington Consensus', referring to the Washington-based international institutions such as the World Bank and the International Monetary Fund. In the 1980s and 1990s, the Washington Consensus was based around the view that good economic performance required 'fiscal austerity, privatization and market liberalization' (Stiglitz, 2002, p. 53). What developing countries required was to greatly reduce government and rely on private markets. Stiglitz argues that much of this was a failure. Alternative approaches may have been market-based but also gave government important roles; a 'short, sharp shock' may be appropriate for some circumstances, but more often careful consideration and sequencing of implementation issues would be more effective.

It could be argued that the original mission of the IMF is no longer relevant as most of the major countries operate a floating exchange rate. It has become a financial bail-out agency for developing countries, one that is often controversial. As will be discussed later (Chapter 7), the WTO has major problems, including limited popular support, while the World Bank is heavily criticized, in particular, for loans made to projects resulting in environmental and cultural problems in developing countries.

Mathews (1997, p. 50) argues that there is a decline in the power of states and a sharing of power with other players, notably NGOs:

> The end of the Cold War has brought no mere adjustment among states but a novel redistribution of power among states, markets, and civil society. National governments are not simply losing autonomy in a globalizing economy. They are sharing powers – including political, social, and security roles at the core of sovereignty – with businesses, with international organizations, and with a multitude of citizens' groups, known as nongovernmental organizations (NGOs). The steady concentration of power in the hands of states that began in 1648 with the Peace of Westphalia is over, at least for a while.

It is certainly the case that other actors are being brought into governmental organizational structures. NGOs are consulted, involved as participants in forums, as are other interest groups of various kinds, but it is only government that has the jurisdiction and the coercive power of the state to bring about major change. Slaughter has argued that there is a continuing role for states, notably states working together. In her view the state is not disappearing, 'it is disaggregating into its separate, functionally distinct parts' and these parts 'are networking with their counterparts abroad, creating a dense web of relations that constitutes a new, transgovernmental order' (1997, p. 184).

Transgovernmental solutions to problems do not reduce the power of government itself, rather there is a sharing of power and expertise with similar organizations in other governments. Specialists at lower levels get together to solve problems in this way. In the international sphere, then, there is no real diminution of the role and power of states. It is the case that states are working with each other, but they are cooperating, working together as nations, and they are using the powers that governments have retained.

Despite difficulties with particular international institutions, the idea of the multilateral system is largely still in place. Countries do work together to solve issues much more than they once did; they set up institutions and even, as is the case of the WTO, commit to binding agreements.

Conclusion

There are some indications of a return to government. Following the terrorist attack on the World Trade Center in New York in 2001, approval of government institutions rose to high levels. Shortly after that the collapse of large businesses in the United States, notably the energy company Enron, led to calls for more government involvement to keep the private sector honest. There may be some turning towards government or at least some re-establishment of the worth of government in the eyes of citizens.

In the 1970s and 1980s, free market advocates such as Stigler (1975) and the Friedmans (1980) argued that the best government was no government at all. Perhaps this was a reaction against a time where government and the public sector appeared much more important than business and the private sector. The period since has not seen a great diminution in the role of government, but has seen a change in the kinds of things governments do. The debate over the role of government may have been useful in focusing attention on those things that government does well and those things it does badly (Hughes, 2003).

Government involvement in any particular area is a matter of debate rather than being fixed, and there is less ideological heat over economic roles than was once the case. It is simplistic to say that minimization of government would be best for business; in some instances government action can assist business, in others it may harm it. Even if government is appreciated again, we are most unlikely to see a return to large-scale, bureaucratic solutions to problems. Following some experimentation with a minimalist state, it does appear that by the turn of the twenty-first century a new age of pragmatism about the role of government had emerged. Rather than the best government being one that is reduced to the barest minimum, government is more often seen as an important and powerful institution which can facilitate the role of the private sector instead of being its axiomatic competitor.

Chapter 4

Regulation

Introduction

Regulation is at the core of the relationship between business and government and is perhaps the main reason why a perpetual state of tension exists between the two. Government regulation of business activity is constantly debated in terms of purpose, scope and means. In this debate, two issues are generally prominent: first, the extent to which government should use the coercive powers of the state to regulate economic activity; and second, whether it is legitimate for regulation to have social as opposed to economic objectives. Neither of these issues is ever completely resolved.

This chapter will discuss how the regulatory relationship between business and government is evolving. Although it is fashionable to suggest that the overall trend is for governments to regulate less, this does not always seem to occur. It is true that there is an international trend for governments to disengage from some forms of regulation, but this has generally been accompanied by a corresponding increase in other forms of regulation. In this sense, regulation may seem as pervasive as ever. But concern about the *amount* of regulation tends to distract attention from what is perhaps of greater significance – namely, the *effectiveness* of regulation. Regulation can take many forms and it cannot be assumed that all of these will be equally effective. Indeed, it is possible that a regulatory instrument will exacerbate or compound the problem it was meant to address. Knowing *when* to regulate, *whom* to regulate and *how* to regulate are surely some of the most difficult challenges confronting any government.

What is regulation?

There are so many forms of regulation that a universal definition initially seems elusive. The OECD (2000, p. 9) defines regulation as 'the diverse set of instruments by which governments establish requirements for enterprises and citizens'. Regulations thus include 'laws, formal and informal orders, subordinate rules issued at all levels of government, and rules issued by non-governmental or self-regulatory bodies to whom governments have delegated regulatory powers'. This definition is supported by Gow and Maher (1994, p. 114) who define regulation as the rules 'effected by departments and statutory authorities through the use of statutes and subordinate legislation (including regulations, rules, by-laws and ordinances)', and Weidenbaum (2004, p. 32) who defines regulation as 'agency statements that implement, interpret, or prescribe a law or policy'.

Other definitions of regulation focus upon the role of regulation in constraining economic activity. Majone (1996, p. 9) defines regulation as 'rules issued for the purpose of controlling the manner in which private and public enterprises conduct their operations', while Vogel (1996, p. 9) sees regulation as 'public control over private sector behaviour'. Stigler (1975, p. 145) has a similar focus, describing the regulatory agency as 'an inevitable instrument in the public control of industries, occupations, and other particular branches of economic activity'.

The emphasis on the role of the regulatory agency, as suggested by Weidenbaum and Stigler, supports Majone's view that there are different understandings of regulation on either side of the Atlantic. In Europe, 'there is a tendency to identify regulation with the whole realm of legislation, governance and social control' (Majone, 1990, pp. 1–2). This contrasts with the US where regulation is generally seen as 'a sustained and focused control exercised by a public agency over activities that are generally regarded as desirable to society'.

Forms of regulation

The OECD (2000, p. 9) suggests that there are three categories of regulations:

1. *Economic regulations* – intervening directly in market decisions such as pricing competition, market entry or exit.
2. *Social regulations* – protecting public interests in such areas as health, safety, the environment, and social cohesion.

3. *Administrative regulations* – so-called 'red tape' through which governments collect information and intervene in individual economic decisions.

However, most commentators generally see regulation as having only two main purposes – *economic* and *social*. As the OECD suggests, economic regulations usually take the form of overt barriers to entry and exit, licensing and tariff laws, and price and wage control in specific industries. Social regulations, on the other hand, are rules or statutes directed at social objectives, such as protecting citizens, worker health and safety, environmental goals or promoting civil rights. Examples of social regulations include public access requirements for disabled people, mandating smoke alarms in homes, equal opportunity and affirmative action requirements, and environmental protection.

Whether its purpose is economic or social, what all regulation has in common is the intention to use the unique coercive powers of the state to control, or regulate, activity of some description. When governments regulate there is usually some effect on economic activity, whether that activity is undertaken by the private sector, the public sector or both sectors. Even social regulation impacts upon economic activity. Indeed, it is very hard to think of any forms of social regulation that do not have any economic implications. For example, the ratings given to films by classification boards may be intended to ensure that only designated groups within the community see particular films. However, such ratings inevitably affect the financial interests of film producers, distributors and cinema owners, sometimes positively, sometimes adversely. Restrictions on stem cell research, or a prohibition on abortion, might also appear to have a purely social purpose, but even these forms of regulation will at some point affect economic activity and economic interests.

Corporate charters and company laws

Much significant economic activity involves incorporated bodies more commonly known as companies. These bodies have their origins in medieval times. As individuals pooled their resources in response to commercial imperatives and opportunities (thus effectively forming partnerships), a need arose for legal recognition of such arrangements. As discussed in Chapter 2, the earliest form of the modern company evolved in order to facilitate state-approved foreign trade. The Hudson's Bay Company and the East India Company were both set up by Royal Charter as monopolies to exploit foreign territories on behalf of the British Government. From bodies such as these the concepts of jointly owned stock and profits developed, together with a distinct body of law concerned with the specific requirements and structures of companies (Lipton and Herzberg, 2001, p. 2).

As companies became more numerous, so the need for effective regulation grew. Company law has evolved to provide a regulatory framework in which companies or corporations operate. While the scope and application of company law vary, they typically include: the obligations of officeholders within the company to shareholders; the duties of directors; financial reporting; members' remedies; the laws governing takeovers and insolvency, and the forms of protection afforded to shareholders and stakeholders.

Financial regulation

Although there has been a general trend in recent years for governments to intervene less in financial markets, governments continue to take a keen, if sometimes indirect, interest in interest rates, exchange rates, foreign investment rules and other aspects of monetary policy. At the end of the day, if inflation spirals, or interest rates make credit unaffordable, or the declining value of a national currency puts imported goods out of reach, or a building society goes to the wall, there will be a political price to pay. Seen in this light, government intervention is bound to happen.

One of the main instruments governments use to effect financial regulation is the central, state-controlled bank. The US has the Federal Reserve, the UK the Bank of England, and Germany the Deutsche Bundesbank, although most of its functions have been transferred to the European Central Bank. These bodies have effective responsibility for monetary policy and are usually technically independent of government. But the reality is that they are also creations of the state, with key appointments and general policy direction determined by government. Apart from supervising 'policies that affect the supply of money and credit and the terms on which credit is available to borrowers' (Stiglitz, 1997, p. A14), the role of the central banks can also include responsibility for supervising and regulating banking institutions, protecting the credit rights of customers, maintaining the stability of the financial system and providing financial services to the government, the public, financial institutions and foreign institutions.

Another fairly common form of financial regulation can be seen in the limitations and constraints imposed by governments upon foreign investment. These can take a number of forms: restrictions on the right to private ownership; compulsory partnerships with local enterprises (as is required in China); specific exclusion of some sectors from foreign investment (such as the media in Australia); restrictions on the number of foreign firms that can operate in specific sectors; restrictions on the size of foreign firms; limitations on land ownership; higher tax rates for foreign investors; compulsory sharing of technology with local companies; restrictions on repatriated profits; and performance requirements linking investment approval to export or employment targets. Sometimes some of these provisions are enforced by the central bank, but governments also use other means, notably legislation and dedicated agencies, to pursue their objectives. As instruments of international governance develop and assume a greater role in matters relating to foreign investment, however, the capacity of individual governments to restrict this form of investment is likely to become more constrained.

Corporate regulation

Governments regulate corporate activity by a variety of means. Governments may impose constraints upon pricing by putting a ceiling on the *price* of a good or service. Governments commonly intervene to regulate housing rentals when property values soar, leaving existing tenants unable to meet rising market demands. Conversely governments might inflate the price of a good whose consumption they wish to ration or limit. In Australia, the price of leaded petrol was increased to encourage car owners to switch to more environmentally friendly cars, before leaded petrol was phased out altogether. Governments may also intervene when the price of a good declines to the point where there is a risk that producers may cease production. Agricultural subsidies are a common example of this form of regulation, with governments guaranteeing a minimum price for a commodity which the market is unable or unwilling to meet.

Another form of corporate regulation occurs when governments place limits upon the *quantity* of goods to be traded. The imposition of controls may reflect environmental concerns – such as the need to conserve a particular breed of fish whose stocks are being depleted by over-zealous harvesting. In such cases, there is no alternative to government intervention as business cannot be expected to take such actions of its own volition. Other forms of quantity regulation include zoning controls and pollution controls. Sometimes, quantity restrictions are imposed to safeguard existing industries. An example of this occurred in the 1980s when the Japanese imposed voluntary export restraints on automobiles as a strategy to fend off more restrictive measures from the US.

In addition to regulating the *quantity* of production, government may regulate the *quality* of production. This often occurs in response to consumer demands for better or more consistent quality in the goods they purchase. But quality regulation can also have the intention of maintaining and protecting competitive advantage. The enforcement of the *appellation d'origine contrôlée* prevents winemakers outside France from using the names of France's distinctive (and highly marketable) wine regions. Winemakers in South Africa, Australia and elsewhere cannot label their sparkling white wines as 'Champagne', their dry white wines as 'Chablis' or their red wines as 'Burgundy' or 'Bordeaux'. Instead, they must find other terms to promote their products. This ensures that the substantial marketing advantages associated with long established and much admired winemaking regions remain with the winemakers in those regions.

Corporate regulation can also be achieved through the use of *tariffs* – one of the most highly visible forms of government intervention. Tariffs increase the price of imported goods by the application of a government levy. They are both a source of revenue to government and a means of addressing the concerns of particular constituencies, usually domestic producers and their employees. Critics of tariffs argue that they represent an indiscriminate tax on consumers and prop up uncompetitive domestic producers. However, nearly every country imposes some form of tariff and although many countries have reduced tariffs as members of the World Trade Organization, other less visible forms of protection have sometimes been substituted.

Another form of corporate regulation is the application of *product and packaging standards*. The range of products for which standards may be imposed is endless but as with some other aspects of regulation, international pressures are being exerted upon individual governments, specifically with the advent of the

ISO 9000 quality standard developed by the International Organization for Standardization. This organization has now promulgated over 16,000 international standards for business, government and society as part of its overall brief to facilitate the international exchange of goods and services. International harmonization is also evident in packaging regulation. In early 2002, the European Union decreed that consumers should pay an additional fee for plastic bags at supermarkets in an effort to reduce the quantity of plastics consumed and then discarded. In this instance, the EU was responding to an environmental issue, just as many businesses have in removing ozone-depleting chlorofluorocarbons (CFCs) from spray cans and replacing non-degradable polystyrene fast-food packaging with less polluting forms of packaging.

Workforce regulation

From the time of the Industrial Revolution, governments have been under pressure to regulate the workplace and the conditions of working people. Many aspects of work can be subject to regulation: hours worked; minimum pay; workplace conditions (ventilation, lighting etc); work-related entitlements (leave, superannuation etc); occupational health and safety; equal employment opportunity, and affirmative action. As Box 4.1 explains, the International Labour Organization has played a significant role in regulating workforce practices although the degree of regulation varies from country to country. In recent times, there has been a trend towards the deregulation of labour markets so that market forces operate more freely. These moves have been both vigorously resisted (usually by workers and their representatives) and welcomed (generally by employers and their representatives).

Competition regulation

Over two centuries ago Adam Smith observed that markets are not naturally competitive and are thus susceptible to anti-competitive practices including collusion, predatory pricing, takeovers, resale price maintenance and exclusive dealing arrangements. As a consequence, many governments now vigorously pursue pro-competitive regulation with the objective of realizing free, fair and open markets. Some governments have embraced this form of regulation only relatively recently, but the US enacted some of the

Box 4.1   The International Labour Organization and workforce regulation

Created in 1919 at the end of World War I, the International Labour Organization (ILO) is the agency of the United Nations that works to promote employment creation, social protection, social dialogue and rights at work within UN member states. At its first International Labour Conference in 1919, the ILO adopted six International Labour Conventions addressing hours of work in industry, unemployment, maternity protection, night work for women, minimum working age and night work for young people in industry. In 1926, a Committee of Experts was established to supervise the application of ILO standards in member countries.

While national governments continue to devise their own workplace and industrial relations policies, the Committee of Experts still exists today and reports annually on member nations' observance of International Labour Standards (ILS), which are either legally binding *Conventions* or non-binding *Recommendations*. By the end of 2006, the ILO had adopted 187 Conventions and 198 Recommendations addressing: freedom of association and collective bargaining, equality of treatment and opportunity, abolition of forced and child labour, employment promotion and vocational training, social security, conditions of work, labour administration and labour inspection, prevention of work-related accidents, maternity protection, and the protection of migrants and other categories of workers such as seafarers, nursing personnel or plantation workers.

Source: Data from International Labour Organization website, www.ilo.org/global/ lang—en/index.htm, accessed May 2007.

strongest and earliest antitrust (anti-monopoly) legislation with the Sherman Antitrust Act of 1890. In 1904, the crusading journalist Ida M. Tarbell exposed the anti-competitive behaviour of Standard Oil and its owner, America's wealthiest man, John D. Rockefeller. The legacy of this case is still evident in the US where strong antitrust legislation continues to empower government regulators against powerful business interests. Pro-competitive regulation, or competition policy, will be discussed further in the following chapter.

Licensing

Governments use licences to regulate many activities. Cars must be registered, and their drivers licensed. Fishermen must have a permit before casting a line off a pier. Alcohol may only be sold by licensed vendors, usually from licensed premises. In each case, government requires the licensee to comply with certain conditions (which usually include the payment of a fee) before it permits the licensee to conduct a particular activity. In return, government exercises a degree of control over – and responsibility for – the licensed activity. Thus car-owners expect to drive on safe, well-maintained roads. Fishermen expect that clean waterways and effectively policed limits on catches will ensure that they take home a good supply of fish to fry. And publicans and bar-owners expect that governments will root out illegal competitors, together with their pot-stills and moonshine. But in reality, licence fees are often seen by government as another useful source of income and are rarely fully reinvested back in the licensed activity.

Occupational licensing

A specific form of licensing concerns the regulation of occupational categories to control entry and practice in a particular field. Governments typically justify this form of regulation in terms of public safety. Electricians and plumbers clearly fall into this category, as do doctors, dentists, and pharmacists. In other forms of occupational licensing the broader concept of the public interest may be invoked. In recent times, government licensing has expanded beyond the traditional confines of trades and professions. In some jurisdictions, it is necessary to be licensed by government before practising as an interior designer, selling time-shares in resorts or acting as an agent for burial agreements. This growth in regulation is not always opposed, even by those it seeks to regulate. Occupational licensing can confer considerable financial benefits on the recipients of licences and there can be vigorous competition (and even profiteering from the trading of licences) when the number of licences issued – such as those to operate taxis or to fish for deep-sea tuna – is restricted.

Consumer protection

Supporters of consumer protection argue that this form of regulation is essential in the public interest. According to this view, without adequate regulation consumers lack sufficient information about goods and services and are at risk from faulty or hazardous goods and services. Advocates of consumer protection argue that government must intervene because business will not voluntarily do so. This assumption is disputed, most notably by Friedman and Stigler whose arguments are discussed below. Despite their opposition, consumer protection has been one of the fastest-growing areas of regulation since the 1960s and a contentious by-product of this trend has been the emergence of large bureaucracies to administer the regulations promulgated by government.

When regulating for consumer protection, governments have several options. One is to ban certain goods from entering the marketplace – such as an unsafe child restraint or highly flammable children's clothing. Another is to restrict the sale of some goods – such as tobacco and alcohol – to minimize the potentially harmful effects of their use. A third option is to require sufficient product information to enable consumers to make an informed choice at the time of purchase. The labels on many supermarket goods now contain considerable details (for example, ingredients, nutritional qualities, date and place of production and use-by date), so that consumers can read this information prior to making a purchase.

Environmental protection

The environment represents a classic case of what Garrett Hardin (1968) termed 'the tragedy of the commons' – when common property (such as air and water) is exploited because it is freely available and no individual has an economic interest in its preservation. Instead, businesses benefit, at least in the short term, by taking as much as they need. In these circumstances, environmental advocates argue, only government can act decisively to protect the environment from potentially adverse activities.

Like consumer protection, environmental regulation has attracted widespread support since the 1960s. With global warming and climate change now firmly on the international agenda, this support has only intensified in recent years. Initially, governments tended to regulate to prevent or limit pollution or environmental degradation. Under this approach, businesses that exceeded the limits imposed by regulation either to take from the environment or to discharge into it were punished. More recently an alternative regulatory approach has been for governments to reward businesses for *reducing* pollution. In this alternative to command-and-control regulation, an improved environmental record translates into the economic performance of the business. So a business that adopts environmentally friendly technology or practices can price its goods more favourably than its polluting competitors. Environmental regulation, including market-based forms of regulation, is discussed in greater detail in Chapter 9.

Utility regulation

Governments have traditionally attempted to regulate apparently monopolistic markets (the so-called 'natural monopolies') for power, water and telecommunications. In the US, governments preferred to regulate private service providers to prevent monopolistic exploitation. The rationale for this form of regulation was that it retained the benefits of monopoly production (cheaper costs), while avoiding the disadvantages of monopoly provision (exploitative pricing and poor service) (Weidenbaum, 2004). Elsewhere, notably in the UK, Europe and Australasia, government regulation of monopoly markets took the form of public ownership. Under this model, government assumed total control of virtually all aspects of planning, production, sale (pricing) and delivery of utility services. Underpinning this approach was the central assumption 'that public ownership would increase government's ability to regulate the economy and protect the public interest' (Majone, 1996, p. 11).

When governments have opted to exercise control through monopoly ownership, the organizational form of the public enterprise has usually been employed. This involves the creation of a dedicated agency operating at arm's length from government, although legislation usually ensures a degree of political accountability. Over the course of the twentieth century, but particularly in the aftermath of the Second World War, public enterprises were created to produce and deliver an increasingly broad range of goods and services – including water, power, telecommunications, transport, financial services and infrastructure.

More recently, it has been suggested that the benefits of regulating an industry through monopoly government ownership have been outweighed by the disadvantages of non-competitive markets, bureaucratic management and lack of accountability (especially to consumers). Initially, such views were largely confined to classical economic theory. But as these opinions gained wider acceptance, public ownership – once supported across the political spectrum in many Western countries – lost favour. The result was the deregulation of many industries, the privatization of many public enterprises and the emergence of collaborative relationships – or partnerships – between government and the private sector to deliver goods and services which were once the exclusive domain of monopolistic public enterprises.

Why do governments regulate?

Although it is undeniable that governments regulate extensively, there is trenchant debate as to *why* governments regulate. Cynics suggest that governments regulate because it is politically expedient and rarely involves any direct taxation or expenditure. Seen in this light, regulation is a relatively painless means of government intervention. But this analysis obscures a deeper debate which focuses upon two key propositions. The first is that governments intervene in economic activities to promote what is broadly understood to be the common good or the *public interest*. The counter-argument is that government decisions are linked not to the public interest but, as Adam Smith argued, to 'the clamorous importunity of partial interests', or in other words, the *private interests* of powerful groups. This latter interpretation has much in common with *public choice* theory – a theory derived from neoclassical economics – which argues that governments are inherently inefficient and wasteful because they lack the discipline of the market to restrain self-interested and utility-maximizing behaviour (Downs, 1957; Niskanen, 1968; Stigler, 1972). The application of public choice theory to explain the role of government in regulation has been termed the *private interest* model (Quiggin, 1996).

Advocates of the *public interest* model argue that governments intervene when confronted by market failure – when 'markets fail to produce either economically or socially desirable outcomes' (Gilpin, 2001, p. 68). Under ideal conditions, markets ensure an efficient allocation of resources, meaning that consumers get good products at a reasonable price. But in reality market conditions are often sub-optimal. Competition may be less than perfect. Private providers may not find a market for some essential services. Information between buyers and sellers may be less than complete. Undesirable 'spillover' effects for third parties may occur. Scarce resources may be exhausted due to indiscriminate exploitation. In each case, the consequences may leave government no option but to intervene in the public interest. Examples of market failure, or the considerable discrepancy between the theory and practice of the marketplace, generally fall into four categories: natural monopoly, public goods, imperfect information (or information asymmetry), and negative externalities. These were discussed in Chapter 3.

Criticisms of regulation

An alternative to the *public interest* model as an explanation of government regulatory intervention is the *private interest* critique offered by Stigler, Friedman and others. In some respects, it is understandable that regulation should have its critics, given its breadth, scope and impact. The OECD (2000) reports that regulation may fail for many reasons – the design of rules may be flawed, policy instruments may be inappropriate, and those being regulated may not understand compliance requirements. But government may too readily employ regulation as a substitute for direct expenditure; regulation may be overly prescriptive or insufficiently accountable. There may be little attempt at cost/benefit analysis or retrospective evaluation of regulatory effectiveness, and public participation and consultation on regulatory issues may be inadequate.

While some criticism of regulation is specific to particular instances of failure or under-performance, other criticism is more general – suggesting that problems in regulation stem from larger issues in the management of the public sector. According to this view, ineffectual, inefficient or costly regulation simply mirrors the bureaucracy which created it. However, other criticism of regulation is even more fundamental than this – arguing that because *all* forms of regulation are flawed, governments should keep regulatory activity to the absolute minimum, and regulate only when market failure is clearly demonstrated, only when regulation is the best method of correcting this failure and only when the benefits of regulation outweigh the cost.

The private interest critique

The private interest critique argues that regulation is flawed because it cannot be what its proponents claim it to be – that is, in the public interest. Instead, the private interest critique asserts that all regulation is prompted by self-interest and should be avoided wherever possible. Two of the most prominent advocates of the private interest model are the Nobel laureates George Stigler and Milton Friedman.

In *The Citizen and the State* (1975), Stigler rejects the notion that regulation results from government concern for the public interest or from demand from the community for government action. While he concedes that government is capable of 'acts of great moral virtue' (1975, p. 114), Stigler argues that where government is concerned less noble instincts will often prevail, with regulation a case in point. 'As a rule', he states, 'regulation is acquired by the industry and designed and operated primarily for its benefit' (p. 114). According to this view, industries will try for a direct subsidy to improve their profitability. Or they may try to control the entry of rivals to protect the interests of those already in the industry, as dairy producers did in severely constraining margarine producers for many years. Or they might attempt to engage in price-fixing agreements to restrain the amount of competition they have to face. This self-interest does not end with the establishment of regulations. Stigler argues that a regulatory regime, once created, acquires its own momentum and will constantly seek to extend its power and influence. It will do this regardless of its capacity to discharge its duties effectively and is unlikely to be made fully accountable for its performance.

Friedman, too, is a severe critic of regulation. In *Capitalism and Freedom* (1962), he argues that governments make a critical mistake intervening in markets when market forces are superior. If Friedman had his way, government would no longer engage in: parity price support programmes for agriculture; tariffs and restrictions on exports; control of output such as pro-rationing of oil; rent control; minimum wage rates; maximum prices; detailed regulation of industries; control of TV and radio; compulsory social security programmes; licensing of many occupations and professions; public housing; military conscription; national parks; the prohibition on carrying mail for profit; and publicly owned and operated toll roads (1962, pp. 35–6).

Friedman shares Stigler's view that regulatory agencies are captured by the very interests they are supposed to regulate and end up suppressing competition, preserving monopolies and harming both consumers and potential competition (Friedman, 1983, pp. 130–1). Referring to occupational licensing, Friedman reports (1962, p. 140):

> [T]he pressure on the legislature to licence an occupation rarely comes from the members of the public who have been mulcted or in other ways abused by members of the occupation. On the contrary, the pressure invariably comes from members of the occupation itself. Of course, they are more aware than others of how much they exploit the customer and so perhaps can lay claim to expert knowledge.

The case against consumer protection

The opponents of regulation reserve some of their strongest criticism for those regulations justified on the basis of providing consumers with protection from the marketplace. As noted earlier, this form of regulation has grown enormously since the 1960s, when Ralph Nader's *Unsafe at Any Speed* (1965) revealed an alarming absence of safety standards in the US car industry and led to the passing of consumer safety laws. Consumer protection generally takes the form of making goods and services safer or redressing the information imbalance (or asymmetry) which typically disadvantages the consumer. But far from providing essential safeguards, these regulations – nearly always promoted as being in the public interest – are dismissed by critics, including Friedman and Stigler, as unnecessary and wrong.

Friedman is particularly dismissive of the consumer movement in the US. He reports that by 1975 consumers in the US were 'protected' by a raft of regulatory agencies administering some 60,000 pages of rules or proposed rules in the *Federal Register* and no less than 72,000 pages of regulations in the Code of Federal Regulations (1983, p. 162). In Friedman's view, all this activity did not bring about better consumer protection, but simply fostered the interests and career ambitions of bureaucrats. Friedman even disputes the role of government in banning potentially harmful goods such as saccharin and cyclamates. These artificial sweeteners were believed to carry the risk of causing cancer. The preferred alternative for Friedman is for consumers to be told of the risks associated with particular products (as occurs with the sale of tobacco and alcohol) and then allowed to make their own choices, even if it means choosing something that might be harmful. For Friedman (1983, pp. 164–5),

> The most effective protection of the consumer is free competition, free competition at home and free trade throughout the world. It is the free market, the free private market, with free competition everywhere that is his best protector. The great danger to the consumer is from monopoly whether it be private or public. The great protection to the consumer is having alternative sources of supply.

Friedman believes it is in the self-interest of entrepreneurs to protect consumers, leading him to conclude that there is no role for government in preventing the sale of adulterated products or weeding out false advertising. Consumers are, he argues, considerably smarter than the regulators realize, and the common sense of consumers when combined with contestable markets will always produce a better outcome than government regulation.

For Stigler, the alternative to consumer protection regulation is *caveat emptor* or letting the buyer beware. Instead of creating extensive and ineffectual bureaucracies to protect consumers by regulating product safety, advertising standards, packaging and labelling, Stigler argues that it is 'the great engine of competition' which leads companies to improve quality, reliability and safety in order to become more profitable. In this view (1975, p. 188):

> The superiority of the traditional defences of the individual – reliance upon his own efforts and the power of competition – lie precisely in the characteristics which distinguish them from public regulation. Each of the traditional defences is available and working at all times – self-interest and competition are never passing fads. Each of the traditional defences is available to individuals and small groups – changes in policy and adaptation to new circumstances do not require changes in the ponderous, expensive, insensitive machinery of a great state. It is of regulation that the consumer must be aware.

Regulatory failure

Critics of regulation point to the many instances of unsuccessful government regulation and the costly consequences for the community. Medical boards may fail to prevent rogue (or simply incompetent) doctors from continuing to practise. Prudential regulation may be inadequate, leading to costly corporate collapses of which the Enron disaster is but one example. Company law may fail to ensure that directors always act in the interests of shareholders. Occupational health and safety standards may be breached with tragic results, as occurred in Bhopal, India when a gas leak from a Union Carbide India plant caused nearly 4,000 deaths in 1984. Environmental regulation may fail to halt the extinction of species. In all of these cases, it is evident that regulation is as susceptible to human error and fallibility as any other activity.

Government failure

Critics of regulation also employ the concept of *government failure* to explain sub-optimal results from government intervention (Stiglitz, 1997; Weidenbaum, 2004). The underlying assumption is that just as markets are prone to failure, so too are governments. However, this possibility is rarely entertained by governments contemplating regulatory action and so regulation proceeds even though there may be a strong likelihood of failure.

It is certainly tempting to categorize much regulatory failure as government failure – it is government after all that fails to provide regulatory agencies with adequate resources to do their job and government that fails to monitor diligently all aspects of regulated behaviour in the economy. Government also is clearly responsible when those it appoints as regulators fail to meet expectations and when regulations impose an additional financial burden upon consumers. In all this there is a risk that government failure may have worse consequences than market failure. Further, there may be insufficient mechanisms to curtail government intervention even when it proves unsuccessful.

The notion of government failure is consistent with the public choice perspective on government – that without the discipline of the market, government and its employees will be inefficient, self-serving and oblivious to the cost of regulation. According to the Competitiveness Enterprise Institute, a US think tank, federal regulations cost the US economy US$1.127 trillion in 2005, the equivalent of 9 per cent of US gross domestic product (Crews, 2006). Just as public choice theory leads inevitably to the conclusion that government should leave as much as possible to the market, so the government failure model concludes that governments should minimize their role in regulation.

The case against public ownership

State-owned or public enterprises delivering power, water, telecommunications, postal services, transport and various other goods and services were once commonplace in many Western economies in the twentieth century, with the notable exceptions of the US and Japan. Some public enterprises emerged as a consequence of market failure – private providers had failed and there was strong pressure from the community for government to intervene. Other public enterprises were created because of a prevailing belief that the market they operated in was a natural monopoly and monopoly provision by government was preferable to monopoly provision by the private sector. Others were established because of a preference for public, as opposed to private, provision. Regardless of the underlying motive, there was in many countries a broad consensus supporting the regulatory role and functions of public enterprises.

For a while, it seemed as if governments, through their public enterprises, would always play a role in the mixed economy. But gradually confidence in this form of government intervention eroded to the point where many public enterprises were split up and sold to the private sector. Stretton and Orchard (1994, p. 80) summarize the origins of this change as the 'theory of public incompetence'. According to this theory, public enterprises neglect their customers' wants, allocate their resources inefficiently, produce inefficiently at unnecessary cost and resist necessary modernization or replacement. They can do this because (Stretton and Orchard, 1994, 80):

- administrative planning is a poor substitute for the customers' market demands;
- public investors and managers lack profit-seeking discipline and incentives;
- public employees can use industrial muscle to get more pay for less work than market-disciplined employers could afford; and

- governments are inclined to finance inefficient and unnecessary activities when market discipline would reform or stop such activities.

Majone (1996) also reports a litany of reasons why regulation via public enterprise is doomed to failure. He cites interfering politicians meddling in pricing and personnel matters, exemptions from antitrust legislation, failure to protect consumer interests, vague and inconsistent objectives, capture by interest groups and trade unions, overstaffing, poor coordination, and lack of effective control by the legislature, the courts or the responsible minister. Majone concludes (1996, p. 23):

> The great paradox of nationalization is that public ownership has weakened, instead of strengthening, the regulatory capacity of the state. By confusing the roles of manager and regulator, and effectively subordinating the latter to the former, public ownership has impeded the development of specialized regulatory institutions.

Even defenders of public enterprises concede that there is substance to many of these criticisms. Self (1993, p. 216) reports that state-owned banks in Australia suffered disastrous consequences in the 1980s when they strayed from their traditional role as conservative lenders for housing, small business and public works and engaged in speculative and rash lending. Stretton and Orchard (1994, p. 88) refer to public housing in the US, the UK and Australia in the 1950s and 1960s when the public enterprises concerned failed to consider adequately, let alone consult with, the very people who would be expected to live in the high-rise ghettoes that became a symbol of that period. Ernst (1994, p. 79) acknowledges that the industries nationalized by Thatcherism were strongholds of a trade union movement which had used its monopoly negotiating power to win award improvements without any necessary corresponding increase in productivity.

Deregulation or re-regulation?

Since the early 1980s, public enterprises around the world have been largely abandoned by governments of all political complexions and have been dismantled, disaggregated and sold off to an eager private sector. The term applied to this process is *deregulation*, signifying the liberalization of markets (by introducing greater competition into the market) and the reduction or elimination of government rules and regulations constraining competitive markets. For many governments, the idea of deregulation – with its implication of government relinquishing control – has undoubted appeal. Even a country like the US, traditionally seen as a country of minimal government, experienced extensive deregulation in the transport, energy, finance, agriculture and telecommunications sectors in the late 1970s and early 1980s.

However, it is not apparent that deregulation necessarily equates with less regulation. Niskanen (1999, p. 319) observes that declining regulation in some aspects of the US economy has been accompanied by increasing regulation in other areas of economic activity, citing occupational health and safety, the environment and employment relations as examples. Even within specific areas of economic activity, it is debatable whether deregulation has led to less regulation. According to Kay and Vickers, deregulation more often than not leads to 'new and generally more explicit regulatory structures simultaneously erected in place of what went before' (1990, p. 223). Moran and Wright support this view, arguing 'that the creation of an economy in which free exchange and private property are supreme demands an extensive apparatus of state power'. In their view, 'the "freer" the economy the more extensive and powerful the state has to be' (Moran and Wright, 1991, p. 243). Vogel's study of regulatory reform in the United Kingdom and Japan provides further support for the argument that deregulation has not resulted in less regulation but *re-regulation* – or 'the reformulation of old rules and the creation of new ones' (1996, p. 3). In Vogel's study, the United Kingdom and Japan were found to have reorganized their control of private sector behaviour, but not to have substantially reduced the level of regulation. This was because creating more competition in previously highly regulated markets inevitably led to the creation of more regulations. So far from facilitating the retreat of the state, regulatory reform 'has involved a fundamental restructuring of the core functions of the state: finding new ways to raise revenue and to service debt, and developing more effective mechanisms of policy implementation' (Vogel, 1996, p. 269).

Responsive regulation – an alternative approach to regulation?

As many of the economic reforms promoted by governments since the 1980s illustrate, the debate about regulation has largely been conducted between those who seek greater regulation of economic activity and those who would prefer to see less. In the rhetoric of this debate, regulation is effectively a zero-sum game. To Sparrow, deregulation represents 'yet another swing of a now familiar regulatory pendulum' between two apparently irreconcilable regulatory styles – one adversarial and punitive and the other more inclined to persuasion and negotiation (2000, p. 34). However as Sparrow and others argue, the one extreme of the regulatory pendulum need not rule out the other, and the swinging of the pendulum is not necessarily inevitable.

One alternative to the conventional view of regulatory policy is suggested by the advocates of 'responsive regulation' (Ayres and Braithwaite, 1992). According to the supporters of responsive regulation, regulatory institutions must be moved away from 'the simplistic and mechanistic models of economic rationalism, legalism and government command and control' (Braithwaite, 1993, p. 97) to adopt a more versatile and constructive approach to their role. Central to this is the progressive application of a graduated hierarchy of responses to non-compliance which is represented by the pyramid in Figure 4.1.

According to Braithwaite (2006, p. 886):

> ... our presumption should always be to start at the base of the pyramid first. Then escalate to somewhat punitive approaches only reluctantly and only when dialogue fails. Then escalate to even more punitive approaches only when the more modest forms of punishment fail.

Several assumptions underpin this approach. First, for every object of regulatory intervention there must be more than one regulatory mechanism so that the weakness of one may be complemented by the strength of another. Underpinning this approach is the conviction that 'regulatory agencies are best able to secure compliance when they are benign big guns' (Ayres and Braithwaite, 1992, p. 19). Second, the cheapest and most respectful option (self-regulation) should always be considered and used where possible.

Figure 4.1   Hierarchy of responses to non-compliance

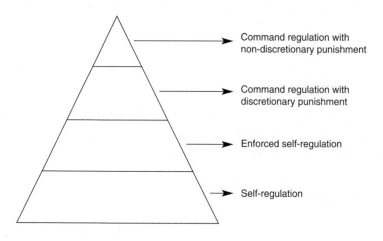

Command regulation with non-discretionary punishment

Command regulation with discretionary punishment

Enforced self-regulation

Self-regulation

Source: Ayres, Ian, and Braithwaite, John (1992) *Responsive Regulation: Transcending the Deregulation Debate* (Oxford and New York: Oxford University Press), Figure 2.3, p. 39. By permission of Oxford University Press, Inc.

Third, those who are regulated should be required to comply only with a just rule or standard.

With its emphasis on trust, transparency and professionalism, responsive regulation represents an attractive alternative to 'the polarised choice between punishment and persuasion' (Healy and Braithwaite, 2006, p. S56). However, as Sparrow argues, 'carefully structured sanctions' will not always decrease the risk of law-breaking and other strategies must also be considered. These include (Sparrow, 2000, pp. 42–3):

- tri-partism – involving non-government entities in the regulatory process;
- information strategies – the communication of risks and risk factors to affected parties and to others in a position to bring pressure upon them to act in a socially responsible way;
- self-regulation – allowing regulated parties deemed relatively trustworthy to conduct and report upon their own audits and inspections, subject to some risk of verification;
- positive incentives – influencing behaviours within and beyond

the scope of regulations by the use of praise, prizes, awards, and marketing advantages arising from government approval;
- use of negotiated rule-making procedures – which focus on establishing consensus early to avoid conflict later;
- partnerships – between and among regulators, industries, industry associations, communities, advocacy groups and other government agencies.

To Sparrow, 'regulators face no shortage of strategies, methods, programs and ideas. Rather, they face the lack of structure of managing them all' (2000, p. 49).

Conclusion

In many countries it is no longer automatically accepted that regulation is always in the public interest. As a consequence, there has been much deregulation of markets and privatization of economic activity previously undertaken by the state. However, it would be a mistake to interpret regulatory reform as evidence that governments are now regulating less. Although it is probably true that regulation is greeted with more scepticism than in the past, governments continue to regulate and to do so 'in the public interest'. To many, the perspective represented by Stigler and Friedman is simply too extreme, relying upon an imperfect marketplace to safeguard the community's interests.

The challenge for both business and government in the twenty-first century is not, then, to abolish regulation but to make it more effective. The massive experiment of extensive state intervention through public ownership has been largely discarded and anti-competitive restrictions and industry-specific regulation have generally lost favour. With these changes, new forms of regulation have emerged. Where governments once attempted to regulate prices, products and services through direct production and provision, they now rely increasingly upon regulatory regimes to monitor the performance of private firms. For the time being at least, it would seem that is where the future of regulation resides. But this shift alone will not guarantee success. Effective regulation demands a balance between an array of competing interests – persuasion and force, punishment and forgiveness, voluntary compliance and state intervention, customer service and mission accomplishment, delegation and control, discretion and obligation, to name but a few. The enduring challenge for both business and government is to somehow reconcile these interests.

Chapter 5

Competition Policy

Introduction

Competition policy is an important, if contested, area of govern-ment–business interaction. At its broadest, it is the use of govern-ment laws or regulations to force or encourage competition to occur in the private marketplace. Competition policy can be defined as 'those policies and actions of the state intended to prevent certain restraints of trade by private firms' (Doern, 1995, p. xi). Without competition policy, its advocates argue, firms would collude; behave in a predatory manner or merge with com-petitors, all with the aim of reducing competition and keeping prices and profits high. Competition policy operates at the very border between government and business, with government action being intimately concerned with the operations of the market. Its role can become controversial, with businesses not always particu-larly happy with the way competition authorities go about their work. Not surprisingly, businesses and business groups often object to the results of particular cases and to restrictions on their freedom of action.

The contest over competition policy is given extra spark by there being no consensus within economics as to the desirable scope of government actions to force private businesses to compete. It is noteworthy that competition laws have extended their applicability in recent decades at the same time as there have been attempts to generally reduce economic regulation due to theoretical change and the problems of over-regulation. This is somewhat paradoxical. How is it possible to justify, on the one hand, deregulation and, on the other, an increase in regulation? If we have a free-market system, what is wrong with letting it work?

It is usually assumed that competition is the driving force leading to greater efficiency in market systems and, therefore, policies that enhance competition should be good for the consumer and the economy. At the same time, many economists argue that the biggest constraint on markets is the dead hand of government. Some argue that all regulation imposes costs and competition policy is just another form of regulation and is inherently ineffective. There are arguments that markets themselves sort out the problems of cartels or other forms of concentration, and that competition policy by an individual government is not needed if there is free trade between nations. Some argue that competition policy leads to a decline in national competitiveness, if it means, for example, that firms are prevented from merging to acquire the necessary economies of scale or scope to compete internationally. Critics of competition policy claim that such action is unnecessary, that markets are robust and competition works its magic by itself, and that monopolies or cartels fall apart even without ill-conceived competition laws.

On the other hand, advocates of competition policy argue that without government action private markets will seek ways of avoiding competition and only government, through the legal system, can achieve genuine competition in the marketplace. There are many examples from business history of collusion and monopoly leading to higher prices for consumers. In the late nineteenth century, Jay Gould and other 'robber barons' colluded through trusts that controlled a large part of the American economy. At the same time, John D. Rockefeller and his Standard Oil company managed to corner the market in oil in the US – owning three-quarters of the entire industry – before being broken up by government action. It seemed that only government action could deal with this form of capitalism and the antitrust movement in the US led to the Sherman Act of 1890.

Competition policy is becoming more of an international phenomenon. There have been some conflicts over merger policy between the EU and the US, with the former being more willing to oppose mergers even between US companies if they have an effect on competition within the EU. Rather than signalling a new era of competition, it could be argued that globalization will lead to the dominance of international cartels in some products and only by governments getting together can consumer interests be protected.

The policy area is a contested one, even if there are, in general, better arguments in favour of competition policy than against. Recent years have shown increased attention being paid to governments intervening in markets to make competition actually occur. The existence of laws regulating business behaviour in this sense can be seen as giving confidence to the citizens that the market system operates in a fair and reasonable manner.

The problem of competition

A free-market system is based on several premises, one of which is that competition between providers will drive down prices, force competitors to provide better services and increase innovation, all to the benefit of consumers. In the real world it does not necessarily work like that. There are many instances where a business facing a difficult competitive environment will find it more advantageous to get together with its competitors and agree to fix prices or to engage in a merger or other anti-competitive practices than to compete vigorously. As Graham and Richardson (1997, p. 11) argue:

> No firm prefers competition in its output market. However successfully competition may deliver efficiency and fairness to a market system as a whole (sellers, buyers, and final consumers), each firm would rather have less competition as a seller; a monopoly would be most preferred. This is true of market-leading firms and for those hanging on for survival.

A business faced with a need to ensure its survival will look at any legal alternative including that of reducing competition.

In 1776, in *The Wealth of Nations*, Adam Smith noted there was a propensity for businesses to collude or restrict the extent of real competition that they face. As he argued (1976 [1776], p. 144):

> People of the same trade seldom meet together, even for merriment and diversion, but the conversation ends in a conspiracy against the public, or in some contrivance to raise prices. It is impossible indeed to prevent such meetings, by any law which either could be executed, or would be consistent with liberty and justice. But though the law cannot hinder people of the same trade from sometimes assembling together, it ought to do nothing to facilitate such assemblies; much less to render them necessary.

The first sentence of the quotation from Smith is often cited as it shows that businesses are likely to collude. The remainder is quoted much less often, but points to the real and enduring difficulties in doing anything about the conspiracy against the public.

Smith argues that meetings of people from the same trade cannot be prevented as the law to do so could not be executed and would not be 'consistent with liberty and justice'. The remainder of the quotation counsels government to avoid assisting such meetings, 'much less to render them necessary', presumably by not agreeing to, or not imposing, some kind of statutory monopoly on a trade. Smith sums up the problems very well. Without government action business will collude in a 'conspiracy against the public' and to the likely detriment of the whole market system. On the other hand, laws regulating business conduct cannot be so onerous that they threaten liberty and justice.

Doing something about competition inevitably becomes a matter of action by government. What competition policy seeks to do is recognize that businesses will collude if allowed and then try to do something about it through the imposition of laws. Those who complain most vociferously about restrictions argue that their liberties are being infringed and have a point consistent with that made by Smith. However, governments could argue that business freedom is not an untrammelled right. Although the government extends protection to the market, this does not mean that the market can do anything it wishes. After all, competition policy is a relatively light form of regulation compared to alternatives such as nationalization.

The aim is to make the market work better, not to supplant it; to make businesses actually do what they are supposed to, which is actively compete. There are other benefits, as the European Commission (2000, p. 4) argues:

> The competition policy implemented by the Commission and by the Member States' authorities and law courts aims to preserve and develop a state of effective competition in the common market by impacting on the structure of markets and the conduct of market players. Requiring firms to compete with each other fosters innovation, reduces production costs, increases economic efficiency and, consequently, enhances the competitiveness of the European economy, particularly *vis-à-vis* its main trading partners. Firms stimulated by competition thus offer products and services which are competitive in terms of price and quality.

Governments cannot allow the perception that the market is biased in some way. Consumers will not support a market and economic system they regard as being unfair. One of the main features of a free-market system – and a generally positive one – is that of 'creative destruction' and the freedom to fail. The costs of failure are high, even the jobs of managers may be at stake and a company facing difficulties is more likely to try to reduce its effective competition if that is possible. This is likely to mean that without government regulation, companies may form cartels, restrict access to their products and fix prices. Competition policies around the world 'seek a blend of efficiency and fairness in their markets' (Graham and Richardson, 1997, p. 8). They may or may not be justifiable in terms of economic theory, and the particular circumstance would need to be looked at. But the market system itself requires political support in order to persist. Competition policy can help to do this.

The beginnings of competition policy

Statutes prohibiting monopolies go back as far as ancient Babylon. In the fifth century AD the Eastern Roman Emperor Zeno 'prohibited and exiled monopolists in terms remarkably similar to those used in modern statutes' (Clark and Corones, 1999, p. 1). The Tang Code in China in the eighth century AD prohibited a buyer or seller from creating a barrier to entry or fixing or misrepresenting prices (Liu, 1995). In 1602, under English law, a monopoly granted by the Crown for the importing, making and selling of playing cards was found to be invalid; and in 1759, an agreement between salt producers to fix prices was found to be unlawful. And, as already noted, from the late eighteenth century, Adam Smith and others were well aware of business attempts to avoid competition.

In the modern era, the US was not the first Western industrialized nation to enact legislation to prevent firms from forming agreements in restraint of trade. That honour belongs to Canada in 1889, although the Canadian legislation could not be considered a great success. It was rarely enforced, with only nine criminal merger cases laid between 1910 and 1986 and with none being successful (Goldman, Bodrug and Warner, 1997, p. 50). The US was, however, the first country to take competition policy seriously.

The Sherman Act in the US

In the late nineteenth century, large 'trusts' – cartels by another name – used their market power to restrict competition and raise prices. Seventy-one industries in the United States were so organized into trusts as to have no effective competition, including not only the well-known examples of steel and oil, but also lead, rubber, paper, chemicals, tobacco products, bricks and leather (May, 1997, p. 43).

Following political agitation from groups such as farmers, particularly affected by hikes in freight rates for rail transport, the Sherman Antitrust Act was passed in 1890. There were two key provisions of the Act:

1. Every contract, combination in the form of trust or otherwise, or conspiracy, in restraint of trade or commerce among the several States, or with foreign nations, is declared to be illegal. Every person who shall make any contract or engage in any combination or conspiracy hereby declared to be illegal shall be deemed guilty of a felony.
2. Every person who shall monopolize, or attempt to monopolize, or combine or conspire with any other person or persons, to monopolize any part of the trade or commerce among the several States, or with foreign nations, shall be deemed guilty of a felony.

The penalties were a 'fine not exceeding $10,000,000 if a corporation, or, if any other person, $350,000, or by imprisonment not exceeding three years, or by both said punishments, in the discretion of the court'. Speaking to Congress in favour of his Bill, Senator Sherman argued (*Congressional Record*, vol. 21 (1890), p. 2457):

> If anything is wrong this [industrial combination] is wrong. If we will not endure a king as a political power we should not endure a king over the production, transportation, and sale of the necessaries of life. If we would not submit to an emperor we should not submit to an autocrat of trade, with power to prevent competition and to fix the price of any commodity.

The Sherman Act is clearly broad in its sweep. By deeming combination – forming a cartel – a felony and with the potential for very high fines and terms of imprisonment any offence was clearly regarded as a very serious one from the start.

The Sherman Act was somewhat vague, but its intent and framework still stand today. Although there was no administrative mechanism for enforcement until the Clayton Act was passed in 1914, restraint of trade and monopolization were thenceforth regarded as illegal. The Clayton Act also increased the scope of the Sherman Act by making some mergers, price discrimination and interlocking directorships unlawful if they substantially lessened competition (Trebilcock, 1998, p. 91).

Restraints on trade

National laws differ, but there is general agreement as to the practices that are to be declared against the law. Among the practices outlawed by the Sherman and Clayton Acts were resale price maintenance; price fixing by cartels, and mergers resulting in a substantial lessening of competition. The European Commission points to four areas of action: the elimination of agreements which restrict competition, and of abuses of a dominant position; the control of mergers between firms; the liberalization of monopolistic economic sectors such as telecommunications, and the monitoring of state aid. The last point is really in response to the EU's own circumstances and is not a general part of competition policy. The following are more generally regarded as the main parts of competition policy.

Price agreements

This area includes a wide range of possibilities including outright collusion and price-fixing. Price agreements are where competitors get together to restrict competition. They may make an agreement to fix prices or form a cartel. A single firm in an industry is able to make greater profits, so if an agreement can be made between the competitors to collude and raise prices it may be possible for all in that industry to gain the benefits. The intention is to make an agreement to reduce competition and to make greater profits for all the participants.

Price-fixing and cartels are generally prohibited by the competition policies of different countries. The offences listed in the

Canadian Competition Act include 'conspiracies, combinations, agreements or arrangements to lessen competition unduly in relation to the supply, manufacture, or production of a product' (Canada, Consumer and Corporate Affairs Canada, 1992, p. 18). This sets out quite concisely what is involved in price agreements. These are universally regarded as detrimental to the operations of the market and the discovery of such an agreement would, by itself, be evidence of breaking the law. Where other parts of competition policy might allow some discretion by the regulator, this is not the case with regard to price agreements in their various forms.

Competition authorities may set up mechanisms, such as in Europe, where firms in an industry may seek an exemption from prohibitions but this is unusual.

Misuse of market power

This is where a firm uses its market power in order to damage a competitor or prevent one from entering its market. Misuse of market power could arise where the dominant player in a market acts in such a way as to stifle effective competition, for example by lowering its prices below cost to drive a competitor out of business and then increase them again when effective competition has gone. Misuse of market power is difficult to determine in practice, as it can be hard to distinguish between vigorous and desirable competitive activity and economically inefficient and monopolistic practices which are undesirable. Firms do attempt to outperform competitors in a manner which, if successful, could have adverse consequences for those competitors. A new and better product might put competitors at a disadvantage or in extreme cases even put them out of business, but that is not necessarily the sort of conduct which should be prohibited.

Misuse of market power involves conduct which exceeds the limits of vigorous competition, and can thereby entrench a firm's market position to the detriment of the competitive process. It is, in practice, difficult to define 'excessive' conduct, in predatory pricing or refusal to deal. This has not stopped regulators from doing so in particular instances.

In 1998, the US Justice Department brought a case against software provider Microsoft over misuse of market power and a ruling was made against the company two years later. The court found that Microsoft had misused its position by neutralizing competitors through making its internet browser available free of charge. It was not so much the dominant position of Microsoft that led to the case but rather allegations about its conduct towards competitors. In 2001, the case was overturned on appeal and, following some undertakings by the company, the Justice Department announced it would no longer be seeking to break it up. In practice, misuse of market power is difficult to prove. Although Microsoft products dominated software for the personal computer market, this could be argued to be merely the result of a good product becoming dominant and to be not related to illegal market conduct at all.

Unlikely agencies can become involved in competition policy actions. In France in 1993 an appeals court found that the National Weather Bureau had abused its dominant position by refusing to supply a potential competitor with meteorological data. In Australia, the Bureau of Meteorology similarly attracted attention by its decision to provide a free service in colour weather information as this was seen as an abuse of market power.

Resale price maintenance

This practice involves individual suppliers seeking to force distributors or retailers to charge fixed prices for their products. Resale price maintenance is the practice whereby a supplier requires retailers to sell at or above a minimum price and has been associated with collusive retailing practices and the raising of consumer prices. It is not at first glance obvious why a supplier would wish to do this, given that the supplier would normally be thought to want to increase sales, and dictating prices after the wholesale stage by nominating a retail price would not maximize sales. But there are some reasons given for the imposition of minimum resale prices. The producer may wish to have some control over the retail price that is charged by the dealer and this can be a way of protecting retailers from competition. Producers may wish to refuse to supply goods unless the retailer agrees to charge the final price the producer wishes to maintain, and could do this prior to legislation prohibiting the practice. Resale price-fixing may be a form of price-fixing in an industry, although it may be argued to enable better service provision through after-sales service. Certain luxury items might be regarded as more exclusive if they are not discounted. In 1996, in Australia, a men's clothing manufacturer, importer and wholesaler specified minimum prices below which certain lines of suits could not be sold or advertised for sale and was fined for resale price maintenance.

There are generally no good arguments for resale price maintenance; it stifles discounting by retailers, and, it follows, reduces competition in the economy. Dictating of the final sale price by manufacturers or wholesalers means that competition is not occurring throughout the economy. The practice was prohibited in the UK in 1964, fifty years after the United States, and in Australia in 1971.

Mergers

Mergers need to be examined as part of competition policy as they may have the effect of reducing competition. If firms that are dominant are permitted to merge without restriction they may be able to become effective monopolies or, at least, monopolies for a time and able to charge higher prices. On the other hand, there can be advantages for firms in merging by gaining economies of scale. Part of the logic of a market system is that poorly performing firms should face the possibility of being taken over; the threat of merger can be a way of improving the performance of management. But mergers may also be anti-competitive if the merged firm is sufficiently large to have a degree of market power.

Merger policy needs to allow the possibility of takeovers if they are in the public interest, but not if they go so far as to significantly reduce competition. This is clearly not easy to do, and when prospective mergers occur there is a lot at stake for the various parties. The wording of the relevant statute is crucial in deciding the point beyond which a merger is regarded as being against the public interest. International treatment of mergers is evenly divided between a 'substantial lessening of competition' test and a 'market dominance' test. In the United States, the Clayton Act of 1914 uses the words 'substantial lessening of competition' and some other countries use the same phrase, such as Australia and the UK, while others in Europe use the words 'market dominance'. In Germany, for instance, the Cartel Office can prohibit mergers that create or strengthen a dominant position. It is easier to show that competition will be reduced than it is to make a case that a merged entity will be dominant. In the United States, mergers which substantially lessen competition are prohibited, unless authorized. In New Zealand, mergers which result in or strengthen a dominant position are prohibited, unless authorized. In the UK mergers are dealt with administratively and may be prohibited where found to be contrary to the public interest, having regard to matters such as competition, consumer interests, efficiency, regional employment and export growth. In Canada mergers may be prohibited if they are likely to prevent or lessen competition substantially, but will not be prohibited if they are likely to bring about efficiency gains which outweigh any lessening of competition.

In Australia, the Trade Practices Act of 1974 originally used a 'substantial lessening of competition' test. In 1976, following a change to a conservative, more business-friendly government, the test was changed to 'market dominance' and several mergers occurred in airlines, retail shopping and newspapers which would probably not have been allowed under the 'substantial lessening of competition' test. With a further change of government the wording was changed back to the original.

It is usual for there to be a threshold established for concentration in a market beyond which a merger may not be permitted. In some countries mergers may need to be notified to the regulator and permission may be sought.

Regulation of natural monopolies

As argued earlier (Chapter 3), natural monopolies arise in markets where an established provider can provide service to a new customer at a lower price than any new entrant to the industry can. In many countries, natural monopolies – electricity, gas, water supply – were often provided by governments through public enterprises. The first wave of privatization in the 1980s led to the realization that merely changing ownership did not by itself provide for competition to occur in such industries and that there still needed to be regulation. Industry-specific regulation of the former public enterprises in the UK was widely seen as a failure as the regulator tended to become captured by the industry being regulated. In Australia, where privatization occurred later, the regulation was provided through the general competition policy regulator and generally worked better than did the industry-specific kind of regulation.

Consumer protection

Another role for competition authorities can be to provide for protection of the consumer. Instances of misleading behaviour have often led to political demands to set in place fair-trading laws. The role of competition authorities is to make rules for the provision of information, as part of the general policy of allowing competition to occur. Advertising should not be misleading. If claims are made in advertisements they need to be substantiated. Advertising cannot misrepresent the price at which a product is sold and also, if being sold at a bargain price, it needs to be available in reasonable quantities so that a retailer cannot advertise a product at a very low price and a potential buyer finds that there are insufficient stocks. Also, if prizes are available in a promotion then information about the chances of winning and the total value of prizes needs to be made available. The safety of some products is also an important consideration – children's clothing which readily catches fire or toys with small parts, or even food or food additives that can be lethal to those with allergies – and laws exist essentially to provide information. The labelling of the contents of food is required by law in some countries, with the United States for one requiring quite stringent listing of food contents.

Without such laws there would always be some companies that would perceive an advantage in being misleading, and while companies may prefer to not comply, the requirements are not usually a major burden. There can be more prescriptive consumer protection laws that the trader must satisfy, or less prescriptive fair-trading laws which 'merely outlaw misleading or deceptive information to allow the consumer to make a rational judgement – the "*caveat emptor*" approach' (Bollard and Vautier, 1998, p. 127).

Penalties

Even if there are laws against anti-competitive conduct, they can be ineffective if not implemented or if penalties are low. It could be less costly for a company to deliberately flout the law and to take its chances on not being found out, or of paying relatively low fines if they are prosecuted. The US Sherman Act did provide for jail terms but this was generally unusual among countries and, indeed, it was rare in that jurisdiction that such a penalty was invoked.

In recent years, competition authorities have persuaded governments to increase penalties and have more vigorously enforced the penalties already in place. In October 1996, a prominent US agribusiness company agreed to pay \$US100 million in fines for participating from 1992 through 1995 in a conspiracy to fix the prices of its lysine and citric acid products. An FBI informer for the case recorded one of its executives saying, 'Our competitors are our friends, our customers are the enemy' (*The Economist*, 31 October 2002). Later two senior executives went to jail.

In 2001, manufacturers of vitamins in an international cartel were fined €900 million for price-fixing, after an investigation involving competition authorities from a number of jurisdictions. The cartel had earlier been fined in America, and several executives had served time in American prisons. In Germany, a price-fixing cartel for cement incurred fines of €700 million in 2003. And in changes announced in 2000, the European Commission has the power to levy fines which may be as much as 10 per cent of the firm's worldwide turnover (European Commission, 2000, p. 9). It is increasingly that case that executives and individual company directors face prison if they participate in cartels.

The increase in penalties is such that engaging in anti-competitive activity is risky for both companies and individuals. As *The Economist* (18 April 2002) notes:

> Bosses beware: price-fixing and other dodgy dealings are under fire from governments everywhere, as regulators cast a wider net for culprits ... The costs of collusion should make any boss think twice, though ... Dawn raids are running at about one a month in the European Union. In America, fines are based on the size of the market affected, but private lawsuits can be far more costly: Sotheby's was hit by a $45m fine by the American government, but its customers' lawsuits have cost it hundreds of millions more.

Such high penalties and prison terms for individuals should mean that executives will rethink any strategy involving anti-competitive conduct. In addition, competition authorities are using a leniency policy, meaning that penalties can be waived for the first member of a cartel to become an informer on the other members. This increases the risk in engaging with other firms to form a cartel. Even having a meeting with executives from another firm in the same industry could be risky, as not only is there a chance that emails, phones or the meeting itself are under surveillance, but, in addition, the executives present from the other firm might already be informers for the competition authority.

National differences

From differing views about competition policy, the different national approaches have largely converged. The US has the longest case history of antitrust. Antitrust has had somewhat inconsistent application depending on the attitude of particular governments to such questions. Antitrust policy in the US was introduced for political reasons, not economic ones as the apparent power of cartels 'resonated badly against a political philosophy with uniquely deep roots in America' (Scherer, 1994, p. 21). For a long time the basic principles of antitrust were generally supported, but from the 1970s they came under attack as part of the movement against government intervention of any kind, as will be discussed later.

In the Reagan years there was less enforcement than either before then or since, but from the Bush, Senior presidency onwards antitrust activity returned. There was some revival during the Clinton years, the most celebrated case being that of Microsoft, and in the second half of the Clinton years a very active approach from the Department of Justice. In the US, governments have generally recognized that antitrust policy does have public support.

Antitrust policy over the years has had powerful effects in controlling collusion, stopping cartels, preventing anti-competitive mergers, eliminating resale price maintenance, and encouraging entrepreneurship. Then, too, the antitrust laws have constituted a formal expression by the American government that the interests of the people come before those of any company, however powerful (McCraw, 1997a, p. 330).

Not only is there public support for the US antitrust enforcers but 'in general they have managed to move toward outcomes that have been economically effective' (McCraw, 1997a, p. 330). Other developed countries did not follow the US example until much later. Their different experiences and more recent convergence point to the need for effective competition policy becoming recognized in different countries.

In Germany, for instance, cartels were actively encouraged by governments for a long period of time. From around 1870 to 1945, much of German industry was organized around cartels. The cartels had three goals: '(1) to ensure producers an "adequate" return on their investments by avoiding "excessive" competition; (2) to coordinate supply and demand ... and (3) to represent the marketing interests of the industrial sector as a whole' (Fear, 1997b, p. 148). They were found to be legal, with the highest German court ruling in 1897 that 'cartels did not violate the right of other parties to do business' and 'interpreted the freedom to do business as the right of business to be free from interference by the state in a classical, liberal sense' (Kuhn, 1997, p. 116). Combinations were allowed as a way of increasing economies of scale and competition with the companies of other countries.

Cartels were linked to industry protection in Germany. Using high tariffs against external competition, cartels could maintain artificially high domestic prices while 'engaging in virtually unlimited exports to foreign markets' even at prices below domestic costs of production in some circumstances (Cameron and Neal, 2003, p. 243). Cartels became an instrument of government policy, including during the period of the Nazis in the 1930s. After World War II, the occupying powers set out to break up the cartels, not only to emulate US antitrust law, but also to 'curtail the political power of German industry, which was seen as detrimental to the development of a democratic political system' (Kuhn, 1997, p. 117). Fear also argues that the strength of most cartels should not be exaggerated as in practice they were 'neither monopolistic nor particularly solid' and did not prevent competition. As he argues (Fear, 1997b, pp. 148–9):

> Even within cartels, industrialists could still attempt to increase the differential between cartel-set prices and production costs through greater economies of scale and scope, or higher technical efficiency, or both. Cartel members haggled over quota shares, chased after productive efficiency, and attempted to reduce transaction costs arising from the cartels that they had erected themselves. German industrialists and bankers largely considered cartels 'children of necessity' designed to save entrepreneurs from 'ruinous competition'.

In 1957, cartels were prohibited in West Germany and controls placed on firms with dominant market position. In 1973 a further Act prohibited collusion and resale price maintenance, and instituted controls over mergers.

The German experience makes it more difficult to argue that competition policy is unnecessary. Allowing cartels was tried in effect and failed; companies did find it easier and more profitable to collude but at a cost to the consumer. In 1997 there were still more than 300 legal cartels (Kuhn, 1997, p. 124). Since 2002, though, in part due to the need to implement domestically European Commission policy on competition, the Federal Cartel Office has become much more like a competition authority in other countries.

The UK provides an example of a country where competition policy laws were enacted but rarely and only half-heartedly enforced, at least until recently. As Wilks argues (1999, p. 339):

> The theoretical underpinnings of policy were virtually absent in the 1940s and competition was regarded with scepticism or even hostility. In the 1990s economic theory was host to several schools of thought about competition and there was a widely shared commitment to free competition in an open economy. The theoretical and economic environment had been transformed. In the 1990s competition policy had become a constituent of the British market economy and a defining feature of the new, post-Thatcher, form of British capitalism.

The Fair Trading Act was passed in the UK in 1973 but was not very effective. Only after 1998, when a new Competition Act was passed designed to work with European law, could the UK be argued to have joined the ranks of countries serious about competition policy. The 1998 Act prohibited agreements which restrict competition and set in place substantial penalties of up to 10 per cent of turnover.

Australia's experience is similar to that of the United Kingdom in that it took a long time to enact serious competition laws. There were some early attempts at passing legislation in the 1960s, but business lobby groups stopped these. Business was uncompetitive and many industries operated agreements that effectively fixed prices. In 1961 there were over 600 trade associations in Australia of which an estimated 58–66 per cent operated restrictive trade practices (Australia, Independent Committee of Inquiry into Competition Policy in Australia, 1993, p. 9). Many industry associations set prices for their members; discounting was rare as retail prices were fixed. In 1974, the Trade Practices Act was passed and with similar provisions as those in the United States, although enforcement was more consistent.

Like the United Kingdom, though, it took many years for the benefits of competition to become accepted even within the business sector.

Many of the issues around competition policy are the same ones argued about for more than a century. It is the case, however, that the historical record does show what can happen in the absence of laws to force competition to occur. Compared to business in the US, Germany showed some of the costs associated with a system of cartels; the UK showed that ineffective legislation was almost as bad as none, while after 1974, Australian business had to change its ways quite dramatically. In the US, as Adams and Brock argue (1994, p. 508):

> The trust movement demonstrated that, as a system of governance, the competitive market is neither a self-perpetuating nor an immutable artefact of nature. Without strictly enforced rules of the game, the competitive market can be subverted from within – through agreements not to compete, as well as through consolidations of industrial control in the hands of dominant firms and private power complexes.

There has been substantial convergence over competition policy in more recent years. European Union provisions are comprehensive and have been important in reducing barriers between its constituent nations, as well as requiring national governments to adopt the same, quite stringent, standards.

There even seems to be at least impressionistic evidence that countries with good competition policy prosper more than those where this is not the case. Also, the transition to market economies in Eastern Europe following the fall of communism showed the need for good institutional arrangements in order for markets to function optimally. Monopolies and collusion did spring up in Russia, rather than genuine competitive markets. It does appear that institutional safeguards, including adequate competition policy, are needed for markets to work well.

International competition policy

Monopolistic practice is more easily found within a given nation. Indeed, opening a national economy to international competition can reduce the need for competition authority action in many

Box 5.1   Competition policy in Europe – a coordinated approach

While all members of the European Community have their own competition authorities, the European Commission established the European Competition Network (ECN) in order to strengthen the development and enforcement of competition policy within the EC's (then) 25 members. A discussion forum that encourages cooperation between competition authorities, the ECN addresses competition policy issues in the areas of antitrust, mergers, cartels, liberalization, state aid, and international cooperation. The Network's discussion of these policy areas spans a number of sectors: agriculture, consumer goods, energy, financial services, motor vehicles, professional services, and sports. As well as identifying common policy concerns within these sectors, the ECN aims to encourage consistent application of competition legislation within the European Community, foster information-sharing among members, and provide assistance with investigations into suspected anticompetitive practices.

Source: http://ec.europa.eu/comm/competition/index_en.html.

areas. Freer trade in goods and services may mean that international competitors appear for the most concentrated of industries. Trade can be an alternative to competition policy in areas that are able to be traded; some goods may be uneconomic to trade through their size or weight or if consumer preferences are entrenched. If an industry is open to international competition those pressures by themselves may be enough to obviate oversight by competition regulators. However, in some industries there are relatively few players and competition may decrease; in some products there can be international cartels; there can be international mergers that are anti-competitive and against the public interest.

The most famous international cartel is OPEC, the association of oil-producing exporters. It was formed in 1960 to 'to coordinate and unify petroleum prices among Member Countries, in order to secure fair and stable prices for petroleum producers; an efficient, economic and regular supply of petroleum to consuming nations; and a fair return on capital to those investing in the industry'. Originally it had five members – Iran, Iraq, Kuwait, Saudi Arabia and Venezuela – and in 2007 had 12 members with 40 per cent of the world's crude oil and 55 per cent of the crude oil traded internationally (OPEC, 2007, p. 13). The history of OPEC shows both the positive and negative aspects of international cartels. At times of strong demand OPEC countries have been able to keep a higher share of the money earned from oil than they did in the past. However, in times of lower demand it has been difficult to maintain discipline within the cartel and to agree on reductions in production.

Over recent years there has been more of what could be termed international competition policy where the competition authorities of different countries act together. It is already the case that mergers of US companies – approved in the US – have been opposed by competition authorities in Europe. Competition policy authorities cooperate to overcome the formation of international cartels (see Box 5.2).

In 2000, investigation of auction houses Christie's and Sotheby's involved authorities in the US, UK and Europe. In August 2007, a US court accepted an agreement made between the Department of Justice and British Airways and Korean Air, where the two airlines pleaded guilty and were sentenced to pay separate US$300 million criminal fines for their collusion over passenger fuel levies and cargo rates. This case was one where there was transatlantic cooperation between the UK and US authorities. In addition to the fines, passengers would be able to sue the airlines for damages estimated at a further £300 million. Virgin Atlantic, which revealed the conspiracy in return for not being prosecuted, still faced class actions from its passengers.

Within the EU, competition policy has the role of enforcing the common market itself (see Box 5.1). For example, the vehicle manufacturers Opel and Volkswagen were prosecuted for putting in place systems that made it difficult for consumers in one European country to buy their vehicle in another. This role of competition policy reinforces the political decision made to remove impediments to cross-national trade within Europe. The rules against some forms of state aid in the European context are similar in their aim.

Criticisms of competition policy

For a long time the basic principles of antitrust were generally supported in the United States, even though, as noted earlier, they were little used in other countries. Competition rules were thought

Box 5.2   The International Competition Network

Launched on 25 October 2001, the International Competition Network (ICN) is a network of competition authorities and competition experts representing numerous jurisdictions. Senior antitrust officials from Australia, Canada, the European Union, France, Germany, Israel, Italy, Japan, Korea, Mexico, South Africa, the United Kingdom, the United States and Zambia established the group, which now comprises 80 member states.

The ICN addresses issues around antitrust enforcement and competition policy, with an emphasis on international cooperation and increasing consistency of approach. Its members meet as part of working groups to develop recommendations regarding issues of common concern, and agree on 'best practices'. Competition authorities in member countries then decide whether and how to implement these. Current working groups of the ICN focus on: cartels, competition policy implementation, mergers, and unilateral conduct by large corporations.

Source: www.internationalcompetitionnetwork.org.

to be a reasonable compromise between allowing the market and companies to do what they would wish and the wider public interest. However, with the demise of Keynesian economics in the 1970s and the rise of neoclassical economics, competition policy began to be questioned anew in the United States. Big business had never been happy with what it saw as restrictions placed on its freedom of action by unwarranted government attention. With the new economics making similar assertions, theoretical arguments emerged to back up this view.

In the 1980s, notably in the United States during the Reagan era, the 'Chicago economists' – named after the University of Chicago where some such as Stigler and Friedman were professors – achieved some prominence in policy circles and, as a result, antitrust policy was little enforced for a time. As Trebilcock (1998, p. 93) argues of these theorists:

> They argued that the purpose of antitrust policy should be to maximize efficiency; other goals of social policy should be pursued, if at

all, through other instruments. As a result of this efficiency-oriented analysis, corporate concentration and mergers leading to high levels of concentration were viewed as likely to reflect, or to be likely to realize, superior efficiencies, while many vertical and some horizontal arrangements that had been condemned in the past were viewed by the Chicago School as socially desirable.

There are three main arguments made against competition policy or antitrust policy. First, a firm with market power was argued to have achieved that by its superior efficiency. Chicago School economists argued that the existence of monopoly is relatively uncommon and does not justify government regulation. Monopolies were argued to only arise through government action in creating them, not through free-market activity. They also believed in free trade. If there were monopolies in particular markets, opening the area to international players would provide competition without government involvement being necessary. Mergers were argued to allow better managers to take over and should not be restricted. They also argued that market entry is not difficult and that large scale or size was a sign of efficiency not of anti-competitive practice.

Second, a related argument is that markets are resilient rather than fallible, and the distortions that result from monopolies or effective monopolies are rare and do not deserve the full weight of the law. In Chicago School economic theory a monopoly does not last long before competitors arise; the opportunity to gain excess profits attracts other players. Even if there is one supplier high prices can be deterred merely by the chance that a competitor could appear. Cartels are unstable in theory as it is necessary to restrict supply in order to keep the price high, but to voluntarily restrict supply can be difficult for any one of the participants who has an incentive to break the agreement.

For example, at the end of the 1970s, the Hunt brothers' attempt to corner the world silver market resulted in higher prices to start with, but then increased production from new or previously marginal mines led to the Hunts eventually going broke. Only by controlling production can a cartel work. Even then it is very hard to keep such a grouping together. The Chicago critics may have a point when they say that markets are resilient. As Stigler argued, 'More and more economists have come to believe that competition is a tough weed, not a delicate flower' and 'the enthusiasm for antitrust has diminished, although it has not disappeared' (1988, p. 104).

Third, and perhaps as a part of the return to the wisdom of Adam Smith favoured by many of the Chicago group, the argument was made that intervention by government in the market is against the principles of liberty and justice. As this argument applied to all government intervention, it also needed to be made against competition policy, which was to be regarded as wasteful, unnecessary and against economic freedom and property rights. As Armentano argues (1994, p. 932):

> The economic and normative case for free markets without any antitrust regulation grows stronger. Since the laws inevitably interfere with the discovery and dissemination of market information, they must tend to make the competitive market process less efficient. And since the laws inevitably interfere with individual property rights and voluntary exchange, they must restrict liberty and freedom. In short, antitrust regulation appears to have lost all of its claim to political legitimacy. In a rapidly changing information and technological world, with an inevitable internationalization of markets, the burden of proof is clearly now on those who would retain the law to demonstrate why all antitrust regulation should not be abolished.

There are criticisms of competition policy, and markets are strong, at least up to a point. But the economic argument against competition policy has not been substantiated. Competition authorities have found their actions supported by the courts and in the even more important court of public opinion. The existence of economic arguments against competition policy does mean, however, that competition authorities do not have untrammelled freedom of action.

Arguments in favour of competition policy

Despite the criticisms within the economic literature, recent years have seen more concerted competition policy rather than less. It was noted earlier that competition policy is controversial; it is a contested area of government involvement, despite the theoretical (and ideological) arguments coming from economics. There are three main arguments in favour of competition policy.

First, perhaps the main reason for having competition policy is that markets are not infallible. It can be as profitable for business to collude with rivals, or buy them out, as to compete with them. A free-market system relies on relentless competition to drive efficiency by business and to respond to consumer preferences. Competition is fundamental to a market system and to private enterprise so, to the extent that competition is constrained by collusion, the free market must be less effective than if there really was competition.

The ideal of perfect competition is difficult to find in real markets. It occurs when there are many producers, free entry into and exit from the market, identical products, and where there is perfect information for both sellers and buyers. In the real world such conditions are rare and, although the interactions in less than perfect markets are studied, there is likely to be a need for some action to make sure that competition actually occurs. Government is the only player that can insist, through its monopoly on laws, that competition be real. As perfect competition is hard to find, competition policy can be used to make businesses operate with a reasonable level of competition.

In real markets, as opposed to theoretical ones, unlimited competition can lead to there being one player. It is also possible for competition to cease through merger or collusion. There is ample historical evidence for both of these eventualities. Perhaps a truly competitive market is '*not* an immutable artefact of nature' and does not always perpetuate itself as it is 'susceptible to destruction from within by private interests who chafe at its discipline, who refuse to submit to its control, and who aspire to arrogate its planning function unto themselves' (Adams and Brock, 1989, p. 4). From this perspective, government action preserves competition and the market system and leads to better aggregate economic outcomes than would its absence.

A second argument used to justify competition policy comes from empirical work on the sources of business and national competitiveness. Porter (1998) found that companies facing strong domestic competition were then able to be more successful in international competition. Business had often argued for there to be 'national champions' in some industries by allowing companies to merge to create a single large company that would be able to compete on the world stage. Porter argued against this. It was vigorous domestic competition – between, for example, camera and consumer electronics companies in Japan, luxury cars in Germany, pharmaceuticals in Switzerland – that equipped companies to become vigorous competitors internationally. It followed that the competitiveness of a nation requires strong competitive companies in the domestic market supported by competition policy. As he argued (Porter, 1998, p. 189):

> Deregulation and privatization on their own, however, will not succeed without vigorous domestic rivalry. That requires, as a corollary, a strong and consistent antitrust policy. A strong antitrust policy – especially for horizontal mergers, alliances and collusive behaviour – is fundamental to innovation. While it is fashionable today to call for mergers and alliances in the name of globalization and the creation of national champions, these often undermine the creation of competitive advantage.

Porter argued that governments should promote competition by disallowing mergers, acquisitions and alliances. His work on competitive strategy was very influential in providing intellectual support for countries to strengthen their competition policy. In addition, competition policy can be linked to trade policy, with several WTO agreements containing provisions related to competition law.

The third argument in favour of competition policy is that a market system will not work without broad political support. If there is a demand to restrain business in some way, for it to be 'fair' whatever that means, politicians need to respond. There is no basis for the strict separation of business and government. They are not separate entities at all. Markets rely on the system of law, especially contracts, provided by government. Individual property rights are not sacrosanct – they are subject to government and operate within governmental rules. As Eisner (1991, p. 237) argues:

> Most arguments regarding antitrust reform (and deregulation in general) rest on a false distinction between a naturally efficient and responsive market and an inefficient and inflexible bureaucratic state. Whether markets function efficiently is not determined by whether or not they are free from state intervention, since this 'intervention' provides the very foundation for market transactions.

The best argument for the existence of competition policy is that it can assure the general community that business is operating within the rules provided by society. The original antitrust laws in the US in the 1890s came about as the result of dissatisfaction within the wider community; by combinations and other anti-competitive practices, businesses were not actually competing with each other. And, without vigorous competition, 'the private sector probably would not attract and maintain sufficient public support for its continuance' (Weidenbaum, 1995, p. 157). Should the perception arise that markets are unfair or biased in some way, that the ordinary consumer's interests are not being served, there will be political demands to make markets work. As Wilks argues, 'competition policy has made a minor contribution to the efficiency of the economy, but a major contribution to the legitimacy of the market' (1999, p. 346). This is no small achievement.

Arguments about *caveat emptor* or the folly of hobbling companies with competition policy requirements miss the key point that the market system needs continuing support from the populace. In turn, competition policy as a political instrument needs to be reasonably limited in scope in order to maintain support in the business community. As Trebilcock (1998, p. 89) argues:

> Competition policy is ... primarily concerned with protecting consumer welfare, not with preserving some given state of competition or number of competitors. Conceived of as consumer protection legislation, competition laws should not be encumbered with other policy objectives such as protecting small business or industrial policy concerns such as promoting 'national champions'. This view of the purposes of competition policy has now won wide acceptance amongst antitrust scholars and enforcement authorities in the United States, Canada and the European Union ... This has been an important advance over earlier and widely divergent understandings as to the purposes of competition policy.

Competition policy has become harmonized in large measure. There might be differences of detail but not of kind in the competition policy statutes in different jurisdictions. The more than a hundred years since the Sherman Act have been years of policy learning.

Conclusion

Competition policy has become more important in recent years as other regulatory regimes have been reduced. There has been some impact on policy from the critiques of the Chicago economists even if their precise recommendations have not been followed. It is often the case that cartels break down on their own, and, providing there is free entry into and exit from markets, monopolies are rare. Granting favoured companies a statutory monopoly – by law there will be no competitors – is now rarely used as a policy. However, despite these points there is no diminution in the need for competition policy.

The best argument for competition policy is that the market system is itself a political creation and, as such, depends on public support for its continuance. If there is a demand to restrain business in some way, for it to be 'fair' whatever that means, that has to be lived with. But by the same token, competition policy and its agencies operate in a political environment as well and will be constrained if they go too far.

In many sectors and in many markets, competition does occur. In others competition occurs only through intervention by the government. Competition policy provides a compromise. Government can regulate markets at relatively small cost to itself, given that competition authorities are relatively small, and by forcing competition to occur the community at large can gain benefits.

Chapter 6

Competitiveness

Introduction

Each year two significant reports on international competitiveness are published. One is the *World Competitiveness Yearbook* released by the International Institute for Management Development (IMD), a business school based in Lausanne, Switzerland. The other is the *Global Competitiveness Report*, published by the World Economic Forum (WEF), a Geneva-based foundation best known for its annual meetings of the rich and powerful. Prominently featured in both reports is a competitiveness index or 'scorecard', ranking selected countries on the basis of criteria broadly linked to economic performance. According to one observer, the concern with competitiveness, as exemplified by the production of these and other 'scorecards', has 'spawned a large industry aimed at policy makers, analysts and enterprises ... feeding an insatiable appetite for benchmarking competitive performance and providing guidelines for strategy' (Lall, 2001, p. 1501).

The existence of competitiveness 'scorecards' undeniably promotes the idea that nations compete against each other in economic terms in much the same way the East and the West once competed militarily at the height of the Cold War. To put it another way, the 'scorecards' suggest that competitiveness is a zero-sum game – that one nation's improvement is at the expense of another's. But does the concept of economic competition between countries make sense? Michael Porter, internationally renowned as a commentator on competition, acknowledges that 'while the notion of a competitive firm is clear, the notion of a competitive nation is not' (1998, p. 158). Krugman (1994b, p. 44) goes even further, arguing that 'competitiveness is a meaningless word when applied to national economies'.

But the debate about competitiveness tends to overshadow a much more fundamental issue – namely, that competitiveness now

114

predominantly refers to *productivity*. In this sense, the current focus upon competitiveness is essentially concerned with achieving competitive advantage through improvements to productivity. This chapter discusses why competitiveness 'has become one of the central preoccupations of government and industry in every country' (Porter, 1990, p. 1), the significance of productivity and the role of business and government in creating and improving economic performance.

What is competitiveness?

Competitiveness in relation to business is relatively straightforward. As Krugman observes (1994b, p. 31):

> The bottom line for a corporation is literally the bottom line: if a corporation cannot afford to pay its workers, suppliers and bondholders, it will go out of business. So when we say a corporation is uncompetitive, we mean that its market position is untenable – that unless it improves its performance, it will cease to exist.

Competitiveness in relation to nations, on the other hand, is more problematic. In contrast to private firms, countries, regardless of their financial travails, 'do not go out of business' (Krugman, 1994b, p. 31). So if competitiveness in relation to nations does not refer to financial survival, what then can it mean? Porter, who acknowledges that there is no accepted definition of competitiveness as applied to a nation, concludes that 'the only meaningful concept of competitiveness at the national level is national productivity' (1990, p. 6). There is little disagreement from Causa and Cohen (2006, p. 15):

> A company can be less competitive than another and be under threat from bankruptcy because, for example, its cost structure prevents it from keeping up with its direct competitors. A nation, in contrast, can always devalue its currency to restore its 'competitiveness' in relation to its costs. What counts is its productivity, which is to say the volume of goods produced by its inhabitants. From this point of view, the only ranking that counts, if any ranking is really required, is that of productivity.

The distinction between the competitiveness of a firm and that of a country had been noted by the *Report of the President's Commission on Competitiveness* (1984, cited in Cohen, 1994, p. 195), prepared for the Reagan administration:

> Competitiveness has different meanings for the firm and the national economy ... A nation's competitiveness is the degree to which it can, under free and fair market conditions, produce goods and services that meet the test of international markets while simultaneously expanding the real incomes of its citizens. Competitiveness at the national level is based on superior productivity performance.

This focus upon productivity – 'the value of the output produced by an input of labour or capital' – is echoed by the WEF which refers to competitiveness as 'that set of factors, policies and institutions which determine the level of productivity of a country' (2006, p. xiii). The significance of productivity is promoted by the OECD which also defines competitiveness as 'the degree to which a country can, under free and fair market conditions, produce goods and services which meet the test of international markets, while simultaneously maintaining and expanding the real incomes of its people over the longer term' (1992, p. 237). This linking of competitiveness to rising living standards is reiterated in the EU definition of competitiveness as 'a sustained rise in the standard of living of a nation and as low a level of involuntary unemployment as possible' (European Commission, 2001, p. 9). The IMD also links competitiveness to living standards, defining competitiveness as 'the facts and policies that shape the ability of a nation to create and maintain an environment that sustains more value creation for its enterprises and more prosperity for its people' (International Institute for Management Development, 2006). The consistent motif that emerges in all these definitions is *productivity*, so perhaps the last word should go to Boltho (1996, p. 5) whose advice is 'to avoid the word competitiveness and concentrate on the word productivity'.

How is competitiveness achieved?

Originally, competitiveness between nations was understood in terms of relatively static or passive factors – land, location, natural resources (such as minerals and energy), labour and population size. Ricardo's theory of *comparative advantage* attempted to explain how and why one country could be more successful than another in the production of a particular good. According to this theory, relative efficiency led a country to increase production and trade in the areas where that relative efficiency, or comparative advantage, applied. This increased production was also associated with specialization, which in turn enhanced productivity. More recently, other factors more amenable to human influence have been identified as explanations of competitiveness. As Porter (2001, p. 22) reports:

> Competitiveness is rooted in a nation's microeconomic fundamentals and manifested in the nature of company operations and strategy and in the quality of the microeconomic business environment.

Porter thus sees microeconomic phenomena, government policy and management practices all having the potential to impact upon national competitiveness. This view has proved to be extraordinarily persuasive. Many if not most countries now have councils and boards responsible for advising government upon competitiveness and how it can be improved. Implicit in the role of these bodies, which usually bring together representatives of government, business, labour and academia, are two key assumptions. The first is that the economic competitiveness of a nation matters, and that the relative standing of a nation cannot be ignored or dismissed. The second is that government – rather than business – now plays a critical role in shaping national competitiveness.

The imperative of national competitiveness is now widely accepted. According to Causa and Cohen (2006, p. 13), 'a country's industrial productivity is one of the key determinants of its prosperity'. They calculate that 'poor countries are four times less productive than rich countries' (p. 29). High productivity can thus be linked to the redistribution of national income to the young, old, disabled and unemployed, the alleviation of poverty, the promotion of employment and even economic democracy. Prestowitz (1994, p. 188) argues that 'loss of economic competitiveness can weaken national security and cause greater vulnerability to political regimes and cartels that may severely constrain a country's economic potential'. With such high stakes, it is little wonder that 'competitiveness has become one of the central preoccupations of government and industry in every nation' (Porter, 1990, p. 1) or that there should be such intense interest in competitiveness and how it can be achieved. The *World Competitiveness Yearbook* identifies ten 'golden rules' that governments must follow if they are to sustain and enhance national competitiveness (IMD, 2000):

1. Create a stable and predictable legislative environment
2. Work on a flexible and resilient economic structure
3. Invest in traditional *and* technological infrastructure
4. Promote private savings and domestic investment
5. Develop aggressiveness on the international markets (exports) as well as attractiveness for foreign direct investment
6. Focus on quality, speed and transparency in government and administration
7. Maintain a relationship between wage levels, productivity and taxation
8. Preserve the social fabric by reducing wage disparity and strengthening the middle class
9. Invest heavily in education, especially at the secondary level, and in the life-long training of the labour force
10. Balance the economies of proximity and globality to ensure substantial wealth creation, while preserving the value systems that citizens desire

All of these are fairly self-explanatory – with the exception, perhaps, of the tenth with its reference to 'economies of proximity and globality'. An economy of proximity provides goods and services close to the end user, such as construction, health and education. Many of the jobs in this economy add social value but have little mobility. In an economy of globality factors of production need not be close to the end user. The economy of globality has much more to do with the differing comparative advantages of countries and the impact of this upon performance and productivity. Thus 'balancing the economies of proximity and globality' refers to a country's need to balance that part of the economy which mainly generates employment and social cohesion with that part that mainly generates revenues and technology.

The essence of the IMD's ten 'golden rules' is also to be found in the nine 'pillars of competitiveness and productivity' promoted by the WEF: institutions, infrastructure, macroeconomy, health and primary education, higher education and training, market efficiency, technological readiness, business sophistication, and innovation. Both the IMD 'rules' and the WEF 'pillars' imply that competitiveness is largely a product of government, whose policies create 'a friendly business climate, supportive of private sector activity' (World Economic Forum, 2006, p. xiii). The global proliferation of national competitiveness councils and committees would seem to explicitly accept that there is a role for government in national competitiveness. But what should this role be? When establishing his Presidential Commission on Industrial Competitiveness in 1983, the late President Reagan was very clear about what government should and should not do (Reagan, 1983):

> Now some believe that the Government should try to read ... trends to determine which products, services and industries have a place in our future and which do not. They would have government planners divert resources away from traditional industries and channel them into new fields. But the history of progress in America proves that millions of individuals making decisions in their own legitimate self-interest cannot be out-performed by any bureaucratic planners. Government's legitimate role is not to dictate detailed plans or solutions to problems for particular companies or industries. No, government serves us best by protecting and maintaining the marketplace, by ensuring that the rules of free and fair trade, both at home and abroad, are properly observed, and by safeguarding the freedoms of individual participants.

President Reagan's point was that while the role of government is crucial, firms also play a critical role in gaining competitive advantage. As Porter (1990, p. 71) argues, it is firms, rather than nations, that trade. Competitiveness thus requires strong, world-standard firms:

> Firms gain competitive advantage where their home base allows and supports the most rapid accumulation of specialized assets and skills, sometimes due solely to greater commitment. Firms gain competitive advantage in industries when their home base affords better ongoing information and insight into product and process needs. Firms gain

competitive advantage when the goals of owners, managers and employees support intense commitment and sustained investment. Ultimately, nations succeed in particular industries because their home environment is the most dynamic and most challenging, and stimulates and prods firms to upgrade and widen their advantages over time.

For Porter, competitive firms are essential to the competitive advantage of nations. Of course, government policies contribute considerably to competitive advantage. Education policy, tax policy, health care policy, antitrust policy, regulatory policy, environmental policy, fiscal and monetary policy – all of which are set or influenced by government – are all relevant to the economic performance and competitive advantage of individual firms. Clearly then, both business and government are critical to national competitiveness.

Porter's diamond

To illustrate his argument that competitive advantage can be created, Porter employs a diamond to represent the environment in which all firms operate (1990). The four points of the diamond – factor conditions; demand conditions; the strategy, structure and rivalry of firms; and related and supporting industries – summarize the key determinants of the comparative advantage of firms. Each of them can be created or at least significantly influenced by government. *Factor conditions* such as skilled labour, capital and infrastructure are created not inherited. *Demand conditions*, in which the more demanding the customers a firm has the more likely it is to improve its competitiveness through innovation and better quality products, are also amenable to external influence. *Firm strategy, structure and rivalry* are influenced by the conditions in which firms operate and the belief that it is competition, or rivalry, that impels firms to increase productivity, innovation and quality. *Related supporting industries* are those upstream or downstream industries which have the capacity to promote exchanges of ideas and innovations.

Porter's diamond, which emerged from his study of ten leading trading nations and the successful industries within them, asserts that the sustained economic success of some countries has little to do with the passive factors traditionally ascribed to comparative advantage. Instead, a far more complex interplay of factors is involved in the creation of competitive advantage. Far from denying a role for government, Porter's diamond promotes a role for government as both catalyst and challenger, encouraging and pushing firms to higher levels of competitive performance.

As discussed in Chapter 5, one of Porter's more contentious propositions relates to domestic rivalries. According to Porter, economic reforms such as deregulation and privatization will fail without strong domestic rivalry supported by a strong and consistent antitrust (or pro-competitive) policy. Going against the tide of popular opinion in at least some smaller countries, Porter stands firm in the face of those who argue for the emergence of 'national champions', arguing 'real national competitiveness requires governments to disallow mergers, acquisitions and alliances that involve industry leaders' (1998, p. 189).

While critical of some aspects of government regulation and intervention (such as overlapping authorities and inconsistent policies), Porter envisages a proactive role for government in creating competitive advantage, which challenges the more conventional view that governments should effectively allow markets to operate with minimal intervention. For Porter, the agenda of nearly every government agency touches upon national competitive advantage in some way, although as he observes, it is the principal agenda of few bodies in most governments. However, the adoption of pro-competitive policies in the years since Porter's landmark work does suggest that the diamond framework and the theories that accompanied it have had a significant impact.

The role of the competitiveness 'scorecards'

The interest in the *World Competitiveness Yearbook* and the *Global Competitiveness Report* relates primarily to the rankings these reports give to an ever-increasing number of countries. These rankings emerge from the application of complex methodologies involving a range of quantitative and qualitative criteria. In each case, advanced industrial economies dominate the top end of the rankings, with less developed economies clustering at the bottom. Box 6.1 explains in greater detail the workings of both the IMD and the WEF scorecards.

With the scorecards, one country's movement up the rankings comes at the expense of another country. For those that move up, the point of the scoreboards is clear. Upward mobility sends out an

Box 6.1   The IMD 'World Competitiveness Yearbook' scoreboard and the WEF Global Competitiveness Index

How is competitiveness defined?
The IMD assesses data on economic performance, government efficiency, business efficiency, and infrastructure in order to determine an overall competitiveness ranking on its World Competitiveness Scoreboard. The WEF takes a similar approach, considering institutions, infrastructure, macroeconomy, and market efficiency, but also evaluates data in a number of additional categories: health and primary education, higher education and training, market efficiency, technological readiness, business sophistication, and innovation.

Who is ranked?
Since its publication of the inaugural *World Competitiveness Yearbook* (WCY) in 1989, the IMD has been assessing data on economic performance, government efficiency, business efficiency, and infrastructure in order to determine an overall competitiveness ranking on its scoreboard. The numbers of countries participating in the *Yearbook* varies from year to year. In 2007 all OECD countries participated, plus: Argentina, Brazil, Bulgaria, Chile, China Mainland, China Hong Kong, Colombia, Croatia, Estonia, India, Indonesia, Israel, Jordan, Lithuania, Malaysia, the Philippines, Romania, Russia, Singapore, Slovenia, South Africa, Taiwan, Thailand, Ukraine, Venezuela. The WEF's Global Competitiveness Index also ranks these countries, but includes a further 70 nations, comprising developing economies from Africa, Central and South America, South East and Central Asia, as well as the Middle East.

implicit but none the less powerful endorsement of that government's macro and microeconomic policies, public institutions, and business environment and practices. Governments and their agencies eagerly seize upon high scorecard rankings or upward movement in the rankings as approbation of their economic management and policies, as the case study in Box 6.2 illustrates.

If a high ranking or upward movement on a scorecard is taken as proof that a country's economic policies are working well, a low

Which countries are the most competitive?

There has not been much movement in the top ten rankings in the WCY over recent years. Since 2004, the US has held the number one ranking, Singapore has remained in the top three, and Denmark, Hong Kong, Iceland, Canada and Luxembourg have all been ranked within the top ten most competitive countries. In contrast, the United Kingdom has spent the past four years ranked at or just below 20, and France, Spain and Italy have consistently ranked below 25, lower in fact than a number of developing countries. The WEF's ranking does not differ significantly – the United States, the Nordic countries, Singapore and the Netherlands remain at the top of the index.

The top ten ranked countries in the 2007 WCY scoreboard and the 2007 Global Competitiveness Index are listed in the accompanying table – a ranking of 1 indicates that a country has been assessed as the most competitive, and so on.

WCY scoreboard 2007 rankings (2006 ranking in brackets)		WEF Global Competitiveness Index 2007 rankings (2006 ranking in brackets)	
1 United States (1)	6 (8)	1 United States (1)	6 Finland (6)
2 Singapore (3)	7 Iceland (4)	2 Switzerland (2)	7 Singapore (7)
3 Hong Kong (2)	8 Netherlands (15)	3 Denmark (3)	8 Japan (8)
4 Luxembourg (9)	9 Sweden (14)	4 Sweden (4)	9 UK (9)
5 Denmark (5)	10 Canada (7)	5 Germany (5)	10 Netherlands (10)

Source: IMD (2007) *World Competitiveness Yearbook*. Geneva: IMD, www.imd.ch/research/publications/wcy. Copyright © IMD 2007.

Source: Porter, Michael. E., Schwab, Klaus and Sala-i-Martin, Xavier (eds) (2007) *The Global Business Report 2007–2008*. Basingstoke: Palgrave Macmillan. Reproduced with permission of Palgrave Macmillan.

ranking or downward movement is generally considered to indicate an underlying concern or weakness in a country's economic circumstances. With the very specific data presented in the yearbooks, it is possible in many cases to pinpoint the cause of the declining ranking on the scorecard. Changing demographics (such as an ageing population), political instability, labour market shortages or any other obstacle to growth can be identified as causes of declining competitiveness.

Box 6.2   Marketing competitiveness – a case study

The Australian government's foreign investment agency, Invest Australia, extensively cites the *World Competitiveness Yearbook* to promote foreign investment in Australia. Promotional material published by this agency asserts that:

• Australia has been ranked the most resilient economy in the world for 5 of the past 6 years (*WCY*, 2007).
• Australia has been ranked in the top three countries in the Asia Pacific region for its economic competitiveness (*WCY*, 2007).
• Australia has the lowest risk of political instability in the region and 4th lowest in the world (*WCY*, 2007).
• Australia is ranked third in the world for understanding by political parties of today's economic challenges (*WCY*, 2007).
• Australia's justice system has been rated second best in the region (*WCY*, 2007) and its competition legislation has been ranked fifth best in the world for facilitating competitive business (*WCY*, 2007).
• Australia ranks second in the world for the effective supervision of the management of companies by corporate boards (*WCY*, 2007).
• Australia ranks first in the region and third globally in managing shareholder value efficiently. It also ranks third in the world for the ethical practices of companies (*WCY*, 2007).
• Australia ranks first in the Asia Pacific region for labour, agricultural and industrial productivity per person employed (purchasing power parity) (*WCY*, 2007).

Source: Invest Australia (2007)

In recent years, more countries have been added to the competitiveness rankings. Many of these countries do not have highly developed economies and languish at the bottom of the scorecards. Sri Lanka was included in the WEF's *Global Competitiveness Report* for the first time in 2002 when it was ranked 61st out of 75 countries on the Growth Competitiveness Index and 57th on the Current Competitiveness Index. Some might question the value of a country participating in a process when it has such an outcome, but the proponents of competitiveness rankings disagree.

According to Walker, 'Sri Lanka's low rankings should not lead to despair, but should provide added incentive for the country's leadership to more thoroughly understand policy issues and implement effective reforms' (2002, p. 10).

The *Global Competitiveness Report* analysis of Sri Lanka's performance indicators highlighted a number of policy reform issues and recommendations derived from the indicator rankings including (Walker, 2002, p. 10):

• Urgently regaining control of the government deficit and debt to reduce the risk of financial instability and economic collapse
• Considering tax and regulatory incentives for technology diffusion through FDI in manufactured exports
• Promoting reverse migration of Sri Lankan scientists and engineers working abroad
• Giving priority to government programmes in support of ICT, reforming regulatory climate in support of increased sector competition, and expanding internet access in schools
• Encouraging continuing support of education and health care as essential investments for broad-based development and poverty alleviation
• Increasing emphasis on port, air transport, telecommunications and infrastructure
• Introducing reforms to deal with lack of judicial independence, weak property rights, favouritism of government officials and organized crime
• Instigating legal or regulatory reforms to reduce bribery associated with tax collection and public utility connections
• Strengthening antitrust enforcement in support of local competition
• Encouraging firms to collaborate as clusters
• Implementing legal and regulatory reforms to promote free-market determination of hiring, firing, salaries and improved labour–employer relations
• Promoting effective and rigorously enforced environmental regulations in support of environmental quality and sustained economic growth

The prescriptive tone of these recommendations and the orthodox economic thinking they reflect highlight a contentious aspect underpinning the competitiveness rankings. To their supporters, the scorecards and their accompanying reports simply measure the comparative strengths and weaknesses of national economies and recommend suitable strategies to address any deficiencies and improve overall performance. To put it another way, they give governments in countries that are ranked low a freer licence to change their policies, while giving governments that are ranked high a justification to continue with particular policy directions (Amsden, 1996). At the very least, according to one supporter, 'public and private sector analysts and decision makers concerned with the various sector reform issues could try to use the indicator rankings as partial guides to determining reform priorities within and across sectors' (Walker, 2002, p. 11). Lall (2001, p. 1505), who is critical of both major scorecards, acknowledges that there is a useful role for competitiveness indices:

> Indices can help policy makers to evaluate the shortcomings of their economies, in the same way that technical benchmarking helps enterprises to assess themselves against rivals and undertake appropriate strategies. Indices can also help investors to allocate resources between countries, researchers to analyse important issues in comparative terms, aid donors and international institutions to judge economic performance, and domestic industries to measure themselves against competitors. The justification for using benchmarks (rather than theoretical norms) is simple: many aspects of performance can only be assessed with reference to actual practice.

But to their critics, the scorecards are seriously flawed. Amsden (1996) argues that the *Global Competitiveness Report* is unduly biased towards Anglo-Saxon assumptions about economic success on the basis that 'the more open a country's markets, the higher its ranking'. Amsden queries why fast-growing economies such as South Korea and China are ranked relatively low on the WEF scorecard compared with countries that are either what she terms 'Anglo-Saxon' (New Zealand and the US), or 'city states that are mainly locations for Western multinationals (Hong Kong and Singapore). She argues that the answer lies at the heart of the *Global Competitiveness Report* and the methodology by which it determines the rankings on its scorecard (Amsden, 1996):

Its 'competitiveness index' is supposed to predict future capacity for growth, not acknowledge past achievements. It does not necessarily give high rankings to countries whose actual 'competitiveness', as that term is usually understood, gained them higher market shares in competitive industries, or created employment and higher wages by successfully introducing new products and processes, and insured price stability and economic expansion by raising productivity.

Amsden dismisses the *Global Competitiveness Report* as a 'fraud', citing 'the lack of association over time between countries' rate of economic expansion, or job creation, or export growth, or rise in per capita income, and their estimated rank' (1996). Amsden may have a point about the ranking of some economies by the scorecards. As the graph in Box 6.3 illustrates, the Chinese economy has grown dramatically over the period 1992–2005. Yet the extraordinary dimension of this growth has not translated into a dominant position for China on the competitiveness scorecards. The 2007 *World Competitiveness Yearbook* placed China 15th in terms of competitiveness, well below such countries as Luxembourg, Iceland and Austria. Its rival, the *Global Competitiveness Report*, assigned China an even lower ranking, putting it in 34th place on the scorecard.

A dangerous obsession?

The most notable critique of the competitiveness scorecards has come from the American economist Paul Krugman. In a landmark essay in 1994, Krugman took aim at the scorecards, arguing that 'the whole concept of competitiveness is at best elusive, at worst meaningless', and concluded provocatively that 'the obsession with competitiveness is both wrong and dangerous' (1994b, p. 30).

Krugman's article challenged the assumptions underpinning the notion of national competitiveness (1994b, p. 30):

> The idea that a country's economic fortunes are largely determined by its success on world markets is a hypothesis, not a necessary truth; and as a practical, empirical matter, that hypothesis is flatly wrong. That is, it is simply not the case that the world's leading nations are to any important degree in economic competition with each other or that any of their major economic problems can be attributed to failures to

Box 6.3   China – three decades of impressive growth

With a current value of US$2.2 trillion, China's GDP is substantially higher than that of most OECD countries, with the exception of the United States, Japan and Germany.[1] Since the late 1970s, China's economic growth has consistently outstripped that of other major economies, including the United States, Germany, Japan and the combined growth of the OECD countries.[2] The accompanying graph illustrates the impressive growth of China's GDP since the early 1990s.

Real GDP growth: average annual growth in percentage, 1992–2005

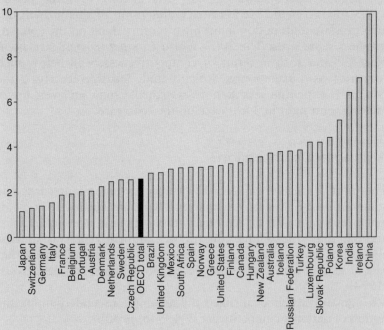

Notes:
1. World Bank. *World Development Indicators database*, accessed April 2007.
2. *OECD Factbook 2007.* © OECD, 2007.

Source: *OECD Factbook 2007.* © OECD, 2007.

compete on world markets. The growing obsession in most advanced nations with international competitiveness should be seen, not as a well-founded concern, but as a view held in the face of overwhelming contrary evidence.

According to Krugman, countries do not compete in economic terms and the struggle to win international markets is not analogous to some form of warfare. As he argues (1994b, p. 34):

> Countries do not compete with each other the way corporations do. Coke and Pepsi are almost purely rivals ... So if Pepsi is successful, it tends to be at Coke's expense. But the major industrial countries, while they sell products that compete with each other, are also each other's main export markets and each other's main suppliers of useful imports. If the European economy does well, it need not be at US expense; indeed if anything a successful European economy is likely to help the US economy by providing it with larger markets and selling it goods of superior quality at lower prices.

International trade, according to Krugman, is not a zero-sum game. When productivity rose in Japan, the main result was a rise in Japanese real wages. American and European wages are in principle just as likely to rise as to fall, and in practice seem virtually unaffected by productivity. While Japanese growth might have diminished US status, this was very different from accepting that it reduced the US standard of living which 'the rhetoric of competitiveness asserts' (Krugman, 1994a, p. 35).

In effect, Krugman was putting forward a classic free-trade view, in which major countries are as likely to be importers as exporters, and often of the same items. Many countries have some form of car manufacturing, while at the same time importing many other makes of cars. Free trade (or a variation of it) offers this choice. Consumers in the UK can choose between UK-made cars (although mostly made by foreign-owned companies), or imported cars from Italy, France, Germany and elsewhere. Some will choose a foreign car rather than a locally made one, but this choice may simply mirror preferences in relation to design and engineering, rather than Britain being competitive or uncompetitive. Consumer preferences for foreign goods can sometimes foster hostility towards foreign competition, but this view may only serve to obscure the real problem (Krugman, 1994b, p. 40):

If you accept the reality that our 'competitive' problem is really a domestic productivity problem pure and simple, you are unlikely to be optimistic about any dramatic turnaround. But if you convince yourself that the problem is really one of failures in international competition ... then the answers to economic malaise may seem to you to involve simple things like subsidizing high technology and being tough on Japan.

For Krugman, there were three inherent dangers in what he saw as the obsession with competitiveness. First, governments could spend money wastefully in efforts to enhance competitiveness. Second, protectionism and trade wars could result, even though (1994b, p. 42):

> Most of those who have preached the doctrine of competitiveness have not been old-fashioned protectionists. They want their countries to win the global trade game, not drop out. But what if, despite its best efforts, a country does not seem to be winning, or lacks confidence that it can? Then the competitive diagnosis inevitably suggests that to close the borders is better than to risk having foreigners take away high-wage jobs and high-value sectors. At the very least, the focus of the supposedly competitive nature of international economic relations greases the rails of those who want confrontational if not frankly protectionist policies.

The third potential consequence of the obsession with competitiveness was that bad public policy could result 'across a spectrum of important issues' (Krugman, 1994b, p. 41). For Krugman, competitiveness is such a poor concept that 'a government wedded to the ideology of competitiveness is as unlikely to make good economic policy as a government committed to creationism is to make good science policy, even in areas that have no direct relationship to the theory of evolution' (1994b, pp. 43–4).

There was, predictably, an emphatic response to Krugman's critique. Prestowitz (1994) challenged Krugman on several points. First, it was entirely possible for international trade to be a zero-sum game. A Saudi order for US$6 billion worth of new planes given to US interests rather than European ones would result in the US gaining jobs and income that Europe might have had but lost. Second, Krugman misrepresented the position of competitiveness proponents on the matter of domestic productivity and ignored the significance of America's imports for the US economy. Third, Krugman underestimated the long-term impact of economic rivalry between nations. Comparing the growth of the British postwar economy unfavourably with that of the US, Prestowitz concluded Britain had 'missed the boat' too many times in commercializing British inventions such as jet planes and radar. It had been the US which had moved quickly to exploit commercial possibilities, with the British losing potential gains in living standards as a consequence. Dismissing Krugman's arithmetic as 'careless and selective', Prestowitz concluded that declining competitiveness did pose a threat to national security and stability, and left a country susceptible to the debilitating consequences of international cartels. As such 'competitiveness, far from being a dangerous obsession, is an essential concern' (Prestowitz, 1994, pp. 188–9).

The link between competitiveness and national security made by Prestowitz was also made by Thurow, who had argued previously that the Cold War threat to the US of military confrontation with the USSR had been replaced by an economic 'battle' between the US, Japan and Europe (by which he meant Germany) (1992). Thurow (1994, p. 192) defended the focus on competitiveness:

> The smart private firm benchmarks itself vis-à-vis its best international and domestic competition. Where it is not the world's best, it seeks to adopt the better practices found elsewhere. A smart country will do the same ... The purpose of such benchmarking is not to declare economic warfare on foreign competitors but to emulate them and elevate US standards of performance. Obsessions are not always wrong or dangerous. A passion for building a world class economy that is second to none in generating a high living standard for every citizen is exactly what the United States and every other country should seek to achieve. Achieving that goal in any one country in no way stops any other country from doing likewise.

There was, however, some support for Krugman. Lall agreed that international trade was not a zero-sum game but something that could benefit all parties, with countries specializing according to their factor endowments. As he saw it (2001, p. 1503):

To focus on competitive gaps in particular activities is partial and mis-leading. Declining US competitiveness in TVs or textiles does not mean that the US economy is less competitive. The decline of these industries may be a manifestation of its changing endowments and a necessary part of resource reallocation from old to new areas of comparative advantage.

However, Lall did not endorse Krugman's scepticism in relation to government's ability to mount selective interventions. Where Krugman had cited unsuccessful US government intervention in semiconductors to argue against strategic trade policies, Lall (2001, p. 1504) noted that evidence did not support such a sweeping dismissal of competitiveness strategy:

> There are many examples in the developing world, particularly in East Asia (and, indeed, in the developed world in its earlier stages of industrialization) of successful strategic intervention. Selective strategies *do* work under specific circumstances, and the rewards in terms of growth and dynamic competitiveness are enormous.

Just as the US, Japan and Europe are no longer 'jousting for economic supremacy' (Thurow, 1992, p. 14), so the debate about competitiveness seems to have receded. But does this mean that debate over competitiveness was, or is, irrelevant? Cohen, who regarded Krugman's critique not as stinging revelations 'but merely oft-repeated truisms' (1994, p. 194), thought the debate was not such a bad thing since it contributed to (p. 195):

> ... a heightened awareness, all to the good, that the United States is no longer supreme, benchmarking is a first step towards serous improvement, and comparative measures – even of economic welfare – have important and legitimate meanings.

For Cohen, the focus on competitiveness posed a sensible question: 'How are we doing compared to the other guys? And why?' (1994, p. 197). Seen in this light, 'competitiveness is a reconsideration of a broad set of indicators, none of which tells the whole story but that together provides a legitimate focus' (1994, p. 197).

Conclusion

Despite more than a decade passing since Krugman's explosive critique was published, there continues to be a very high level of interest in competitiveness and the various competitiveness scorecards. In some respects, the increasing focus upon globalization has only served to reinforce, rather than reduce, notions of competitiveness, and in particular competition between nations. What the US's Council on Competitiveness (1998) documents as the globalization of investment choices, the global availability of human talent, the globalization of demand and the globalization of research, all points to an intensely competitive environment for firms and, for the proponents of competitiveness, nations as well.

In this context, academic debates about whether nations actually compete no longer seem especially relevant. The past emphasis on competitiveness has been effectively supplanted by a focus upon productivity and how it can be enhanced to promote economic well-being in the context of ongoing and increasing globalization. The imperative of improving productivity has now been accepted by both business and government, and the goal of continually increasing productivity pervades much of the relationship between business and government.

Chapter 7

Trade Policy

Introduction

Trade between individuals existed even before there were organized states; before there was any meaning attached to the concept
of a border between states. Once societies became in any way organized, trade occurred in ways quite recognizable as trade in more
recent times. Early empires – Sumerian, Egyptian, Greek and
Roman – were trading empires, precursors of the European maritime empires that date from the late fifteenth century. As Strange
argues, 'trade and war are the two oldest forms of international
relations' (1988, p. 161). And, in the present day, international
trade is central to the interaction of businesses with each other and
with their national governments. Trade has increased faster than
the world economy, almost quadrupling between 1970 and 1997
while over this same period global production only doubled
(Audretsch and Bonser, 2002, p. 5). However, the increases in
trade and the integration of the international trading system have
not been without controversy.

In December 1999, the third ministerial meeting of the World
Trade Organization (WTO) ended in disarray after a series of
violent protests brought the streets of Seattle to a standstill for
more than three days. Protesters representing an eclectic alliance of
environmentalists, organized labour, Third World advocates, civil
society and self-confessed anarchists challenged not only the
authority of the WTO, but the very legitimacy of trade liberalization as a global objective. Inside the meeting room, the situation
for the WTO was little better. Dissension within the ranks of WTO
members meant that the next round of trade talks was delayed. It
appeared that the future of liberalized trade and even the WTO
itself was somewhat clouded, even facing a crisis (Rugman, 2001,
p. 1). The subsequent WTO ministerial meeting was held at Doha
in Qatar in November 2001 – a venue located at some distance

from the centres of protest. Its outcome was rather more positive in starting in train the proposed Doha Round of trade negotiations. However, the fifth ministerial meeting, held at Cancún, Mexico in September 2003, collapsed due to profound disagreements over trade between the rich, developed countries and the developing countries.

After Seattle, meetings of economic ministers faced protests that were often violent – Genoa in 2001, Cancún in 2003, Gleneagles in 2005 – and to such an extent that successive meetings took place in places difficult to get to, such as Doha, or where the governmental apparatus would not tolerate dissent.

How do international meetings focusing upon the intricacies of multilateral trade agreements, and whose activities are normally conducted well away from the glare of the public spotlight, come to be seen as a threat to the environment, labour, food and safety standards and human rights? To the functionaries of the Geneva-based WTO, the debacle in Seattle sheeted home an unwelcome message: economic integration across countries is not universally regarded as the way of the future. There are many in societies who reject the notion expounded by mainstream economists that free trade will bring increased living standards and prosperity to all.

The problems confronting the WTO, an international body with member governments representing most of the nation-states in the world and whose role is to further extend free trade, reflect something of the paradox of the current debate surrounding trade. The vast majority of trade transactions do not involve any national government directly. Trade takes place between businesses or individuals in different countries; it is little more than 'a political accident that governments monitor imports and exports that cross their frontiers more closely than they monitor exchanges that take place within them' (Strange, 1988, p. 165). However, governments have been involved in trade since the beginning of organized nation-states and they remain heavily involved today. Whatever economic theory may argue, trade is, and always has been, intensely political. The circumstances in which businesses may trade with each other across a national border have always been prescribed by either, or both, of the national governments whose citizens or corporations are involved in the transaction. And, as has been demonstrated by the protests in Seattle, Genoa, Cancún and by domestic ructions, international trade can become a significant domestic political issue as well as affecting relations between nations.

Discussions of trade tend to be monopolized by economists, even though much of what actually happens in trade policy falls into the gap between what economic theory postulates and what nation-states actually do. The economic theory of international trade is fairly straightforward, in that it is a rare economist who advocates anything other than unrestricted free trade. But such an ideal has never been seen, nor is it likely, as nations, foolishly or not, against the precepts of theory or not, act to protect their own industries. In the real world of trade relationships between countries, and within countries, political and legal considerations are often more important than the economics. Trade is an important, if difficult, policy area for governments. Some in the society demand unrestricted free trade; others demand protection of domestic industry and restriction of foreign competition on the grounds that the latter may force the closure of domestic businesses, with the loss of jobs. Balancing these conflicting demands is never easy.

Trade and government

It is worth considering why governments feel some responsibility for an activity that is, in essence, part of the private economy. International trade does not take place between governments, or nations. In the abstract, international trade is conceptually no different from domestic trade in that firms or individuals buy and sell goods and services to each other; crossing a border need not be innately important in the transaction. However, there are several reasons why governments involve themselves in matters of international trade.

First, there are legal and jurisdictional issues. National governments have undoubted control over trade, over the circumstances under which goods and services enter and leave the country. Trade that crosses a border must be declared to customs; it can be easily taxed and is more visible than domestic trade. Even if there is no essential difference in the transaction itself, the mere fact of the crossing of a border means that more than one government is affected. The fact that governments have undoubted jurisdiction as they control their borders means that they are necessarily involved in trade; the extent of involvement could vary according to how far a government wishes to exercise its power.

Second, all links with other nations can involve diplomacy. National governments can pass laws for their own jurisdiction, but must rely on forms of diplomacy to influence other jurisdictions. Trade has always been a legitimate topic for diplomacy and international relations. Wars have been fought over trade; disputes between states on trade issues are common, with there being no reduction in trade disputes in the post-Cold War period even between states that are military allies. Even between the European Union and the United States – allies in most senses – there have been trade conflicts over agricultural subsidies, over bananas, hormone-treated beef and many other issues. Such conflicts are common and take up an increased proportion of the time of diplomats. As with the first point, a government can choose how far to exercise its powers over relations with other countries.

Third, governments become concerned about trade deficits. A persistent trade deficit – imports greater than exports – if not addressed can lead to a balance-of-payments crisis. Again, with a floating exchange rate, balance-of-payments crises should not occur. Foreign investment does balance a deficit but at the potential cost of economic sovereignty as more domestic assets pass into the hands of foreigners. There may be flow-on effects on domestic interest rates and other macroeconomic effects.

Fourth, there are issues related to the value of the national currency. The rates at which local currency can be exchanged for foreign currencies is of governmental interest, although with a floating currency there may be little of a direct nature that the government can do. Changes in exchange rates can significantly alter the price of imports and exports and eventually the nation's relative standard of living. A poor trade performance will often mean a decline in the value of the currency while a good one will often mean an appreciation in its value. On the other hand an exchange rate that is too high can lead to uncompetitive industries and higher unemployment. Even if the scope of government is more limited, once a currency is floated, government will remain interested in the exchange rate and how the nation's trade relationships have affected its level.

Fifth, there are taxation matters to consider, for individuals and companies. A large part of international trade – estimated at around 40 per cent (Hoekman and Kostecki, 2001, p. 13) – takes place between branches of the same transnational company. This raises the possibility of tax minimization through transfer pricing, where the company sets the price it charges for its own imports and exports at lower levels in high-tax countries to reduce its overall tax burden. This can affect the domestic revenue in any one country as well as disadvantage purely domestic competitors.

Finally, and most importantly, democratic governments assume responsibility for the prosperity of their citizens. If the paramount responsibilities of government are to defend the nation and provide a system of law, the next must be to maintain a reasonable standard of living. No government could stand idly by while the nation's relative standard of living fell; a governing party is also likely to lose political support in such circumstances. The domestic effects of the nation's international trade are likely to be some of the more important influences on how well the political economy is travelling. Any subsequent policy to deal with a perceived problem might be misguided or incorrect, but no matter how much some economists argue that market forces should prevail, governments will act if living standards decline due to perceived problems with a nation's international trade.

Particular groups may demand political favours because of what is perceived to be their importance to the economy. Groups with concentrated economic interests, such as farmers, often exercise influence over public policy out of all proportion to their numbers (Olson, 1965, 1982). Despite what is usually regarded as a national benefit in participating in international forums to reduce trade barriers, there may be a substantial domestic constituency that objects to such bodies and their influence over domestic economies. These points together mean that, as a national economy becomes more integrated into the international economy, domestic politics is more reactive to international events. To the consternation of many in the society, governments find their domestic powers are limited by their international commitments.

Trade between nations

In practical terms any economy must trade, since it cannot produce all the commodities it needs. Trade can occur between individuals from any area, within a nation or between nations. To begin with, international trade operates the same way as the trade between different parts of the same country. As no nation can acquire all its desired goods from a purely internal market, it makes sense for individuals to buy them from providers in another country.

There are commodities that particular parts of the world specialize in due to the availability of natural resources. No-one in Sweden seriously considers growing coffee or pineapples; farming on Manhattan Island would be quite uneconomic given the price of land. Also, the scale of operations or availability of infrastructure can mean that some parts of the world are simply more suited to some forms of production. It would be unrealistic to imagine that New Zealand could support an aircraft-manufacturing operation capable of building an aircraft like a Boeing 747 at a competitive price. It therefore makes sense for Air New Zealand to buy one from the Boeing factory in Seattle and for the purchase to be balanced by New Zealand's other exports, such as wool and wine.

International trade becomes complicated by all the jurisdictional, exchange rate, taxation and barrier control points mentioned earlier. Still, international trade takes place mainly between individuals and companies, just as in the domestic economy. Before looking at the system of international trade as it now is, it is useful to look at some historical antecedents and trade theories.

Autarchy

Autarchy means self-sufficiency, that is, having a national economy that does not need to trade with others. It requires closing the borders altogether, having a closed economy and only drawing on national resources for everything.

Suppose New Zealand did not trade but still wanted its own aircraft industry. This could only be achieved at high cost, due to the lack of economies of scale. Resources which could be employed in other industries would be virtually wasted on an inherently inefficient one. There have been countries which have tried forms of autarchy, such as those in the Eastern bloc during the period of communist rule, Germany and Italy during fascist rule, Tanzania in the immediate postcolonial period, China from 1949 to 1978, Cuba and North Korea. None of these could be described as complete autarchies, as some trade did occur. However, in each case living standards fell, often quite dramatically.

Two of the most prosperous countries, Japan and the US, have low proportions of imports and exports in their economies. This does not necessarily reflect any closure of borders, but rather that they have economies so large and diverse that they produce most of what they want. However, these two countries are not autarchies, even if they are largely self-sufficient. In such economies, although the amount of trade is not large, the presence of some competition or even potential competition can force domestic industries to be more competitive. But for small countries, autarchy – or even virtual self-sufficiency – is simply not viable. The economy is too small and there are too many goods and services that are not produced at all.

Autarchy is sometimes advocated by those who want a nation's wealth kept within its borders and who are sceptical of the benefits of trade. Environmental extremists are often hostile to trade in principle and sometimes seem to advocate a variant of autarchy in that local sustainability would mean the absence of trade. However, autarchy is not often regarded as a viable solution to societal problems. There are few advantages in this strategy and by most accounts autarchy would lead fairly quickly to a decline in living standards.

Mercantilism

For some two hundred years from around the end of sixteenth century, a nation's trade balance was considered to have a special importance under a theory known later as mercantilism (Hecksher, 1935, 1969). It was thought that the special purpose of trade was for the key nations of Europe – Spain, France and England – to build up a store of treasure, particularly precious metals (gold or silver). This was achieved either by pursuing a favourable balance of trade through regulations such as those requiring goods to be carried in the nation's own ships, or by raiding other nation's stocks and supplies of bullion in the manner of Sir Francis Drake's privateering exploits against the American trade of the Spanish Empire in the late sixteenth century. Large stocks of bullion were seen as the sign of a strong economy, not least because they provided the essential resources for war. The focus of mercantilism was on a state's accumulation of wealth, and the consequent increase in its political power compared to other states. The wealth generated could be used 'to equip armies and navies and thus defeat rivals'; as such, the 'accumulation of wealth made power possible and power led to more wealth' (Overbeek, 1999, p. 1).

European countries enacted various regulations to restrict the loss of gold or silver from the country, in order to enforce strict regulations governing trade for the purpose of benefiting the home government. The English Navigation Acts, for instance, first passed in the fourteenth century and extended after that, required that all goods imported into the country needed to be transported in either English ships or ships from the country where the trade arose. All coastal trade was reserved for domestic ships. The targets of this kind of law were particularly Dutch traders. The aim was not only to strengthen the economy through gaining, or at least not losing, precious metals to pay for freight, but to supply manpower and ships for the navy in case of war.

In the British North American colonies in the late eighteenth century one of these mercantilist rules, the imposition of a tax on tea, became a major rallying point in the dispute leading to the American War of Independence. The Boston Tea Party, by seriously questioning the right of metropolitan nations to regulate their colonial trade, symbolized the beginning of the end of mercantilism.

While plausible at the time, mercantilism makes little sense as an economic doctrine. It has been argued that for Spain in the sixteenth and seventeenth centuries, silver and gold from its American colonies led to inflation and eventual decline rather than enriching the country (Hamilton, 1934). Trade surpluses and political power are not closely linked and there is no innate virtue in gaining bullion or in keeping it within national borders.

The Scottish philosopher David Hume (1711–76) had earlier criticized the illogicality of mercantilism, but the key critique was delivered by a fellow Scot, Adam Smith (1723–90). Smith's *The Wealth of Nations*, published in 1776, the same year as the American Declaration of Independence, criticized the mystique which, Smith argued, wrongly surrounded bullion or treasure. As he pointed out, gold and silver are really no different from any other commodity (1976 [1776], p. 436):

> A country that has wherewithal to buy wine, will always get the wine which it has occasion for; and a country that has wherewithal to buy gold and silver, will never be in want of those metals. They are to be bought for a certain price like all other commodities.

There is great insight in this comment. Smith argued that the close control of trade restricted the expansion of commerce and confined the benefits to a few. Gold and silver did not necessarily benefit the nation that gained them, whereas the free exchange of goods would. Precious metals were not to be valued above all other goods and unfettered trade in all kinds of goods benefited both buyer and seller. He suggested that regulation should be replaced by a system of free trade.

Smith's writings most influenced the expansion of the international trading economy in the nineteenth century, and his ideas still provide the basic intellectual authority for those who believe in free trade and deregulation today. Autarchy and mercantilism are essentially premodern ideas, to be contrasted with that of free trade, which, even if never fully implemented, led to the modern capitalist system.

Free trade

Adam Smith argued that the path to national wealth and prosperity was to encourage individuals to specialize in producing those things for which their talents or resources were best suited, and then to promote free trade, or an unfettered exchange between individuals. He believed that allowing individuals to specialize in producing goods, extending the principle of occupational specialization or the division of labour to the productive process, would increase efficiency immensely. Allowing people to buy and sell freely would be advantageous to both buyers and sellers.

These same principles, he argued, should also be applied to trade between nations. In other words, international trade would be best if there was no essential difference from domestic trade. According to Smith, 'were all nations to follow the liberal system of free exportation and importation, the different states into which a great continent was divided would so far resemble the different provinces of a great empire' (1976 [1776], p. 436). It followed that the best role for government was to stay out of market transactions, either national or international.

The nineteenth century, particularly in Britain, was the highpoint for theories of free trade that became known as *laissez-faire* capitalism. Government stayed out of the market at home and did not intervene in international trade. In what is now seen by some neoclassical political economists as a 'golden age', the century has been represented as one of peace, rising prosperity, and minimal government.

As an economic system, free trade has some undoubted attractions. There is an underlying logic to what is being argued. As Irwin argues (2002, p. 39):

> Free trade contributes to a process by which a country can adopt better technology and exposes domestic industries to new competition that forces them to improve their productivity. As a consequence, trade helps raise per capita income and economic well-being more generally.

But as a political system its efficacy has been more problematic. Free trade is simultaneously praised and yet not followed, usually for political reasons. The unfettered *laissez-faire* capitalism of the nineteenth century is often seen as having led to social problems, many of which subsequently became the focus of the burgeoning state apparatus represented by the welfare state. Despite more recent attempts to roll back, or retrench, the welfare state, governments have never really attempted to stay away from all market transactions, national or international.

Comparative advantage

An important refinement to Adam Smith was the theory of comparative advantage, a theory that arose in the early nineteenth century. Smith had argued that some countries have absolute advantage in some commodities. It was possible, he said, to grow grapes for wine in Scotland by artificial heating, but at thirty times the expense of foreign wine (1976 [1776], p. 480). Trade to exchange other goods for wine therefore made sense. As with Smith's 'foreign' grapes, there are still some commodities in which particular countries have a clear advantage; but absolute advantage does not explain much of foreign trade.

The theory of comparative advantage is usually attributed to David Ricardo (1772–1823), writing in 1817. Using the example of two countries and two commodities – England and Portugal, cloth and wine – Ricardo showed that trade can still occur even if one country has absolute advantage in both commodities. Even if one nation can produce a commodity more cheaply than another, it may still be advantageous to import it as the nation can then specialize in another commodity for which it can receive a higher price.

Comparative advantage was initially based on differences in natural resources and labour productivity between nations. Each country then exports the commodity in which it has a comparative advantage. For example, even if German coal-miners were more efficient than Australian ones, the resources used to mine coal invested in, say, making pharmaceutical chemicals, would earn Germany more. It is in Germany's interests, then, to specialize in chemicals and to import coal from Australia, which also benefits. In other words, international trade 'does not depend on the absolute levels of economic efficiency of the trade partners but merely on the differences in their relative costs of production' (Overbeek, 1999, p. 54).

Ricardo's theory depended on the costs of labour. Under the Hecksher-Ohlin theory of the twentieth century, other factors such as natural endowment, land, and cost of capital can be included along with labour costs. This is a refinement of Ricardo but the principle is the same, that is, trade will occur even when absolute advantage favours the firms and workers of one nation over another. The comparative advantage of the less endowed nation can still lead to it being able to trade.

The theory of comparative advantage explains more trade than simple absolute advantage, but has limits, as will be discussed later. It was originally devised for resource-based trade, but much more trade now is in manufactured commodities without identifiable national advantage, comparative or otherwise. Of course, the theory of comparative advantage has been refined but the basic point still stands – there is much trade that is not explicable by this theory.

Trade theories are still argued about, rather than one superseding another. Autarchy, mercantilism and free trade form part of current debate. Many of the arguments for and against free trade have advanced little since Ricardo. Even autarchy is occasionally advocated. In some respects, theoretical concerns have come full circle. Mercantilism was the first of the modern theories of trade; what has been termed 'neomercantilism' is, in some ways, mercantilism revisited. Like mercantilism, the aim is to benefit the economic conditions of the nation by regulating aspects of foreign trade.

The multilateral system

If one government acts to safeguard its country's trade it can invite retaliation from other countries and a general escalation of trade barriers can occur. Any individual nation may be able to benefit itself to a degree by raising barriers against outside trade, but to the general detriment of the whole trading system. A key reason for the Depression of the 1930s lasting so long was the tariffs raised to very high levels by different nations, mainly in retaliation against others. Instead of assisting local industries, the whole trading system spiralled down, making more people in more countries worse off. If nations act collectively – multilaterally – they can overcome the political problems involved in domestic industries demanding protectionism. If a large number of nations all agree to reduce trade barriers, then all may benefit in the long term.

Bhagwati (1997, p. 18) argues the multilateral trade system operates through

> the rule of law, which means that one does not take the law into one's own hands even if one finds the law to be inappropriate to one's needs; the principle of non-discrimination embodied in the MFN (most-favoured-nation status); and a rules-based 'fixed-rules' approach to trade in place of an outcome-based 'fixed quantity' approach, so that we set the rules and let quantities emerge from the market-place instead of prejudging and prefixing the results of such competition.

Countries agree to abide by their multilateral undertakings, even if rulings go against them. Most-favoured-nation status means that an agreement is open to all other countries on the same basis and cannot be discriminatory. What is established is a rules-based system for trade so that all trade complying with the rules is allowable and nations cannot arbitrarily impose other conditions. These principles started with the GATT and have been continued by the WTO.

The General Agreement on Tariffs and Trade (GATT)

One of the outcomes from the Bretton Woods conference in 1944 (see Chapter 3) was the General Agreement on Tariffs and Trade, more commonly known as the GATT. The delegates recognized that international trade tensions had contributed to instability and that the rapid increase in tariffs in many countries with the onset of the Great Depression had only made matters worse and contributed to international conflict.

Box 7.1   GATT 'Rounds'

The General Agreement on Tariffs and Trade began as a series of negotiations around tariff reduction in the leadup to the United Nations 1947 conference on trade and employment in Havana, Cuba. Fifteen countries participated in the first round of talks. The 47 years of the GATT's existence saw eight rounds of negotiations, encompassing an increasingly broad range of issues, and attended by a growing number of nations.

Year	Place/name	Subjects covered	Countries
1947	Geneva, Switzerland	Tariffs	23
1949	Annécy, France	Tariffs	13
1951	Torquay, UK	Tariffs	38
1956	Geneva, Switzerland	Tariffs	26
1960–61	Geneva, Switzerland – Dillon Round	Tariffs	26
1964–67	Geneva, Switzerland – Kennedy Round	Tariffs and anti-dumping measures	62
1973–79	Geneva, Switzerland – Tokyo Round	Tariffs, non-tariff measures, 'framework' agreements	102
1986–94	Geneva, Switzerland – Uruguay Round	Tariffs, non-tariff measures, rules, services, intellectual property, dispute settlement, textiles, agriculture, creation of WTO	123

Source: World Trade Organization. Table by permission of WTO Publications.

Most countries eventually became signatories to the GATT and thereby undertook to meet their trade obligations in their own jurisdiction. The treaty was in existence for more than forty years and presided over a major reduction in average tariff levels in manufactures, which in the main world markets declined from 35 per cent in 1946 to less than 5 per cent in 1986. The GATT progressed through 'Rounds', as shown in Box 7.1, negotiations often lasting several years and culminating in an agreement.

Changes arising from GATT 'Rounds' were sometimes quite dramatic; for instance, the Kennedy Round reduced industrial tariffs by 35 per cent.

From the first meeting in Geneva in 1947 of 23 countries through to the Uruguay Round of 1986–94 with more than 120 countries, negotiations continued. Over the long period of the Uruguay Round – named after the country where negotiations commenced in 1986 – it seemed at times that no agreement would be made. The credibility and relevance of the GATT were challenged as protectionism increased. Non-tariff barriers were increasingly implemented; trade tensions increased among the large players – the US, Japan and the European Union (EU) – and the GATT was often bypassed by bilateral agreements instead of multilateral ones. However, eventually, in April 1994 in Marrakesh, Morocco, the Uruguay Round ended as ministers signed the Final Act.

The World Trade Organization

The most important outcome of the Uruguay Round was the creation of the World Trade Organization (WTO) as the successor body to the GATT, as shown in Box 7.2. Hoekman and Kostecki argue (2001, p. 41):

> There are many similarities between the old GATT and the WTO. The basic principles remain the same. The WTO continues to operate by consensus and continues to be member-driven. However, a number of major changes did occur. Most obviously, the coverage of the WTO is much greater. Moreover, in contrast to the old GATT, the WTO is a 'single undertaking' – all its provisions provide to all members. This implies it is much more important for developing countries than the GATT was. In the dispute settlement area, it became much more difficult to block the formation of panels and the adoption of panel reports (through the adoption of a 'negative consensus' rule: all must oppose a finding). Finally, much greater transparency and surveillance

Box 7.2   From the GATT to the WTO

By the mid 1980s, it was clear that reforms to the GATT were necessary to address significant changes in the world trade environment during the years since the Agreement had come into effect. The increasing complexity and importance of world trade, along with the globalization of the world economy and the development of trade in services, posed significant challenges to the GATT. In addition, the exploitation of loopholes in the existing system and concerns about the GATT's institutional structure and dispute settlement processes prompted calls for an overhaul of the Agreement. These issues were discussed during the GATT's Uruguay Round, which resulted in the creation of the World Trade Organization (WTO). Established on 1 January 1995, the WTO and its agreements cover trade in goods, and trade in services, as well as traded inventions, creations and designs (intellectual property).

As of July 2007, the WTO had 151 members, which included most members of the United Nations.

functions were granted to the secretariat through the creation of a Trade Policy Review Mechanism.

Other key achievements of the Uruguay Round were inclusion of agriculture for the first time and agreements on intellectual property rights, such as copyright protection for books, CDs and computer software. In the years since then, the vast majority of nations have signed up for the WTO, even including the ostensibly communist countries of China and Vietnam.

Principles of the multilateral system

There are five main principles embodied in the GATT and WTO: (1) non-discrimination; (2) reciprocity; (3) enforceable commitments; (4) transparency, and (5) safety valves.

Non-discrimination – This principle means that a product from one country is treated the same as the same product from any other country. As Article 1 of the GATT states, 'any advantage, favour, privilege or immunity granted by any contracting party to any product originating in or destined for any other country shall be

accorded immediately and unconditionally to the like product originating or destined for the territory of all other contracting parties'.
Associated with this is 'national treatment' in which foreign goods
are treated in exactly the same way as those produced domestically. The principle that countries treat their trading partners
equally is termed 'most-favoured-nation treatment' by the WTO.

Reciprocity – This means that concessions are mutual, including,
for example, the fact that when a country accedes to the WTO it
gains market access from previous rounds of liberalization and will
therefore be required to open its own markets.

Enforceable commitments – Commitments to liberalize need to be
enforceable otherwise countries can ignore them. The WTO has
greater powers to enforce decisions than did the GATT. When any
country that feels that its firms are disadvantaged by another
country breaking its commitments under the WTO, it may take an
action. Dispute settlement procedures can include the establishment of a 'panel' of experts to make a ruling on the case and under
the rules that were agreed to on signing up, these rulings are
binding. If agreement is not forthcoming the injured country may
apply a discriminatory tariff to any of the imports from the
country in breach. It is important to note that only governments
have legal standing in the WTO and not companies or other
private parties.

Transparency – In order for commitments to be made WTO
members must make information available as to their trade regimes
and such transparency is a legal obligation. Transparency is 'vital
in terms of ensuring "ownership" of the WTO as an institution – if
citizens do not know what the organization does, its legitimacy will
be eroded' (Hoekman and Kostecki, 2001, p. 35).

Safety valves – Governments are still able to restrict trade in the
specific circumstances of: 'articles allowing for the use of trade
measures to attain noneconomic objectives; articles aimed at
ensuring "fair competition", and provisions allowing for intervention in trade for economic reasons' (Hoekman and Kostecki, 2001,
p. 36). The first includes policies for public health or national security and to allow an industry to adjust to changed circumstances.
The second includes the right to adopt countervailing duties on

subsidized or dumped imports while the third point includes actions to alleviate balance-of-payments problems or to support an infant industry.

The future of the multilateral system

The future of the multilateral system is problematic, and there is now much uncertainty as to how the system is to work. The operation of free-trade theories relies on other nations to follow agreed rules. More recently, other countries have had their own trade problems and have, in some ways, moved away from free trade. North America, Japan and the European Union have instituted protective policies which impose costs on smaller players in the international system. There is also potential for smaller countries to be excluded by the manoeuvrings of the larger trading blocs. Preferential trade agreements have sprung up around the world: these include the North American Free Trade Agreement (NAFTA) in North America, Mercosur in South America, the Asian Free Trade Area (AFTA) and the EU itself, and many others. Most agreements are to some extent discriminatory against countries not in the bloc. Some trade agreements are open, such as Closer Economic Relations (between Australia and New Zealand); some are quite restrictive 'hub-and-spoke' agreements benefiting one large partner; others such as APEC (Asia Pacific Economic Cooperation) follow principles of open regionalism.

Despite protestations of support for the world trade system, it is clear from the actions of major players that multilateralism may not be followed when domestic political pressures intervene. The US, already quite discriminatory especially in agricultural trade, has used so-called voluntary export restraint (VERs) to restrict Japanese car imports. If they were real constraints there would be a clear violation of WTO rules but their voluntary nature still means there is a restriction on trade. Towards the end of his term, President Clinton was not able to get 'fast track' authority from the US Congress to commence a further trade agreement. Section 301 of the Trade Act of 1974 provides for trade retaliation in ways that later appeared to be against WTO rules, although in 1999 a WTO panel ruled that it was not inconsistent with the WTO obligations of the US. The Helms-Burton Act in 1996 provided for trade retaliation against companies from other countries than the US which trade with Cuba. The EU was clearly unhappy with Helms-Burton and with other WTO decisions that went against it, notably over bananas from former colonies as well as the ruling against it by the WTO with regard to the EU's decision to ban hormone-treated beef imports from the US.

In general, the Uruguay Round – the final round of the GATT that led to the creation of the WTO – was successful but it is still possible that multilateralism has reached its high-point. The US was reluctant to ratify the Uruguay agreement and flirted with forms of protectionism even after the agreement was signed. The Doha Round, started in Qatar in 2001, appeared to make little progress. The WTO has some way to go before being accepted fully as an umpire of the world's trading system, although it is notable how its membership increased from 107 in 1995 to 151 in 2007. These new members, mostly developing countries, must see some benefits in joining the WTO.

An alternative to multilateralism is the making of bilateral trade agreements between countries. It has been suggested that such agreements can be discriminatory to third parties, in that they provide concessions only for the parties to the agreement. Trade theorists usually argue that bilateral agreements are not as beneficial as multilateral ones, but if the world goes increasingly down the bilateral route, some countries may find themselves increasingly isolated. Bilateral deals are less useful than a multilateral agreement, especially for poorer countries, as *The Economist* (24 July 2006) notes:

> These smaller agreements are a poor substitute for global progress. While they improve flows within the deal, they distort markets by favouring certain countries over others, even if their goods offer less economic value. The proliferation of special regulations, which companies must spend time and money to understand, does nothing to free up trade generally. And such deals sap the will for broader progress in multilateral talks. This is particularly harmful to smaller and poorer countries, which lack the economic muscle to win concessions from behemoths like America and the EU unless they are part of a broad negotiating consortium. With the sun finally setting on the hopes for Doha, there may be very dark times ahead for trade.

This risk is heightened for those countries which may have placed too much reliance on multilateralism and which in any event do not have a ready supply of natural partners for bilateral agreements.

In 2001, Rugman argued that the WTO was in trouble and could fail for three reasons: first, 'it is a technical body, lacking in political power and even political understanding'; second, its 'acute lack of political skill led it to make the dreadful mistake of giving standing' to NGOs; and thirdly, that its ruling against the US over export subsidies 'could cause a firestorm of protest in the US Congress and even lead to the withdrawal of the United States from the WTO' (2001, pp. 19–20). As he also argues (p. 20):

> The World Trade Organization (WTO) is in a crisis. This is due to a complex evolution of events in which the protests of its left-wing critics have diverted public and elite attention from the critical issues of interdependent trade and growth … The present crisis at the WTO concerns the status and functions of the organization's secretariat, and the observance of its rules by member governments. The secretariat is an understaffed and overworked technical bureaucracy, facilitating, often opportunistically, bargains by governments to reduce trade barriers.

Some years later the US is still firmly within the WTO, but there appears to be only lukewarm support within the US Congress and some leading presidential candidates for the 2008 elections were quite openly hostile to free trade and the WTO. Perhaps the rules-based multilateral environment is losing its support and credibility, most notably in the land which has done more than most to bring about an open trading system.

The Doha Round was formally suspended in mid 2006 and although later resurrected is hardly healthy. There seemed little prospect of either it reaching a conclusion or another round starting in the near future. This may well mean that the multilateral system has already reached its highest point and that for many countries future trade deals will be bilateral. From 2004 to 2007, as the Doha Round appeared stalled, the US alone negotiated ten bilateral deals, with four more pending.

Problems of the trade system

Current orthodoxy is still based on the theories of free trade and comparative advantage, the latter modified to include costs of other factors than simply raw materials. If every nation followed these precepts, most economists would agree that all would be better off: standards of living would rise and consumers would benefit. However, there is something wrong with an orthodoxy from which there are so many divergences. In addition, even if the system of world trade has never been particularly popular in the public mind, recent years have seen increased opposition to international trade and the process of globalization. Proponents of further integration may regard this opposition as irrational, but it is there and is real and cannot be dismissed so easily.

Declining support for free trade

According to the Friedmans, 'no subject has so united economists since Adam Smith's *Wealth of Nations* was published in 1776 as belief in the virtues of free trade' (1984, p. 129). They add, 'unfortunately, with a few exceptions during the nineteenth century, that professional consensus has not prevented one country after another from imposing tariff barriers. The special interest of producers has overwhelmed the general interest of consumers'. A consensus does exist among economists as to the benefits of free trade; but as the Friedmans say, free trade is not generally practised and never has been. The main reason is that matters of politics, most often domestic politics, intrude.

International trade has always attracted domestic political opposition and where this happens politicians can be found to represent views that are prevalent in the community. As Cohen, Paul and Blecker argue (1996, p. 7):

> The desire of politicians to seek favour with the electorate is incompatible with their placing complete trust in the invisible hand of the market to determine the composition, volume, value of its imports and exports of goods and services. The result, simply stated, is that an interventionist, market-altering strategy dominates the conduct of all countries' trade policies.

In most countries there is usually only a relatively small constituency in favour of free trade. Political and bureaucratic elites are generally in favour but such groups may not be widely trusted in the community at large. Business groups are split: some can see the advantages of global trade; many can only see a relentless drive to lower costs in order to compete and see their market share at home eroding due to the pressure of international competition. Large companies, particularly transnationals, can see the benefits and are strong advocates, but, politically, such players can easily be accused of special pleading.

Appeals to politicians that jobs are being threatened by 'unfair' foreign competition are undoubtedly influential. For all the theoretical advantages of free trade between nations, it is a system simultaneously praised by economists and not honoured by national leaders. All this suggests that the theory itself needs to be questioned, or at least broadened to include those political questions which have always existed. It seems rather odd to rely so heavily on a theory no-one follows very seriously.

Problems with the theory of comparative advantage

Originally intended to account for the different natural resource advantages of nations, comparative advantage no longer explains much actual trade. The amount of trade in commodities in which nations have some differential endowments is now quite small, while the postwar growth in world trade has largely been in manufactures, where comparative advantage is often hard to ascertain. There seems to be no particular resource reason why Japan is good at manufacturing cars or cameras. As Porter points out, 'comparative advantage based on factors of production is not sufficient to explain patterns of trade'; and the theory is underpinned by unrealistic assumptions (Porter, 1990, p. 12):

> The standard theory assumes that there are no economies of scale, that technologies everywhere are identical, that products are undifferentiated, and that the pool of national factors is fixed. The theory also assumes that factors, such as skilled labour and capital, do not move among nations. All these assumptions bear little relation, in most industries, to actual competition. At best, factor comparative advantage theory is coming to be seen as useful primarily for explaining broad tendencies in the patterns of trade (for example, its average labor or capital intensity) rather than whether a nation exports or imports in individual industries.

The theory of comparative advantage now seems an inadequate general explanation for trade between nations. Some countries, notably those of the 'Asian miracle', have seen comparative advantage as something that can be created instead of relying on nature. They argue it should be a dynamic concept and not a static one. It is even argued that comparative advantage is obsolete (Porter, 1998, p. 373).

Problems of agricultural trade

There are particular problems in trade in agricultural and other resource-based products. Agriculture has attracted intervention by governments, so much so that, of all industry sectors, agriculture is the one least amenable to trade liberalization. Due to domestic political pressure governments assist agricultural industries to a greater extent than other sectors.

Over the past century there has been a general decline in the terms of trade for commodities – the value of exports compared to imports. In other words, the value of the export of primary commodities such as wheat or cotton has declined compared to manufactures such as tractors. Despite occasional fluctuations and more recent rises, the real price of wheat, for instance, was less than half in 2000 of what it was in 1960. There are many primary producers from many nations competing with each other and the prices they receive for their commodities do not keep pace with those for other goods.

One of the factors causing price falls has been the major technological changes in agriculture resulting from the 'green revolution', with increasing productivity – most particularly in the developed world – but decreasing prices. Another aspect is the invention and use of synthetic fibres as substitutes for natural fibres.

Agricultural interests in many countries exert political power often far beyond their actual numbers. The three leading economies – North America, the European Union and Japan – provide substantial protection for their own agricultural producers because of the domestic political strength of farm groups. As well as providing direct and indirect assistance they also, by various protectionist means, deny access to competitors. Such support policies have resulted in excess production and have reduced market access for efficient agricultural exporters, and the disposal of surplus production on world markets has had a depressing effect on world food prices.

The traditional arguments used to defend the protection of agriculture include the desire to maintain a fair standard of living for farmers, to preserve rural life, and to ensure food security, particularly in the EU and Japan. In the EU, the greater importance of rural employment – and in France the 'cultural significance' of its farm sector – makes policy-makers more sensitive to the social and political costs of adjustment. The EU Common Agricultural Policy (CAP) has led to large surpluses in wheat, barley, sugar, dairy products and deciduous fruits which are then sold at subsidized prices on world markets. Grain producers in other countries suffer from the general decline in prices resulting from assistance to US farmers through the Export Enhancement Program.

The Uruguay Round offered little on agriculture and the Doha Round was supposed to finalize a deal concerning it. But the key countries again made few concessions while developing countries refused to continue unless there was more offered in this area. The suspension of the Doha Round altogether five years later would owe much to domestic political pressure from agricultural interests in the EU and the US.

The WTO has been active in mediating trade disputes between member countries; see Box 7.3.

A decline in sovereignty?

It is often argued that the international trading system, as moderated by the WTO, diminishes national sovereignty. Critics argue that, having signed up to the WTO, governments have less room for manoeuvre; political parties cannot openly advocate radical solutions for fear of alienating international markets. The scope of allowable action is constrained.

There is an unlikely mix of interests which argue that there is a decline in sovereignty. Far Left and far Right find common cause in opposition to international organizations, such as the WTO, World Bank and IMF. This seems to be most evident in the US, where the Left (Ralph Nader) and the Right (Pat Buchanan) both argue that the US cannot give up its sovereignty to the WTO. Indeed, especially on the far Right, any international body is seemingly suspect with the World Bank, IMF and the UN and its agencies attacked as leading towards a 'world government' and taking away US governmental scope. Perhaps in part due to such sentiments the US has shied away from a leadership role in further extending free trade, despite it being the biggest beneficiary.

Box 7.3   The WTO and trade disputes

Since its establishment in 1995, the WTO has been asked to settle a total of 363 trade disputes, or an average of 30.25 disputes per year. The party bringing the dispute is termed the *complainant*, and the party against whom the dispute is brought the *respondent*. It takes the WTO 12 or 13 months to settle a dispute.

Of the 151 WTO members, 57 have been involved in trade disputes brought before the WTO. The majority of these countries have been involved in fewer than ten disputes each. There are, however, some notable exceptions, as the accompanying table shows.

Country	Cases as complainant	Cases as respondent	Total cases
United States	88	97	185
European Union	76	57	133
Canada	28	15	43
India	17	19	36
Brazil	20	14	36
Argentina	14	16	30
Japan	12	15	27
South Korea	13	13	26
Chile	10	12	22
Mexico	17	14	21

In the main, most complainants have not lodged disputes against a particular country on more than five occasions. Yet the dispute statistics also point to a number of ongoing trade rivalries. South Korea has brought a complaint against the United States on seven occasions, and the US has made six complaints about South Korea. The US has also lodged six complaints about Japan, as well as six complaints about Mexico. Japan has complained about the US on eight occasions, and Mexico has lodged seven complaints about the US. More significantly, Canada has made 14 complaints against the United States, and the US has made five complaints against Canada. However, the most tension seems to lie in the relationship between the United States and the European Union: the US has complained against the EU on 17 occasions, and the EU has lodged 31 complaints against the United States.

Source: Adapted from World Trade Organization. Table by permission of WTO Publications.

Trade and the environment

Some of those against the liberal trading regime argue that trade is incompatible with environmental protection, because corporations either actively seek out countries with lax environmental standards or force greater environmental degradation onto developing countries through unsustainable practices, such as clearing rain forests for timber or clearing land for cattle or other products able to be sold on world markets. Supporters of trade liberalization argue that greater environmental protection occurs as developing countries become more prosperous. It is the case that more developed countries have better standards, and that countries closed to the world have much worse outcomes, but that is not the whole story. There are instances where severely polluting industries, such as ship-breaking or recycling lead batteries, take place in developing countries, where environmental standards are lower, and this might have the effect of making the overall environment worse.

One way of dealing with environmental concerns is to bring such matters within the ambit of treaties between nations. The signing of NAFTA required side-agreements on the environment, as well as labour standards. In addition, such sensitive issues as the killing of dolphins in the harvesting of tuna are the subject of trade agreements, as is the trade in noxious or dangerous products. Domestic governments do have the capacity to act as argued by an OECD paper (1998, pp. 15–16):

> Trade and investment liberalization are not the root causes of environmental problems. Under trade agreements such as the WTO, governments retain the sovereign right to set their own environmental objectives. And they can apply measures to enforce achievement of them within their own territories ... What is needed ... is not a halt to liberalization efforts, but sound environmental policies that are properly integrated with trade and investment policies.

The problem, though, is one of institutional capacity and willingness to act. A developing country faced with having no industry at all if environmental standards are enforced may choose to not impose the developed world's environmental standards. On the other hand, most transnational companies are concerned with their environmental reputation as it can quite directly impinge on their profitability.

Irwin argues that trade and the environment are not linked. For example, environmental outcomes in Eastern Europe were far worse prior to it opening itself to trade. He argues further (2002, pp. 48–9):

> Environmental damage results from poor environmental policy, not poor trade policies. Environmental damage results from the inappropriate use of our natural resources in the land, sea and air. The overuse of these resources is commonly related to the lack of well-defined property rights. When property rights are not well-established, that is, when no one has ownership rights and control over a resource, then open access to the resource frequently leads to its exploitation beyond the socially optimal level.

In the developing world much more forest is cleared for domestic use, such as fuel or grazing, than for trade-related purposes. It would seem that the effects of trade on the environment are not substantial unless another argument is being made; that capitalism itself, or providing goods and services to consumers willing to pay for them, is the root cause of environmental damage. In general, trade is 'only indirectly related to environmental problems, and therefore trade policy is an indirect, inefficient, and often inefficacious way of addressing environmental problems' (Irwin, 2002, p. 49).

Trade and intellectual property

Nations have for a long time provided for some protection of intellectual property rights (IPRs), such as copyright for written works or music, and patents for inventions. Extending such rights to other countries has been problematic in practice even if there are fewer concerns about it as a principle.

If there was no recognition of intellectual property across borders, there would be no way of stopping unauthorized copying. Patented products could be copied without any compensation to the holder of that patent. Companies in developed countries get upset with imitations or counterfeits of their products and the US, in particular, has been assiduous in trying to reduce such piracy. Some developing countries were less concerned given that non-recognition of intellectual property might mean cheaper generic medicines or seeds for agriculture. Also, given that most patents are held in the developed world, recognition of these means a flow of revenue from developing countries.

The Uruguay Round recognized IPRs through the Trade-Related Intellectual Property agreement or 'TRIPs'. The agreement was not easy to achieve. As Hoekman and Kostecki argue (2001, p. 283):

> The negotiation on TRIPs was one of the more difficult of the Uruguay Round, both politically and economically. The issue was relatively new to GATT and involved a North–South confrontation. Industrial countries, led by the US, sought an ambitious and comprehensive agreement on standards for protection of IPRs ... Developing countries sought to draw a firm distinction between work on trade in counterfeit goods and IPRs more broadly defined. They were willing to cooperate on the former, but opposed the latter ... There was a general concern that greater protection of IPRs would strengthen the monopoly power of multinational companies, and detrimentally affect poor populations by raising the price of medicines and food.

In the end agreement was reached and TRIPs is one of the main parts of the WTO to which every new member must agree as part of the single undertaking. The agreement includes copyright over literary and performance works, trademarks, industrial designs, integrated circuits and patents. Copyright and patents were standardized at a fairly lengthy period, indeed, 'in a number of instances, TRIPs established norms that go beyond existing international norms' (Hoekman and Kostecki, 2001, p. 287). Acceding to the TRIPs agreement meant substantial change in the domestic economies of many nations and became something of a political issue.

Trade and labour standards

One of the most common forms of protest against free trade is action by unions and international associations of workers who fear that their jobs will be traded away to workers in other countries, who are willing to work for much less money. There are demands for a 'Social Clause' in the WTO covering such things as minimum labour standards (see Box 7.4), a call that comes from the US as well as a number of NGOs. A social clause may also include conditions of employment, especially in the developing world where child labour, prison labour and other forced labour may be used. However, demands for some uniformity in labour standards may be another form of protectionism by developed countries to prevent a transfer of jobs to developing ones. Some disruption of employment may occur for some low-level jobs, such as assembling shoes. But supporters of liberalization argue that wages by themselves are not necessarily a major factor in the decision to invest in a location and that greater productivity through infrastructure, know-how and capital – human, financial and physical – can 'more than offset the effects of higher wages' (OECD, 1998, p. 59). For these reasons countries such as the US and Germany, which have very high labour costs, are still able to be competitive even in areas such as manufacturing. In addition, given that a large proportion of developed economies is based on services which are not traded, the wage effects caused by developing countries are not likely to be severe. Also, most trade is between the countries of the developed world, all of which have high wage rates, rather than with the developing world where wages are lower. It is true that jobs have been lost in the developed countries in manufacturing over recent decades, but mainly through technological change rather than trade. But even if the 'overall effect of trade on the number of jobs in an economy is best approximated at zero' (Irwin, 2002, p. 71), there are likely to be localized areas of unemployment to which governments will be required to respond. This is best done through adjustment programmes allowing transition to those jobs which have been created elsewhere, notably in services.

Developed and developing countries

If allowed to work, the WTO could be an avenue for greater equity in the application of a rule-based system. But developed countries had the greatest say in how the international trading system was put together, including the negotiations that led to the formation of the WTO. As a result, there is justifiable suspicion from developing countries that continuing restrictions on their own trade with the West – in agriculture, in services and access to low-end manufactures such as textiles – are due to the rules of the game being stacked against them.

As most decision-making in the WTO occurs by bargaining, consultation and consensus, there are opportunities for smaller coun-

Box 7.4   The WTO and international labour standards

At its 1996 Ministerial Conference in Singapore, the World Trade Organization acknowledged concerns about the effects of a more liberalized global trade market on workers' conditions and job security. Item 4 of the Singapore Ministerial Declaration states, 'We renew our commitment to the observance of internationally recognized core labour standards.'[1] The Singapore declaration deferred the responsibility for the development and monitoring of core labour standards to the International Labour Organization (ILO), and affirmed the WTO's support for the ILO's role in 'promoting'[2] the standards. However, the declaration also exposed the tensions that many still perceive between the trade liberalization agenda and workers' rights:

> We reject the use of labour standards for protectionist purposes, and agree that the comparative advantage of countries, particularly low-wage developing countries, must in no way be put into question. In this regard, we note that the WTO and ILO Secretariats will continue their existing collaboration.[3]

In the years since the Singapore Declaration, the WTO has reiterated its commitment to the maintenance of core labour standards: as part of the Ministerial Declaration issued at the 2001 WTO Ministerial Conference in Doha, at the Ministerial Conference held in 2003 at Cancún, and at the Sixth Ministerial Conference in Hong Kong, China in 2005.

Notes:
1. World Trade Organization. Singapore Ministerial Declaration. Adopted on 13 December 1996, WT/MIN(96)/DEC, 18 December 1996, p. 2.
2. Ibid.
3. Ibid.

Sources:
World Trade Organization. *Doha Work Programme Ministerial Declaration.* Adopted on 18 December 2005, www.wto.org/english/thewto_e/minist_e/min01_e/mindecl_e.htm.
World Trade Organization. *Preparations for the Fifth Session of the Ministerial Conference Draft Cancún Ministerial Text Second Revision.* 13 September 2003, www.wto.org/english/thewto_e/minist_e/min03_e/draft_decl_rev2_e.htm.
World Trade Organization. *Singapore Ministerial Declaration.* Adopted on 13 December 1996, www.wto.org/english/thewto_e/minist_e/min96_e/wtodec_e.htm.

tries to participate. However, in practice it is not easy for them. Developing countries have the disadvantage of having less access to legal and other experts well-versed in the intricacies of trade law than more developed countries have. By itself this expertise gap can lead to worse outcomes for developing countries in negotiations. The WTO secretariat can provide technical assistance to developing countries, but this is an inadequate substitute for real expertise.

In addition, there are the so-called 'Green Room' meetings where a smaller group of leading countries attempts to reach consensus. In practice this can exclude developing countries from the crucial, early negotiations. During the Seattle ministerial meeting, many countries that were excluded from critical Green Room meetings 'felt that they were not being kept informed of developments and were not being granted the opportunity to defend their views' (Hoekman and Kostecki, 2001, p. 61). Smaller countries can gain more from rules-based, open trading than larger ones as they are not likely to be in a position to dominate a market or be able to make international public policy for their own benefit. But there is a general view, one that has substantial justification, that the rules militate against the interests of developing countries. What developing countries need is for the developed countries preaching free trade to actually allow foreign competition themselves and effect reform of the rules to enable real developing-country participation. The Seattle ministerial meeting and successive ministerial meetings showed that developing countries would not accept the outright domination by developed countries of the WTO and before that the GATT. The rules may still be biased against developing countries but a rules-based system can be reformed.

One key problem is that the developed countries, most notably the US, which provided leadership on trade in the postwar period, have retreated somewhat from the position they once held. The US and the other two big players – Europe and Japan – are not as committed to a freely trading system as they once were. Where the developed countries are vulnerable to charges of hypocrisy is in simultaneously proposing free trade and shutting their borders to trade from developing countries. As Stiglitz argues, 'How can the advanced economies preach the gospel of competition and free markets, yet turn to managed trade and restricted markets when their own interests are in jeopardy?' (2001, p. 351). Protectionism may be rising, particularly in the US, and with the mood of some developing countries more uncompromising, there is something of a gulf between the views of each group and this is to the overall detriment of the trading system.

It is often argued that developing countries are being exploited by their trade with the developed, that developed countries are engaging in a form of economic imperialism to replace earlier colonialism. In most cases, developing countries actively wish to improve living standards through economic growth. Fieldhouse argues (1999, p. 351), 'the evidence suggests that, in the initial stage at least, the establishment of an export trade was almost invariably the starting point of greater economic growth', and that such trade, even if based on timber minerals or agricultural products enables even least developed countries to increase their incomes.

Trade benefits both parties. No-one is forced to trade, although as discussed earlier not trading – or autarchy – is likely to lead to a decline in living standards. And as Fieldhouse continues, 'There is no evidence to suggest that the Third World was made poorer by the creation of a single world economy and market, though there may well have been undesirable side effects, particularly in cultures and lifestyles' (1999, pp. 353–4). There is a fundamental difference of opinion on this issue between those who see trade as mutually beneficial and those who see it as exploitative, regardless of evidence or the views of developing countries themselves.

In any case, the old arguments about exploitation by the developed world need to confront the emergence of China and India. These are still developing countries by GDP per capita but are so large – each has a population greater than a billion – that their presence in the international trading system means that any such system that excludes developing countries cannot survive. India has been a WTO member since 1995 and China since 2001; their trade and GDP have grown very quickly since they became active traders. In 2005, China was the third largest exporter and third largest importer of merchandise and had a trade growth rate far higher than the first two in each category. The differences between developed and developing countries are less stark than they once were when it comes to trade. Any system of world trade where the long-standing members talk amongst themselves and exclude developing countries from negotiations cannot persist.

NGOs and trade

It could be argued that the intergovernmental form of internationalization is less significant than it once was and other international actors have become important. There has been a rise of non-governmental organizations as global players, an increase in power compared to states. As Rugman argued in the aftermath of the Seattle meeting in 1999 (2001, pp. 20–1):

> As the United States retreats from the global stage, the NGOs take its place ... The NGOs' anti-business activities are fundamentally opposed to the economic interests of poorer countries. The NGOs, by reversing the benefits of multilateralism and free trade, are hindering the economic development of poorer Asian, African and developing countries. Their anti-business activities are profoundly illogical.

The role of NGOs is indeed controversial. They are not elected and could be argued to be less accountable than national governments. Many seek and are granted access to multilateral discussions, even as they are special interests. NGOs are often well organized and global in scope and take advantage of technological change in getting their message across. They have also succeeded in attracting support for their views.

There has been NGO opposition to freer trade for some time. Well-known US activist Ralph Nader argued that the international trade system leads states on a 'race to the bottom' in which corporations will 'profit from the lower wages, pollution standards and lower taxes'. He called for 'community-oriented production' which is 'more flexible and adaptable to local needs and environmentally sustainable production methods, and more susceptible to democratic controls' (Nader, 1993, pp. 6–11). Especially in the wake of the disruption of the WTO ministerial meeting in Seattle in 1999 and subsequent meetings, it was evident that there was real opposition to a more liberal trading environment and that NGOs were in the forefront of this opposition.

Some of the rhetoric against trade is actually aimed at the capitalist system itself, rather than against the world trade system. It is argued that economic growth is harmful and that as more countries develop there will be even greater consumption of resources. It could also be argued that if China indulged in as much conspicuous consumption as the US, the pollution effects would be much harder for the planet to absorb. The problem with this view is that, carried to its logical extension, the fruits of industrialization would be reserved for those countries which have already advanced to that stage and denied to those which have not.

It does not seem to matter that the arguments of those against trade are illogical, since they have attracted an audience; a young and idealistic audience. Through NGOs such as Greenpeace, an anti-trade, anti-business, even anti-capitalist agenda has gained adherents. Such sentiments have evidently attracted their followers and the triumphalism of the defeat of communism by capitalism may have been overstated. One response to NGO pressure has been to invite NGO representatives to the negotiating table at forums like the WTO ministerial meetings. The results have been patchy at best.

Free trade or fair trade?

There is something of a social movement under way advocating 'fair trade' as opposed to 'free trade'. Fair trade means paying a reasonable price, cognisant of environmental concerns, especially for agricultural commodities and handicrafts from developing countries. Such commodities do have special problems of over-supply, long-term decline in price and a very wide disparity between the price paid to producers and that paid by consumers.

Fair trade sets out to provide a fair price to producers, however that might be defined. So we have fair-trade coffee, tea and bananas, and the producers of those commodities get a better return. Consumer prices might be slightly higher but there is an apparent willingness to pay a bit more for coffee if it helps the producer.

The problems from an economic perspective are that fair trade is a distortion of the market that otherwise would find an equilibrium over time. Fair trade is tantamount to paying a subsidy that can, in turn, lead to increased production with the overall effect of even greater dislocation. On the other hand, if consumers are happy to pay a bit more, or international coffee chains such as Starbucks see public relations benefits in being linked with the fair-trade movement, there seems little harm and perhaps some good.

Conclusion

Although trade theory is still nominally based on free trade, comparative advantage and the multilateral trading system, in practice all three are widely disregarded. It is possible that the integration of economies through trade has reached its peak as there is more and more domestic opposition, mainly in the developed economies. There are calls for 'managed trade' or 'fair trade' or for retaliating against unfair competition. The world trade system, as set out by the GATT and continued by the WTO, may have done much to improve the living standards of those countries which participate in it. The economics of trade is relatively simple; there is more benefit to more people, rich or poor, by opening up economies to free trade. And there is more benefit to more people by having binding international agreements on trade. But the politics of trade has been ignored to a greater degree than would be likely to lead to a sustainable trading system for the future. Most people in the domestic polities of the main nations are instinctive protectionists; most are against the global integration that has occurred. The trade system is in trouble, despite its successes over the past fifty years. A new round of trade talks leading to even less restriction in trade seems a long way away.

Chapter 8

Protectionism

Introduction

At their broadest, protection and protectionism are antithetical to free trade. Protectionism involves assisting domestic industries either by imposing barriers to foreign competitors, or by subsidising or compensating domestic industries in some other way to assist them against international competition. Advocates of free trade are explicitly opposed to protectionism; advocates of protection for domestic industry do not like free trade. However, there is more to protectionism than it being merely the obverse of free trade.

Protectionism is essentially about politics. Its benefits are demanded by industries and their workers who fear they are, or will be, damaged by international competition for their products and jobs. Interest groups exert pressure on politicians and political parties to make laws to somehow restrict the imports of goods or services affecting their industry. Any government is in a difficult position. On one side there are demands to allow greater economic integration and more trade. Financial markets, international companies, economic theory and consumers would all claim benefits from fewer trade barriers, as does – for most of the time – the international political system. On the other side, however, is the clamour from domestic companies, workers and unions in threatened industries and most of the population who are, in the main, instinctive protectionists. It seems to many merely a matter of common sense that supporting local industry – however defined – provides for more employment and prosperity. A transatlantic survey carried out in September 2005 revealed that 57 per cent of US respondents believe that freer trade destroys more American jobs than it creates, and 58 per cent of Americans would favour raising tariffs for imported goods if it meant protecting jobs – the latter a higher number than in Germany, France, or Great Britain (*Washington Post*, 15 September 2006). Despite its theoretical attractions to economists, no nation has ever been completely free-trading; all are protectionist to some degree. Even the United States, avowedly in favour of free trade, will be protectionist on a specific issue, such as tariff support for steel or agriculture, if domestic political interests require this. The long-running argument between free trade and protectionism continues, seemingly without either side being able to persuade the other.

Restricting foreign trade has been argued about since there were organized states. More than 200 years ago Adam Smith argued for free trade between nations and his work continues as the benchmark on one side of the perennial argument between free traders and protectionists within politics, economics and public policy. Most ordinary people regard it as a matter of common sense that assisting industries against international competition will provide for jobs and prosperity. A survey carried out across a number of countries found that the share of Americans who believed that trade is good for their country had plunged from 78 per cent in 2002 to 59 per cent in 2007 and was the lowest proportion among the 47 countries included (*The Economist*, 8 November 2007). On the other hand, the overwhelming view of economists and many other parts of the policy establishment is that protectionism is counterproductive, as assistance given has to be paid for in higher taxes and higher prices for consumers. Political parties face the dilemma between, on the one hand, not wishing to alienate the voters, and, on the other hand, not wishing to put forward unsound policies.

Free-trade economists see protection as a distortion of the free market and regard those wanting industry protection as rent-seekers. But the various forms of protection should really be seen as political instruments, carried out in response to political pressures. Protectionism cannot be explained away as simply the resultant of political forces — much protection can only be regarded as bad policy — but it can be understood when one takes account of the *political* economy at work. Free trade and protectionism are not solely matters of economics; they are also matters of politics.

The current status of the long argument between the proponents of free trade and those who advocate protectionism is somewhat uncertain. The sixty years after World War II was a period of genuine reductions in protection around the world and particularly in the more developed nations. The GATT and later the WTO and other multilateral bodies have presided over this freeing up of trade. And yet, protectionism never goes away. The earlier strong support for free trade in the United States seems to be evaporating as the Congress debates various protectionist measures. Japan and Europe have been consistently more inclined to protect industry and if other countries moved towards protectionism they would follow with alacrity.

Protectionism defined

Protectionism is the practice of employing economic devices to restrict or distort trade and to benefit domestic producers. There are numerous forms of protection, notably tariffs, import quotas and other non-tariff barriers, such as preferential procurement arrangements and export taxes. These are described in more detail below.

Tariffs

A tariff is a customs duty on imports – a percentage added to the value of certain classes of goods that the importer pays as a tax to the government. The price that can be charged for an imported good is increased as a result, thereby allowing domestic production to be more competitive with imports. A domestic producer gains an indirect benefit as the tax is only payable on imports, not on local production.

Compared to other protectionist devices, a tariff has some positive features. There is no restriction on quantity and there is some certainty as to the viability of a particular transaction to exporting companies or countries. It also provides some revenue to the government in the importing country that can be used for public purposes and, before the widespread adoption of income taxes, tariffs on imported goods were the main revenue source for most governments. Furthermore, a tariff is easy to collect. As goods must cross borders which are under the control of government, it is relatively easy to require a payment to be made to allow their passage. The GATT and the WTO have had the long-term policy of 'tariffication', that is, changing all forms of protection to tariffs, so that assistance and the conditions applying to the particular transaction are transparent.

Even if tariffs are better than other forms of protection they still present problems. They raise prices and make consumers worse off;

Box 8.1 Tariffs – a closer look

The Uruguay Round of trade talks succeeded in obtaining many tariff cuts across developed and developing economies. In developed countries, cuts were phased in over five years from 1 January 1995, and resulted in a cut in tariffs on industrial products from an average of 6.3 to 3.8 per cent. Many industrial countries also agreed to reduce their tariffs on imports from developing countries. Another important achievement of the Uruguay Round was the 'binding', or fixing, of many tariff rates. Significantly, developed countries have 'bound' the tariffs imposed on 99 per cent of imported products. In developing economies, 73 per cent of tariffs have been bound.

The accompanying table shows that developed and developing societies rely on tariffs for some of their products. Taking as a benchmark the tariffs on transport equipment – a high-end manufacture – it is noticeable that developed countries generally have lower tariffs, but in some areas, such as agricultural production, have quite high levels.

Country (selected)	Average final bound duties (%), 2006			
	Transport equipment	Dairy products	Cereals and preparations	Textiles
Developed countries				
Japan	0.0	176.1	94.3	5.4
Switzerland	2.6	151.2	56.7	6.5
United States	3.1	25.0	3.9	7.7
Norway	3.3	324.3	239.5	7.1
European Union	4.1	56.9	29.1	6.5
Australia	12.6	4.9	2.5	18.3
Developing countries				
China	11.5	12.2	23.7	9.7
Mali	13.4	38.8	59.1	18.4
Brazil	33.3	48.9	43.4	34.8
India	35.8	65.0	119.4	31.4
Central African Republic	38.6	30.0	30.0	42.1

Source: Adapted from World Trade Organization, International Trade Centre and UNCTAD (2007). *World Tariff Profiles 2006*. WTO, ITC and UNCTAD.

they distort allocation within an economy – in their absence industry may move into areas where there is longer-term likelihood of success; and they are politically hard to remove as industry becomes reliant on them.

The WTO has attempted to reduce the overall level of tariffs and achieve greater consistency between tariffs imposed by different trading nations, but there are notable exceptions. It is not only developing nations that have retained higher tariff levels, as illustrated in Box 8.1. The United States, for instance, has low tariffs in transport, cereals and textiles but quite high tariffs for dairy products. The European Union has even higher tariffs for dairy products and for cereals. Developing countries tend to have quite high tariffs across all the categories shown, excepting China.

Import quotas

An import quota is a limit set by the government in the importing country on the quantity of a good or service that is allowed to be imported. This allows room in the market for domestic producers even if they can only produce at a higher price. A quota provides no direct benefit to the government that sets its level, but can provide substantial gains to those in the private economy who succeed in being allocated a quota. Indeed, businesses or individuals may pursue a government-allocated quota instead of trying to actively compete. For these reasons, quotas are not regarded as good policy as 'a quota cuts the link between domestic and foreign prices, is generally discriminatory, does not necessarily allow the changing pattern of comparative advantage over time to be reflected in imports, is less transparent, and is more subject to administrative abuse and corruption' (Hoekman and Kostecki, 2001, pp. 154–5). Quotas are non-transparent forms of protection in that the effective level of protection as a percentage is hidden.

Subsidies to domestic producers

The application of subsidy is another possible form of protection, particularly if it is applied to an industry attempting to compete with imports. Some subsidies can be purely domestic, such as assisting a bus service, but a subsidy applied with the intention of improving the competitive position of an industry is trade-related. To the extent that this subsidy was only given to domestic producers it would have obvious effects on the relative price that could be charged compared to an international competitor. Subsidies are used less often in general and many kinds of subsidy are no longer allowable under WTO rules. Non-specific subsidies – those that do not assist a particular firm or industry – are allowable; however, subsidies that are dependent on export performance are prohibited (Hoekman and Kostecki, 2001, p. 173). Despite the adoption of the rules of the international trading system that apply when a country signs on to the WTO, subsidies that distort world markets are still prevalent in agricultural trade. The farm subsidies common in the United States and Europe affect the world prices of agricultural commodities, in particular those of developing countries.

Export bounties

A government that wishes to encourage exports from particular industries may pay producers a subsidy based on the amount of goods they can export. Instead of subsidizing domestic production a bounty targets only exports. This form of subsidy is no longer greatly used and would be likely to be against WTO rules if it was used. It is also hard to imagine a case where exports from a particular industry are so highly valued that the government would use taxation revenue to assist in their being sent to another country.

Retaliatory action

A nation may decide to retaliate against another nation for real or imagined offences in trade and to do so by restricting trade or applying penalties of some kind. However, retaliatory action can become another form of protectionism. There is an obvious difficulty in working out if another country has actually carried out some action that is against one's own trade. Interest groups often complain that their trade efforts are in some way frustrated by another government and demand that their own government do something, but their arguments are often special pleading. During the Depression of the 1930s retaliatory action by first one country and then another led to massive increases in protection which had the effect of greatly reducing trade and prolonging the economic slump.

A more recent incidence was the long-running dispute between Canada and the US over Canadian exports of softwood from forests. The US maintained that these exports were subsidised by federal and provincial governments in Canada and that this subsidy was unfair, so duties were imposed as a result. After running for twenty years the dispute was settled in 2006 when the US came to terms with Canada after the US lost in a NAFTA arbitration and in a determination made by a WTO panel.

Anti-dumping duties

One allowable form of retaliation is that of anti-dumping duties. Dumping is the practice whereby a foreign firm sells its product in another country at a lower price, however defined, than it sells it at at home and, in extreme cases, at less than the cost of production. Should dumping be proven, countervailing or anti-dumping duties can be imposed. The behaviour that anti-dumping aims to combat is where a foreign producer tries to drive out competition in another country with the aim of increasing prices once there are no effective competitors. In practice, both dumping and measures against it are dubious practices, both theoretically and practically. There is little likelihood that a firm would be able to drive out all competitors by dumping; underpricing for this purpose would be irrational more often than not. The WTO does allow action to be taken against dumping provided that it can be proved and is causing injury. But the incidence of anti-dumping action by advanced countries is much greater than would be expected given the quite rare instances when an outside firm or country would actually benefit from dumping. More often than not, anti-dumping is yet another form of protectionism, as Irwin argues (2002, p. 125):

> The antidumping process involves many arbitrary judgments and is subject to abuse. Can any intellectual defense be mustered in favor of the AD laws? ... The antidumping laws might be worthwhile if they prevented predatory pricing by foreign exporters ... In fact, in the overwhelming majority of AD cases, such predatory motives can be ruled out as utterly implausible.

Anti-dumping is often really a form of outright protectionism and the anti-dumping statute 'is not employed to prevent predatory conduct or preserve competition, but simply to protect the domestic industry from foreign competition' and at the expense of domestic consumers (Irwin, 2002, p. 126). Given that most anti-dumping actions are launched by developed countries and against developing ones, something will need to be done about this practice in order to create a fairer international trading regime.

Voluntary export restraints (VERs)

As the name suggests, voluntary export restraints are targets set by an exporting country with the aim of avoiding more direct action being taken against it later. The best-known example of this is the restrictions placed on the export of cars into the United States from Japan in the 1980s. Under this arrangement, Japanese car-makers 'voluntarily' set an export quota in 1981. Although there was no official trade barrier of any kind forcing them to do this, the US government, under strong pressure from its own automobile industry and the United Auto Workers Union, made it quite clear that if there were no voluntary limit, a more severe one would be imposed. In this type of arrangement, power is being exercised, but not in any overt way. A trade barrier clearly exists, despite US claims that it allows complete free trade in the car industry. A formal quota would have been a breach of trade rules, but an informal system, even if underpinned by the threat of force, is not.

It could be argued that VERs were counterproductive in supporting the US car industry. The quota meant that higher-priced and more profitable models were exported from Japan, further enhancing Japanese competitiveness. Also, Japanese car companies set up highly successful manufacturing operations in the US where they became domestic producers. The new plants were even more efficient than the traditional US producers and were set up away from the traditional homes of car production in the US, in southern states, for instance, and with much less unionization than in Detroit. A case could be made that the introduction of VERs on behalf of the automobile industry in the United States has made that industry worse off in the longer term. This particular VER was phased out in the early 1990s but could recur in other industries.

Quarantine regulations

Quarantine or sanitary and phytosanitary measures (related to the health of plants) are standards established by governments for goods to enter their territory in order to reduce the risk of disease. Countries obviously wish to keep diseases out of their territory, but the rules can become another form of protection. For example, from the 1970s, quarantine authorities in Australia imposed bans on the importation of salmon in order to protect its salmon farms from exotic disease. In 1994, Canada took action against Australia arguing that this ban was just another form of protection. In 1998, a WTO panel found that Australia's ban on fresh, chilled and frozen salmon from Canada was 'not based on a risk assessment, was maintained without scientific evidence and reflected an arbitrary and unjustifiable distinction in levels of protection that resulted in discrimination or a disguised restriction on trade' (WTO, 1998). There have been other long-running disputes between the US and the EU over quarantine regulations. For many years, the EU has opposed the use of hormones in fattening animals prior to slaughter, a common practice in the US. The EU contends that these hormones are unsafe whereas the US insists they are safe. In 1998, the EU agreed that that there was insufficient scientific evidence of harm and allowed the US to impose more than $100 million in punitive tariffs. In addition, the EU has concerns over genetically modified crops that the US regards as unjustifiable. Given the absence of conclusive scientific evidence – both sides are able to cite favourable studies – a trade dispute may arise. An argument over food safety can easily lead to public policy really aimed at assisting domestic industry.

Non-tariff barriers

A non-tariff barrier is 'any government measure that distorts the volume, composition or direction of trade; as such almost any government measure could affect trade and so estimates of their range and effects vary' (Held *et al.*, 1999, pp. 164–5). There are a series of possible non-tariff barriers, such as environmental or health and safety regulations. A requirement to obtain import licences may be a non-tariff barrier, as are domestic standards and certification. Administrative delays or customs procedures may be a form of protectionism, such as the requirement in 1982 that all VCRs imported into France from Japan be sent to a single undermanned customs post in Poitiers in order to delay delivery. Similarly, cargo-handling and port procedures may have the same effect. The WTO tries to reduce the incidence of non-tariff barriers but national governments can be inventive in subverting the rules. Even high domestic taxes and charges could be considered to be non-tariff barriers, as they affect trade. However, virtually any regulation or governmental action has trade effects somewhere in the economy, so it is impractical to imagine that all non-tariff barriers can be removed.

'Buy local' campaigns

It is a common practice for governments and industry groups to try to persuade consumers to buy products made within that jurisdiction. This is another form of protectionism that feeds on and contributes to the perception that domestic products are somehow better for the economy than those produced by foreigners.

The 'buy local' programmes regularly promoted by governments are usually justified in terms of their impact upon domestic employment. But such programmes also undeniably pander to those who believe that purchasing imported goods merely sends money out of the country. Linked to such arguments are those which claim that domestic producers have an inherent 'right' to the domestic market and that consumers owe their loyalty to firms employing local staff. If assistance is to be given, how are the lucky industries to be determined, how does the government 'pick winners'? The US, for example, has a range of 'buy American' statutes giving preference to domestic producers in government procurement. It also has the Jones Act prohibiting foreign-built and foreign-manned ships from engaging in trade between US ports. This means ships constructed in other nations cannot be used in US domestic trade. This mercantilist practice, also known as cabotage, is used by many other nations as well.

As the above examples demonstrate, there are a number of devices available for countries to assist their domestic industries. Even avowedly free-trading countries try to skew their trade in ways that benefit their own domestic industries. Only by acting together can countries try to reduce overall barriers. The GATT and the WTO have tried to do this and to establish a rules-based trading regime. Although the economic argument was won long ago by the free traders, protectionist behaviour continues as political realities are faced by policy-makers. Mercantilism or neomercantilism are ever-present and protectionism persists.

Arguments in favour of protectionism

As discussed in Chapter 7, during the mercantilist period, European countries set up quite elaborate regulatory systems over trade to benefit their own economies compared to others. The very strength of the nation in a military sense was seen as being directly related to economic protection. Held *et al.* argue that 'from its inception the nation-state has used trade protection to raise revenues, manage balance of payments difficulties and promote domestic industry' (1999, p. 187). These three points remain relevant, even if the first two are less important than they once were, particularly in developed countries.

First, as noted earlier, tariffs were an important source of revenue for many countries at least until well into the twentieth century, where other taxes, notably income or sales taxes, require much more infrastructure and compliance mechanisms to work well. Tariffs can be evaded by smuggling or corruption at border posts, but they remain a good revenue source for many developing countries.

Second, the management of the balance of payments through protection was the cornerstone of the mercantilist system. Protectionist regulations attempted to amass the precious metals of gold and silver. A balance-of-payments deficit would result in a loss of precious metals to other countries, thereby weakening the nation. In an age of floating exchange rates, as used now by most trading countries, the use of protection to manage the balance of payments is not likely to be effective.

Third, and most importantly for current debates, the promotion of domestic industry has often been seen as a desirable end in itself, through improving employment and living standards, even if protection is not necessarily a particularly effective way of doing this. Voters often demand industry protection and political parties and leaders often find it difficult to refuse. The revenue and balance-of-payments rationales for protection are now generally unimportant, but the protection of domestic industry remains the main contemporary rationale for protection, with a variety of arguments still being used, as follows.

The infant-industry argument

It is obviously difficult for new firms to establish themselves in the face of international competition against firms with established names, reputations and possibly lower costs. Government assistance may be demanded to allow a potentially viable industry to establish itself, after which further help will no longer be necessary. At that time, in theory, the industry will be a healthy, viable contributor to the national economy, able to more than repay any assistance it may have received. This is usually referred to as the 'infant industry' argument.

The only theorist for protectionism with a role in any way comparable to Adam Smith's as an advocate for free trade is Friedrich List, a nineteenth-century writer influential particularly in Germany and the United States. In 1841, List argued that, without an industrial apparatus, nations like Germany would run the risk of staying inferior to bigger powers if they maintained free-trade policies as the established powers would remain advantaged (1885 [1841]). A protective tariff could allow such a nation to develop and it could then return to free trade. Related to this is the argument that other successful countries were protectionist during their development phase and thus it was unfair for developed countries, once successful, to insist on free trade for everyone else. For List, the predominant power is the one with the power to benefit from free trade, but this policy keeps others inferior. In the nineteenth century, at the same time as Britain followed a policy of free trade, other countries – notably Germany and the US – used trade policies to protect their industries until they became competitive. Britain was thought to be so far ahead as 'workshop of the world' that other nations could not compete in the production of industrial goods.

List argued that free trade was a device through which a strong nation could maintain its strength and hold back the advancement of others, in his case, nineteenth-century Germany. As he pointed out (1885 [1841], p. 368):

> It is a very common clever device that when anyone has attained the summit of greatness, he kicks away the ladder by which he has climbed up, in order to deprive others of the means of climbing up after him. In this lies the secret of the cosmopolitical doctrine of Adam Smith, and of the cosmopolitical tendencies of his great contemporary William Pitt, and of all his successors in the British Government administrations.

Again this is a persistent argument echoing across the last century. Do the advanced countries distort the trade system to hold back the development of others? List is arguing for government to act in order to increase the wealth and power of the nation and economic nationalists still follow this thinking. To him, it is national development that is most important where Smith and the others were only concerned with individual wealth creation.

List argued for a planned national economy for Germany, including protective tariffs, in an attempt to catch up to Britain. And for a time in the nineteenth century, it may have seemed that Britain was the paramount industrial power and that Germany could not compete. But this was only temporary. German companies did compete and to great effect. What cannot be determined is whether industry protection assisted German competition or if it was merely the workings of the theory of comparative advantage as well as intangibles such as the quality of scientific research and education.

Arguments of this kind persist; the infant-industry argument is often used as a justification for protectionism. In the 1970s and 1980s the apparent successes of countries such as Japan, Taiwan and Korea seemed to show that industrial policy and protection could succeed. As McCraw (1997c, p. 528) argues:

> Any late-developing industrializer that wished to become the home base of firms in an industry characterized by large enterprise would likely require a staged program of development involving protection of the home market, financial and other subvention of the industry, and – in those countries with a home market whose size fell below the minimal efficient scale of plants in such industries – export promotion. Many, many countries found it irresistibly tempting at least to try this kind of coordinated development program. Only a tiny number succeeded.

The economic advancement of countries in Asia, seemingly assisted by industry policy and protectionism against the standard prescription that neither should be used, led to a debate in the early 1990s over the value of protectionist policy. Wade's study of Taiwan, South Korea and Japan showed the success of industry policies in those countries. He argued that the three countries have in common 'an intense and almost unequivocal commitment on the part of government to build up the international competitiveness of domestic industry and thereby eventually raise living standards' and that, as a result, 'it is plausible they have created a competitive form of capitalism from which other countries would be wise to learn' (Wade, 1990, p. 7).

Arguments about the success or otherwise of Asian industrialization and the role of government in bringing it about tend to be dismissed by those arguing for a free-market approach. Certainly Asian governments assisted their industries and in ways contrary to standard economic approaches. Even a report for the World Bank – renowned for its free-market approach – argued that 'in a few economies, mainly in Northeast Asia, in some instances, government interventions resulted in higher and more equal growth than otherwise would have occurred' (World Bank, 1993, p. 6). The report goes on to say that such interventions were successful in only a limited number of instances, and that these are not easily replicated by other countries. The fact remained that Japan, Korea and the ASEAN nations did seem to prosper by happily disregarding open-market solutions. Free-market economists argued that such countries would have performed even better if they had created a more level playing field. The Asian economic crisis of 1997–98 seemed to support the view that Asian development was not as robust as had been initially assumed and that it was not possible to generalize protectionist views from the fleeting success of a few countries.

Wade's 1990 book was influential even as it was criticized by orthodox theorists. Writing some years later Wade was unrepentant, even though the Asian economic crisis had occurred in the interim (Wade, 2004, p. xv):

> Almost all now-developed countries went through stages of industrial assistance policy before the capabilities of their firms reached the point where a policy of (more or less) free trade was declared to be in the national interest. Britain was protectionist when it was trying to catch up to Holland. Germany was protectionist when it was trying to catch up with Britain. The United States was protectionist when it was trying to catch up with Britain and Germany, right up to the end of World War II. Japan was protectionist for most of the twentieth century up to the 1970s, Korea and Taiwan to the 1990s ... By and large, countries that have caught up with the club of wealthy industrial countries have tended to follow the prescriptions of Friedrich List.

Again the literature returns to List, although, as Wade argued, 'protection alone is not enough and that it can hinder more than it helps'; there is, rather, a need for it to be 'part of a larger industrial strategy to nurture the capabilities of domestic firms and raise the rate of domestic investment, always in the context of a private enterprise, market-based economy' (2004, p. xlviii).

Advocates of protection for infant industries may claim that once competitiveness is established for the domestic industry, protective measures can be removed, but the likelihood of this happening is uncertain. Assistance, once given, can lead to demands for further assistance. Further, the process requires that governments, rather than markets, should 'pick winners' – a risky prospect fraught with the possibility of failure. A further problem is that industrial assistance appears to disregard the claims of existing domestic players and how they may be affected by selective assistance to a new competitor. It is not altogether persuasive. The infant-industry argument is superficially attractive, but not altogether persuasive. There are established international firms that can seemingly dominate and a domestic competitor is simply not in a position to make a start without some kind of government assistance. However, as Krauss argues (1997, p. 29):

> Infant-industry arguments for protection must be rejected ... because (1) governments have no skill in picking winners and avoiding losers, and (2) even if they did, the effect of protection would be to rob the potentially competitive industry of its incentive to innovate. Notwithstanding these severe limitations, the infant-industry argument survives because it serves as a convenient subterfuge for governments to pass along special-interest money to favoured industries, friends and supporters.

One problem with infant-industry arguments is that only rarely does the infant grow up. Once assistance is given it is hard to take away and an industry may then choose to survive by continuing its subsidy through political means instead of trying to be competitive. On the other hand, it could be argued that the success of Germany and the US in the nineteenth century or of the newly industrializing countries of East Asia in the 1980s and 1990s is at least partly attributable to government industry policy.

National defence

It is often argued that there are some industries that are so necessary for the defence of the nation that they must be supported. A country's security is, it is supposed, potentially vulnerable if it allows itself to become dependent upon imports which may be critical to its defence efforts. Adam Smith allows for this possibility despite his general arguments against protection, referring to positive benefits of protection of shipping to provide a supply of sailors in case of war. It may be worth subsidising a steel or coal industry in case there is a chance of a future blockade. In Japan the rice industry is regarded this way as the issue of food security is seen as fundamental to national survival. Krauss does allow for the possibility of protection on the grounds of national security, as imports of sensitive products can be cut off in times of war. Even there, however, domestic production subsidies are better than tariff or other import restrictions (Krauss, 1997, p. 33).

The national defence argument is not very strong as food and defence equipment can easily be purchased elsewhere. Any threat to Japanese food supplies is insufficiently credible for food security measures to be really necessary, where making consumers pay several multiples of the world price for a staple lowers their standard of living. This line of argument seems, wittingly or otherwise, to be promoting autarchy, since only autarchy will deliver the self-sufficiency claimed as essential to the national interest.

Reciprocity

Proponents of protection also argue that domestic producers should be allowed to compete with foreign imports on a 'level playing field' and that governments should then attempt to equalize costs – by imposing trade barriers – so that the domestic producer is not unfairly disadvantaged. Retaliatory action can be taken if the trading partner is somehow not playing by the rules. The Smoot-Hawley Act in the US in 1930 was essentially of this kind. There were three main parts. First, the tariff was designed to equalize the cost of production in the US and the country of the main competitor; second, the Act allowed for retaliation against 'unfair competition', and third, the President was authorized to retaliate against any foreign country that imposed barriers against US trade (Overbeek, 1999, pp. 428–9). The result was a tariff war with rapid increases in tariffs in many countries and though this Act did not cause the Great Depression there seems little doubt it exacerbated its effects (Bhagwati, 1988, p. 21).

The apparent re-emergence of protectionism in recent years also owes something to the view held by some that countries should only deal with one another on a reciprocal or equal basis. However, retaliatory measures may inflict far greater harm than any gains and may lead to ever-increasing levels of protection.

The difficulty of adjustment

Even if the free-trade case is accepted there can still be protectionism resulting from the difficulty of adjustment for affected industries. A country that decides to reduce trade barriers is likely to find that some established industries are unable to compete with imports and, as a result, highly visible and politically damaging factory closures may follow. These obviously have political ramifications for the government and the party-political debate. It could be regarded as an adjustment problem, in that other jobs are likely to appear elsewhere in the economy, but adjustment may never occur if the political forces opposing cuts in protection are powerful. The social costs of dislocation may be so substantial as to delay or even postpone indefinitely cuts in protection.

Even if protectionism is often not justified, it may make little sense for any one country to reduce its barriers at a faster rate than its trading partners. There have been some examples of unilateral cuts in protection, for example Australia and New Zealand in the 1980s, but these were from very high levels and the results in terms of adjustment have been patchy rather than providing incontrovertible evidence for the benefits of reducing protection.

Strategic trade theory

In the 1980s, a new form of protection appeared in the literature, under the name 'strategic trade theory'. Where protection aims to assist particular industries, often to the cost of consumers, the aim of strategic trade theory is to maximize trade benefits for the nation as a whole. Each country wants its firms to gain the maximum profits in world markets and may be willing to assist through selective intervention. According to Krugman, a key theorist (1987, p. 131):

> The case for free trade is currently more in doubt than at any time since the 1817 publication of Ricardo's *Principles of Political Economy.* This is not because of the political pressures ... [but] because of the changes which have taken place in the theory of international trade itself ... new models call into doubt the extent to which actual trade can be explained by comparative advantage; they also open the possibility that government intervention in trade via import restrictions, export subsidies, and so on may under some circumstances be in the national interest after all.

A strategic intervention could be justified theoretically if either an industry may develop that will garner greater returns and profits in the long run which will overcome the costs of assistance, or if a strategic industry may be developed that will provide for technical knowledge that would not be gathered another way. In turn that technical information would be able to assist other industries to develop.

The classic example of strategic trade policy at work is that of Airbus Industrie. This company was developed as the result of subsidies from several European governments at a time in the early 1970s when the aircraft industry was dominated by US companies, especially Boeing. It is highly doubtful as to whether a viable European aircraft industry would have developed without government involvement, as there is a massive investment necessary before a single aircraft can be built or sold. Developing their own industry in this area would, European governments thought, assist development of other high-technology aerospace industries, both civilian and military. Thirty years later, it could be argued that the strategy actually worked. The other US manufacturers have been subsumed into Boeing and that company and Airbus control the market between them. For a time, Airbus was more successful than Boeing and it could be argued that without Airbus there would not be a competitor to Boeing. The subsidies by European governments amounted to billions of dollars, but they could well argue that the strategic intervention was successful. Europe now has a viable aircraft industry and other related industries have also been assisted.

At its best, strategic trade theory could lead to a significant national advantage. It is also a response to the emerging theoretical problems with free trade and comparative advantage. But the status of this theory is open to much debate. Strategic trade theory is, so far, an interesting area for research in economics. In some circumstances strategic intervention can be successful, but these circumstances may be quite limited.

Strategic trade theory has not supplanted free-trade theory as yet. Krugman, one of the originators of the term, became one of the key critics of those he called 'strategic traders'. He argued (1994a, p. 134):

> There is a better intellectual case for protection than there used to be, and the case for free trade is often overstated. Nonetheless, there is still a good case for free trade as a general policy – not as an absolute ideal, but as a reasonable rule of thumb. American interests would probably best be served by a world of free trade, with the temptations of strategic trade policy kept out of reach by international treaty.

Along with most other mainstream economists, Krugman is now against strategic trade intervention by government.

Strategic trade policy is a political intervention, with its attendant positive and negative features. On the positive side governments can be seen as responding to political demands, but on the negative side much protection is ill-founded and of dubious value. There can be no guarantee that government intervention will be the right amount in the right place at the right time. There is an ever-present risk of wasting resources. Also, a new system of assistance could be subject to abuse from interest groups who would argue that their own industry is one which deserves special government assistance in the guise of strategic trade policy. At its worst, strategic trade theory could be described as 'neomercantilism' or protectionism by another name.

The best that can be said of the arguments in favour of protection is that there may be specific instances or circumstances when some protection can be effective. But the instances where this occurs are so rare when compared with the actual incidence of protection that the arguments for assistance are mostly rationalizations of political intervention rather than being in any way economically justifiable.

Arguments against protectionism

Protectionism has been argued against by economists since Adam Smith and with a high degree of unanimity. They object to several things. The market is seen as more efficient than the government in deciding whether or not to support a particular industry or firm. As Smith argued (1976 [1776], p. 478):

> To give the monopoly of the home-market to the produce of domestic industry . . . is in some measure to direct private people in what manner they ought to employ their capitals, and must, in almost all cases, be either a useless or a hurtful regulation . . . It is the maxim of every prudent master of a family, never to attempt to make at home what it will cost him more to make than to buy . . . What is prudence in the conduct of every private family, can scarce be folly in that of a great kingdom. If a foreign country can supply us with a commodity cheaper than we ourselves can make it, better buy it of them with some part of the produce of our own industry, employed in a way in which we have some advantage.

Protection arrived at through political means most often results from interest group pressure, particularly from small, well-organized groups (Olson, 1965, 1982). Government action resulting from this kind of pressure is more likely to direct resources to the wrong industry than it is to the one where resources can be used to better effect. It is no accident that politically important groups such as farmers receive most protection. For example, assistance to the sugar industry in the US results in consumers paying about twice as much as they should for sugar. Assistance amounts to more than US$1 billion per year, 42 per cent of the benefit going to 1 per cent of all farms and 'the rationale for rewarding a few large sugar producers with hundreds of millions of dollars at the expense of consumers has never been made clear' (Irwin, 2002, p. 55).

It is usually argued that, instead of governments deciding which industries should be supported and doing so politically, the market can do it better. The best role for government in industry is to provide infrastructure and remove barriers, including providing for adequate competition policy (see Chapter 5) and then get out of the way.

A further criticism of protectionism is that it leads to 'rent-seeking behaviour' (Krueger, 1974). Businesses will spend their efforts on trying to persuade the government to assist them rather than working harder to become more competitive. If an entire economy is constrained by government regulations and controls, there are obvious incentives in trying to gain a favourable government decision in some way. Business executives, indeed the best human resources available, will be devoted to seeking rewards from the political system rather than to increasing the production of goods and services, to the general detriment of the whole economy. This wasted effort is bound to have a negative effect on total real growth.

While any government intervention, including taxation, has a distorting effect on the economy, protectionism is argued to be particularly ineffective in achieving its aims. A subsidy, direct or indirect, to one part of the economy must be paid for by someone else. The firms and workers in one sector are supported by taxes paid by those in another. The goods and services produced in the protected sector are likely to be of higher price than if free trade prevailed and those prices are paid by consumers. The presence of international competitors increases competition in the domestic market, as well as providing a greater variety of goods. Even if consumers are willing to pay higher prices, they still have less money to spend on other goods or services in the economy, with flow-on effects on levels of activity and employment. And as import restrictions 'push the domestic price of a good above the world price, domestic firms produce more, while consumers reduce their overall purchases and suffer a real income loss as a result of the higher prices' (Irwin, 2002, p. 55).

In terms of pure economics trade restrictions are damaging, but there still can be reasons for their introduction. The costs of international competition can be seen readily in factory closures and lines of unemployed. The benefits in lower prices are likely to be less visible.

In general, while it is easy to understand how the politics of trade policy can lead to demands for protectionism, the results leave a lot to be desired. Protectionism would result in higher prices, in turn resulting in an economic slowdown; trading partners would be likely to retaliate, and overall, 'increased protectionism is a remedy that is worse than the disease' (Kapstein, 1996, p. 33).

There may be possible benefits in assisting industries where there is some prospect of competitive advantage and where there are information costs or other impediments currently preventing the private sector from taking advantage of such opportunities. The traditional market approach can be criticized for being essentially static – accepting comparative advantage as it is – rather than dynamic, where comparative and competitive advantage can be created. In such circumstances it might be better to provide positive assistance, rather than imposing tariffs, but it is difficult to create positive assistance programmes that are not contrary to WTO rules.

The politics of protection

The standard case for free trade has been the received economic wisdom for some two hundred years. However, historically, protectionism has been more often the policy in place, and in more countries, than has free trade. Even if it is accepted that world economic prosperity is best served by free trade, in some circumstances protection may be of advantage to a particular nation. Domestic political circumstances may demand a protectionist response; even if there is a later cost to the society or adverse international consequences, it may still be in the interests of a national government to carry this out. Protectionist interventions can be for many reasons, but above all else, where a government sees political advantage in making them, as *The Economist* (13 May 2004) argued:

> Mercantilism has been defunct as an economic theory for at least 200 years, but many practical men in authority remain slaves to the notion that exports must be promoted and imports deterred. Over 40% of the European Union's budget is dedicated to defying Ricardo's theory of comparative advantage, subsidising picturesque farms in Burgundy at the expense of efficient farms elsewhere. Tariffs of 500% on rice imports indulge Japan's nostalgia for its lost agricultural past. And protectionists do not stop at subsidies and tariffs. To repel imports of Vietnamese catfish, American legislators were prepared to rewrite the laws of marine biology, the *New York Times* reported. Only the American variety could henceforth count as 'catfish', they ruled.

The most serious attempt to follow the principles of free trade occurred in the middle of the nineteenth century in Britain. At a time in which the ideas of Smith and Ricardo found their greatest governmental influence, there was a real attempt at implementing free trade. Preferences were abolished in the British Empire by 1853 and other than in the self-governing Dominions – Australia, Canada and New Zealand – which imposed tariffs, free trade remained in place in the colonial empire until the mid-twentieth century. The Dominions did allow lower tariffs with Britain under the scheme of Imperial Preference. Britain itself became protectionist in part after 1914 and fully after 1932 along with much of the world as a response to the Great Depression.

Protectionism can become the ideology of an entire society, held as an unquestioned and settled part of public policy. By the late 1970s, Australia and New Zealand had the highest levels of tariff protection in the industrial world (Hughes, 1998). Both relied on agricultural exports and assistance offered to import-competing industries became more and more elaborate. At times a firm experiencing competitive pressures would merely have to make a submission to government to have a suitable tariff applied. In turn the wages of employees were kept high. Companies benefited, as did workers, and political parties across the spectrum accepted the system, indeed, did not think of criticizing it. Over several decades, though, the standard of living in Australia and New Zealand fell behind other countries and the accession of the UK to the European Economic Community in 1973 affected both antipodean countries, especially New Zealand. The old protectionism could not survive and eventually, in the early 1980s, both New Zealand and Australia cut tariffs markedly, opened up their economies and have generally thrived since.

Even if most economists argue against protectionism; even if most policy-makers agree with them in the abstract; it can still be politically rational for instances of protection to occur. One difficulty is that the costs of reducing tariffs in factory closures and apparent unemployment resulting are visible and politically costly, where the benefits are diffused. As Krugman argues (1994a, pp. 123–4):

The benefits of a trade restriction are usually concentrated on a relatively small, well-organized, and well-informed group of producers, while its costs are usually spread thinly over a large, diffuse group of consumers. As a result, the beneficiaries of a trade restriction are usually much more effective politically than its victims.

It is tempting to see many of the current strategies promoted in trade policy as little more than protectionism by any other name. Indeed, the success of the efforts of those promoting protection seems to support Olson's observation (1982) that small groups in society, especially those with collective economic interests, seem to exercise power out of proportion to their actual numbers.

An example of the power of small concentrated groups was the increase in US steel tariffs of up to 30 per cent announced in March 2002. Despite advice to the US government that more jobs would be lost from downstream industries using steel as an input, there were greater political costs in doing nothing at a time at which US steel companies were struggling to compete. But as steel is used to manufacture other items an increase in its price may make those industries uncompetitive with even greater loss of jobs than in the steel industry itself (Krauss, 1997, p. 25). The US steel industry employs some 200,000 workers directly, but there are 8 million employees in steel-using industries (Irwin, 2002, p. 82). If, through protection, steel becomes too expensive it would be fairly easy for more jobs to be lost than those retained in making steel. A year later, in 2003, the US steel tariff was adjudged to be against WTO rules and later still, after less than two years of operation, the tariff was withdrawn by the US. The point of it was never clear, but, politically, perhaps there was some marginal benefit for the Republicans.

The argument between free trade and protectionism is currently in a state of flux. In the US, the European Union, Japan and elsewhere, governments are being assailed by critics of free trade. Some of these critics are merely resurrecting mercantilism, arguing that governments should endeavour to keep their money at home.

After World War II, developed nations tried to reduce protectionism collectively through the GATT and the WTO. The period around 2000 was another high-point of free trade. Perhaps through international action, protectionism became a less favoured policy option for national governments. International institutions such as the WTO require domestic policy to be much more transparent and, as a result, there is much less scope for government assistance as many of the old methods of selective subsidies, cosy government contracts and formal or informal impediments to international competition become impossible to sustain.

And yet, despite the economics and the international agreements against protectionism, there is no certainty that protectionism is defeated forever. The pressures of domestic politics inevitably revive its prospects; political parties are often drawn to the political advantages of reneging on their commitments. While many countries now ostensibly subscribe to free trade, or at least to the dismantling of protectionist barriers, their domestic and international trade practices frequently suggest that protectionism continues to exert an active influence on public policy.

Japan is perceived to be a major economy with an ambiguous commitment to the principles of free trade. There are real impediments to foreign competition in Japan, as rice-growers in other nations would attest, given the Japanese commitment to the maintenance of what they regard as a significant aspect of their rural heritage. Although Japan is a major exporter, it imports low levels of finished goods and maintains a range of non-tariff barriers. What is seen by some as a tendency to exclude foreign competition is exacerbated by the *keiretsu* system in which networks of local firms deal preferentially with one another without recourse to the market. But the Japanese market is just as open as any other market in the industrialized world, if differences in social custom and legal and administrative systems are taken into account.

The European Union presents perhaps the most overt commitment to the selective retention of protectionist policies. While maintaining free trade within the Union, a range of impediments is applied to external competitors. Tariffs, quotas and 'voluntary' restraints are all used to protect sensitive industries and especially agricultural producers. Indeed, subsidies to agriculture under the Common Agricultural Policy now amount to around half the EU budget. To the chagrin of many developed countries, the EU has instituted preferential arrangements with some of the developing economies and has strategically intervened to assist local industries, such as Airbus Industrie, so that they may compete more effectively against external competitors.

The United States prides itself on being the world's leading free trader and in many respects it is. But when it has seen its interests threatened, or rather when lobby groups can persuade the government that their vital interests are in jeopardy, its government can act in ways that are expressly against its overall goal of freer trade. In 2002, for example, as we have seen, very large increases in tariffs were announced for particular kinds of steel production and a new Farm Bill greatly increased the subsidies available to American farmers. As we have also seen, the steel tariffs were later found to be in contravention of WTO rules. In 1999 sheep farmers in South Dakota lobbied their senator with the result that there was a large tariff imposed on lamb imported from Australia and New Zealand. Two years later this was found to be against WTO rules. The continued and very large trade deficit is leading to pressure on the US Congress to revisit various protectionist measures. American agricultural producers have also been very successful in limiting imports from competitors and in having high tariffs selectively applied to particular products. With regulatory barriers aimed at protecting domestic producers, a full third of the US market for manufactured goods is covered by quotas and other voluntary restrictions – such as those outlined earlier for the importation of Japanese cars.

Protectionist sentiments in Japan or the EU, provided they are not too great, could persist even as the world as a whole was becoming less protectionist, and with little effect on policy. But this is not the case for the US. If protectionism takes hold in the US in any substantive way, that may well spell the end of the period of relatively low protectionism that has been present for much of the post-World War II period.

Conclusion

In pure policy terms, rules-based free trade is far better than protectionism. It remains the best overall option especially for small countries. Protectionism, particularly through tariffs, is not likely to lead to efficient export industries although there may be some circumstances where positive assistance may have some benefits, even if these are likely to only be shortlived. The weight of the argument still seems to be against an increased role for government as far as protection is concerned, but it is arguable whether this is a sensible strategy for all countries. Some countries have decided that there are strategic industries which should be developed in the national interest and have done so successfully.

To the frustration of most economists, real policy and politics can be some distance away from pure policy, which certainly favours the removal of protection. Regardless of the purist arguments, governments will act to protect domestic industry if their political interests demand this, as they often do. There has been a reduction in trade barriers, but 'the matter is not settled because the pressures to weaken the commitment to open markets never abate' (Irwin, 2002, p. 228). Protectionism needs to be understood as an understandable political intervention that can arise in some circumstances. There is a big gap between elite opinion and that of most in the community who are likely to be instinctive protectionists.

The demand for protection is part of the democratic process and reflects the fact that government and business operate in a political as well as an economic market. There are advantages in nations acting together to reduce protection through multilateral organizations like the WTO. In effect governments have given up much of their control to a world body and through this may be able to reduce the internal demands for protection. However, it may be too optimistic to see this as occurring without cost and even the more incoherent arguments made by those opposing globalization may lead to some increase in protectionism in developed countries. Some of the arguments made, if accepted, would lead to developed countries shutting the trade doors to developing countries. But, as Krugman argues, 'A protectionist country is usually less productive and thus poorer than it would have been under free trade; a protectionist world economy almost always so' (1994a, p. 126).

Protectionism has been argued about, literally, for centuries. The economic principles in favour of free trade seem so clear and unambiguous that it is almost inconceivable that protectionism would still attract attention. But it does and, indeed, industry protection of one kind or another never really disappears despite the economic arguments. As long as there are specific electoral advantages in deviating from free and open trade, as long as the benefits of protection are concentrated and the costs dispersed, as long as countries can get around the letter or spirit of trade laws, protectionism will continue.

Chapter 9

The Environment

Introduction

Any economic activity must consume resources of some kind. The consequences of this consumption – small or large – can have a considerable impact upon the natural environment, resulting in pollution, despoliation and the irretrievable loss of animal and plant species. Only a few decades ago, concern for the environment in terms of government response focused mainly upon loss of bio-diversity. But this is no longer the case and now the debate about what governments should address incorporates a much broader range of issues that includes climate change, sustainable development, ozone depletion and desertification. As such, the environment is now one of the most pressing and complex issues between business and government.

For its part, business has economic, legal and, arguably, social responsibilities where the environment is concerned. It should not waste or needlessly destroy valuable resources in its quest for economic gain. It should observe the letter of the law enforcing environmental protection. And it should respect the broad consensus in the community that the environment is a fragile resource held in trust for future generations. Government, on the other hand, is increasingly under pressure from an anxious community to minimize, and where possible control, the harmful effects of economic activity. But in doing so, government is brought more and more into conflict not only with business, whose activities it is seeking to curtail, but also with the advocates of environmental protection whose expectations it is rarely able to meet.

This chapter cannot address all the issues arising from environmentalism – one of the great social movements of the twentieth and twenty-first centuries. Instead, the chapter will discuss why governments act to protect the environment from the consequences of market transactions and the various measures governments can employ to minimize the harmful effects of economic activity. In particular, the chapter will focus upon the choices governments and supranational bodies are being asked to make between traditional command-and-control mechanisms to protect the environment and market-based strategies that are seen by their proponents to offer a more effective solution to some of the more pressing environmental problems, including global warming.

Why does government intervene?

When economic activity impacts adversely upon a third party, it is said that a negative externality has resulted. The polluted air in Hong Kong, which all residents must breathe regardless of whether they use a car, bus or ferry, would be seen as a classic negative externality. The oil spill from the *Exxon Valdez* in 1989, when approximately 11 million gallons of oil (38,800 metric tonnes) were spilt along pristine Alaskan coastline with catastrophic results for native wildlife, is another example. Indeed, it is depressing to reflect that it would be impossible to list all the negative externalities affecting the environment. In every part of the world, environmental degradation – much of it irreversible – has occurred, prompting strong pressure on government to correct or at least minimize the impact of business activity.

In Chapter 4 the two main theories that may explain government regulation – public interest and private interest – were discussed. In summary, public interest theory posits that governments regulate because they are responding to the community's expectation that they will do so in the public interest. Private interest theory puts a contrary view, arguing that government intervention is simply a response to the representations of powerful private interests. These private interests 'capture' government regulatory instruments to promote their own agenda. Supporters of environmental regulation claim government intervention responds to community concern. Critics claim that environmental regulation represents the ability of private interests (whose identity depends on the perspective of the critic) to distort public policy for their own gain. Those who argue government has not gone far enough to protect the environment might contend that government has been captured by producer groups seeking to maintain an economic advantage gained from their exploitation of the environment. Those who believe government has gone too far in protecting the environment might maintain that policy has been by snared by groups hostile to any activity affecting the environment.

Regardless of the reasons for government intervention, it is clear that there are few incentives for business to voluntarily restrict or curb its activities. Government, on the other hand, can hardly avoid acting to protect the environment. As Papadakis and Rainbow (1996, p. 108) observe:

> The emergence of green movements and political organizations represents, paradoxically, the expectation by a growing proportion of the population that political institutions, notably those that evolved during the formation of the welfare state in the nineteenth century, become even more involved in regulating the behaviour of powerful groups in society and in shaping the social behaviour of all individuals. Most people expect the government to assume a major role in encouraging industries that help to protect the environment, in educating people and in setting standards.

It was not always so. Until the early 1960s, when the environmental movement gained momentum and started to influence public debate and government action, pressure upon government to protect the environment was sporadic and generally limited to matters of public health. Many of the resources used by business – such as air and water – were viewed as common property, freely available in unlimited quantities and with few if any limitations upon what might be done with them. The consequence was that 'individuals and organizations, both public and private, used the environment as a convenient dump – which of course is the act of polluters polluting' (Weidenbaum, 2004, p. 61). Factories belched out noxious fumes, ships offloaded contaminated bilge, and households used the cheapest, if most inefficient, fuels. All this was possible because the private benefit from polluting far outweighed the social cost, or externality, and the willingness of government to intervene in such matters.

But public opinion and expectations of both business and government dramatically changed. To some the seminal moment in the modern environmental movement was the publication of Rachel Carson's *Silent Spring* in 1962 (see Gore, 1994; Braithwaite and Drahos, 2000; Weidenbaum, 2004). Carson, a former US government marine scientist, provided some of the first

Box 9.1   Milestones in the environmental movement

1962 – *Silent Spring* by Rachel Carson is released, outlining the impact of toxic chemicals on people and the environment.

1968 – UN Biosphere Conference held in Paris, France, to discuss global environmental problems.

1972 – Convention concerning the Protection of World Cultural and Natural Heritage adopted by the General Conference of UNESCO.

1972 – UN Conference on the Human Environment held in Stockholm, Sweden. Delegates lobby for the creation of the UN Environment Program.

1974 – A study on chlorofluorocarbons (CFCs) is published in the scientific journal *Nature*. It finds that CFCs can destroy ozone molecules and may pose a threat to the Earth's ozone layer.

1979 – Convention on Long-Range Transboundary Air Pollution is adopted. The Convention aims to regulate pollution travelling across national borders.

1983 – Prediction of global warming by the United States Environmental Protection Agency and National Academy of Sciences.

evidence of how pesticides used without proper control or knowledge were poisoning the environment. The publication of her book caused a sensation. Pesticides manufacturers sought to discredit the book and its author, but President Kennedy ordered a review of pesticide use and Carson testified before Congress prior to her death in 1964. With *Silent Spring*, public attitudes towards the environment, and what was acceptable in terms of economic activity, changed irrevocably. Environmental activism became one of the most potent political forces in Western society, transcending class and political affiliation. Governments everywhere started to pass laws to protect the environment and created agencies to enforce these laws. See Box 9.1 for a summary of the key developments.

1985 – 'Hole' in the ozone layer discovered.
1986 – Explosion and meltdown of a nuclear reactor at Chernobyl in the USSR sends radioactive particles across Europe.
1987 – Montreal Protocol on Substances that Deplete the Ozone Layer adopted, introducing measures for phasing out the production of some ozone-depleting chemicals.
1989 – The *Exxon Valdez* tanker spills 38,800 metric tonnes of crude oil on the coast of Alaska.
1989 – Basel Convention adopted, with the aim of preventing the shipping of hazardous waste from industrial nations to the developing world.
1992 – UN Conference on Environment and Development (Earth Summit) held in Rio de Janeiro, Brazil, attended by most countries and 117 heads of state.
1997 – Kyoto Protocol developed. Under the protocol, industrial countries must cut their carbon dioxide emissions by 6 to 8 per cent from 1990 levels by 2008–12.
2002 – European Union ratifies the Kyoto Protocol.
2003 – Europe adopts first climate emissions-trading law, paving the way for carbon dioxide to be traded as of 2005.
2004 – European Union releases a pollution register, providing unprecedented public access to data on industrial emissions.

Source: Adapted from Worldwatch Institute.

Government and the environment

When governments first intervened in environmental matters, punitive regulation was the instrument most commonly used. The intention was to change or limit the behaviour of the polluter, so that if a river were polluted those causing the pollution would cease or at least moderate their polluting activity. But the effect of this approach was that governments directed most of their resources to addressing pollution after it was generated, as opposed to encouraging the actual reduction of waste generation. In other words, government regulation acted to punish transgressors but not to prevent pollution. Because of the inherent limitations of this approach, alternative regulatory instruments such as taxes and subsidies, property rights and marketable permits or trading systems are now increasingly being used.

The command-and-control approach to environmental regulation assumes that environmental degradation can be prevented or at least ameliorated by changing the behaviour of polluters. But when regulating for environmental protection, government must first decide whether the purpose of regulation is to ban a form of polluting behaviour altogether or to allow it under certain conditions. Then a choice must be made between technology-based and media-quality regulation. Technology-based regulation uses standards to dictate what kind of technology polluters must install in order to minimize their effluents. Media-quality regulation involves setting a minimum acceptable quality for the receiving medium – air, water or soil. Polluters are then limited to that level of emission. Once a decision has been made, those formulating regulations then typically set environmental quality standards, decide on the abatement actions or methods of achieving the standards (such as permits), inspect and monitor compliance with the standards and abatement schedules, and take enforcement actions against violators.

The command-and-control approach has brought some positive results, even if some style these as 'easy victories' (Demmke, 2001, p. 19). Since the widespread adoption of environmental regulation from the 1960s onwards, its impact has been far-reaching. Also known as the 'end of the pipe' approach because of its focus upon the discharge pipe as the point of regulation, this form of regulation in the US has resulted in the removal of lead from petrol and paint, the reduction of raw sewage discharge into waterways and the banning of DDT and other dangerous pesticides. As a consequence, lead levels in the average American's bloodstream dropped by 25 per cent between 1976 and 1995, fishing and swimming are now possible in some previously polluted waters, and the bald eagle – once close to extinction – has been removed from the list of endangered species (Clinton and Gore, 1995).

Problems with the command-and-control approach

Despite the successes of end-of-pipe regulation, serious environmental problems persist. Many rivers and lakes still do not meet water-quality standards. Many people continue to live in areas where the air does not meet public health standards. The incidence of some illnesses which may be related to environmental pollution

– such as asthma and breast cancer – is increasing. Animal and plant species continue to become extinct at an alarming rate. And disasters – such as the spillage of 100 tonnes of cyanide from the Baie Mare mine tailings pond into Romanian and Hungarian rivers in April 2000 – still occur with appalling consequences. Clearly, end-of-pipe regulation alone cannot address, or resolve, all the problems posed by humankind's interaction with the environment. The reasons for this are both numerous and complex. As Demmke explains, environmental regulation is no simple or straightforward matter. Environmental protection has to take account of complex interdependencies and interrelationships between the environmental media (air, water and soil) and biodiversity, climatic, and seasonal and geographical variations in environmental conditions, in the context of constantly changing states of knowledge and scientific evidence. Environmental law is similarly complex (Demmke, 2001, pp. 18–19):

> Because of the potentially very serious consequences of a lack of foresight, environmental law has to an important extent to be based, both in formulation and interpretation, on preventive and precautionary principles rather than a curative approach. Because it touches everyone, it has to involve a comprehensive set of actors, from government, industry and enterprise to the general public, often implying a very difficult balancing exercise. And finally because it relates to general interests in which there is often not a proprietary stake (clean air and water, a healthy biodiversity), it has to envisage methods of ensuring its effectiveness other than those which are adequate in other fields of law.

For Eisner, Worsham and Ringquist (2000, p. 135), the inherently challenging nature of environmental regulation makes it the most technically complex area of regulatory policy. Regulators must decide on safe exposure levels for toxic and carcinogenic materials in emissions, pesticides and the like. Safe means of disposing of hazardous waste must be found. Emissions from thousands of sources must be constantly monitored. The consequences of global warming must be accurately projected. All this places a heavy reliance upon those with scientific knowledge and technical expertise. Overlaying these challenges is a concern that regulation should be implemented 'without seriously disrupting the existing system of property rights or compromising economic performance'

(Eisner *et al.*, 2000, p. 135). This dual imperative, of protecting the environment while not constraining economic activity or comparative advantage, is at the heart of the tension between business and government in environmental matters.

The command-and-control approach to environmental regulation has also resulted in a vast array of rules. As Demmke (2001, p. 17) observes:

> Regulatory bodies need to have sufficient administrative, scientific and legal resources to issue rules and regulations and to monitor their enforcement but as the number of environmental laws has grown, the capacity of public administrations to administer them has often lagged behind.

Critics claim that the proliferation of environmental rules and regulations has resulted in a regulatory process that is cumbersome, unresponsive and inefficient. DeHart-Davis and Bozeman (2001, p. 474) describe the documentation supporting the US Clean Air Act 1990 as 'typically inaccessible and complex, burying applicable requirements in hundreds of pages of regulatory detail that states rarely distributed'.

A curious side-effect of environmental regulation is the tendency of business to overcomply or 'to spend more money and to commit more resources than are required to comply with environmental regulations' (DeHart-Davis and Bozeman, 2001, p. 471). Overcompliance is more likely to occur where a business has extensive communication with the regulatory authority and where the compliance tasks have been subcontracted, particularly under conditions of regulatory uncertainty. While overcompliance might appear to be an unanticipated bonus for the environment, De Hart-Davis and Bozeman counter that it may also inefficiently use resources that could be better used on alternative pollution abatement activity.

Another problematic aspect of environmental regulation is that it can be as susceptible to rent-seeking as any other form of regulation. According to Adler (1996):

> There is no reason to expect environmental regulations to be immune from the economic pressures that create rent-seeking in other contexts. In fact, by their very nature, environmental regulations are conducive to rent-seeking, for in the environmental context, both regulated firms and 'public interest' representatives

stand to gain from reductions in output and the creation of barriers to entry.

Adler (1996) cites the actions of the US Business Council for a Sustainable Energy Future, a coalition of gas, wind, solar and geothermal power producers, in lobbying for deep cuts in greenhouse gas emissions, to support his claim. The efforts of power utilities in California to require the sale of electric vehicles and representations in the northeastern United States for the introduction of government subsidies for the purchase of electric cars are also mentioned as examples of rent-seeking under the guise of regulation. Apart from the economic consequences for taxpayers and consumers, Adler argues rent-seeking disadvantages smaller firms, while for the larger firms it represents 'a hurdle that can be cleared by reducing profit margins or delaying capital investments'.

There are other limitations of the command-and-control approach. Some regulations may be more readily implemented – and so work better – in some economies than others. For example, emission standards produce few problems for highly industrialized, affluent and pollution-importing countries. They are, however, more problematic for pollution-exporting and less industrialized countries. For these countries, environmental regulation in the form of emission standards involves high costs and low environmental benefits and is unlikely to be an effective form of regulation. Further, once an environmental standard has been reached there is little incentive for the polluter to go any further in reducing emissions by trying new procedures or new technologies. Because all polluters must do is comply with standards, a continuing level of pollution is accepted regardless of the consequences. The fixed nature of regulation means that it is unlikely that all regulations will adequately reflect technological progress. Further, the financial burden regulations place upon the polluter (the so-called 'polluter pays' principle), can often be readily passed on to the consumer (von Weizsäcker, 1990, p. 201). Thus there may be little real incentive for the polluter to change the activity that is damaging the environment or to invest in technologies that might reduce pollution to a greater extent than that stipulated by regulation.

But of all the limitations of the command-and-control approach, the most problematic might be the political environment in which it is applied. It can be politically difficult for governments to prosecute companies for environmental malfeasance, especially if the source of pollution is a major employer or investor in a town or community. Fines and poor publicity in relation to environmental problems can have a detrimental effect upon a company's operations, leading to loss of employment opportunities. At the end of the day, a government and community may prefer to accept a degree of environmental damage if it means jobs are protected in the community.

In summary then, the arguments against the command-and-control approach to environmental regulation suggest that it is essentially a blunt, inefficient and ineffectual tool whose cost, relative to alternative approaches to achieve the desired goal, is excessive (Stiglitz, 1997; Weidenbaum, 2004).

Taxes and subsidies

Pollution taxes, or effluent charges, share with regulation the objective of increasing the cost of, and therefore discouraging, pollution. However, the idea of pollution taxes is that the impost should reduce as the amount of pollution reduces, thus presenting incentives for firms to operate in ways that significantly reduce pollution. Those who pollute least are rewarded in the marketplace, while those who continue to pollute must deal with the higher costs imposed by the taxation system. As Weidenbaum (2004) argues, if prices of goods and services reflect the costs imposed on the environment, consumers will shift to those goods and services that embody lower pollution costs. In this sense, pollution taxes are tools to correct a serious source of market failure – namely, the absence of a 'price' on the careless and/or excessive use of environmental resources. However, if a tax is set high, it has the effect of totally discouraging the polluting behaviour because of its impact upon the price of a product. If it is set low, pollution may not be eliminated but governments will some have funds to clean up the resulting pollution.

Pollution taxes or fees have a long history in Europe. A 'polluter pays' system has been in place in Germany's Ruhr Valley since 1913. France has used fees in conjunction with a permit system as part of its water-quality programme since 1969. The Netherlands charges effluent fees based on volume and concentration of the effluent – an initiative credited with reducing emissions of cadmium, copper, lead, mercury and zinc by more than 86 per cent between 1976 and 1994. In this last instance, it can be argued that the imposition of pollution taxes has contributed substantially to a positive outcome for the environment.

The Greater London Authority charges cars entering the centre of London a congestion tax of £8 and threatened to increase this to £25 for cars it considered environmentally damaging – cars emitting more than 225g CO_2 a kilometre (*The Times*, 13 July 2006). In this, the Authority and its Mayor, Ken Livingstone, had larger, more expensive cars such as the SUVs known colloquially as 'Chelsea tractors' squarely in their sights.

Some political groupings, such as the Greens, support the introduction of carbon taxes (Brown and Singer, 1996, p. 14):

> because they are a way of making the price of energy include the costs it imposes on everyone else: costs reflected in high insurance premiums because of catastrophic weather events, in disruption to agriculture, and in unpredictable changes to the environment, health and society, both in the short term and for future generations.

However, carbon taxes have met stiff opposition from other quarters. Industries most affected have mounted campaigns with some success in the US, the EU and Australia, arguing that such taxes would adversely affect employment and national competitiveness. Sceptics also suggest that carbon taxes will simply drive carbon-intensive production from high-tax to low-tax jurisdictions. If firms relocate on this basis, the effectiveness of carbon taxes is undermined, 'because carbon dioxide contributes equally to climate instability wherever it is emitted' (Hoerner and Muller, 1996). Supporters of pollution taxes counter that these claims are overstated, but concede that such taxes are 'best viewed as one tool in a climate change policy tool kit that includes voluntary agreements, efficiency standards, technology-promoting policies, infrastructure investments, land use policies and other measures' (Hoerner and Muller, 1996, p. 4).

Subsidies, in the form of incentives to firms which reduce pollution, are an alternative to taxes. An example of a subsidy would be a tax credit for the use of pollution abatement machinery. Another example would be government support for recycling programmes. Yet another is a rebate for part of the cost of renewable energy equipment, such as rooftop solar panel systems or wind turbines. *The Economist* (18 November 2006) reports that California has created 'extraordinary incentives' for businesses and homes to adopt what would otherwise be unaffordable technology. Citing the example of a solar panel installation in a Napa Valley winery, *The Economist* explains how US$400,000 of the original cost of US$1.2 million is rebated by the gas and electricity utility, another 30 per cent can be written off as a tax credit provided by the federal government and another tax credit is provided by the state government.

Economists tend to be lukewarm about subsidies – arguing that they are economically inefficient. As *The Economist* (31 May 2007) observes:

> Subsidies are popular with recipient companies; with greens, who reckon that any money used to combat climate change is money well spent; and with governments, which like handing out taxpayers' money. Taxpayers tend not to notice. Some economists also advocate subsidies to particular technologies because they need a kick-start to get them to a market. That may be true in the case of big, risky processes such as CCS ['carbon capture and storage', also known as carbon sequestration]. But subsidies tend to be inefficient because they require governments to pick technologies. And, once in place, they are hard to abolish.

Even so, subsidies are seen to provide a better way than regulation to encourage the behaviour society wants (Stiglitz, 1997, p. 512). *The Economist* (18 November 2006) estimates that California, which aims to generate 20 per cent of its power from renewable sources by 2010, will pay US$2.9 billion in rebates over ten years to households and businesses that install solar panels. In this sense, taxes are the stick, while subsidies are the carrot. Both share the aim of adjusting private costs to account for social costs.

Property rights

The case for assigning property rights as a means of addressing environmental problems is mainly associated with the economist Ronald Coase. In an influential article (1960), Coase challenged the view that negative externalities were best dealt with by government regulation. Coase argued that punishing or restricting the activity of the producer of the externality could 'lead to results which are not necessarily, or even usually, desirable' (1960, p. 2). A more effective approach, he claimed, was to restrict government intervention to the designing and assigning of property rights, so that the market – rather than government – would take care of externalities.

Coase's theorem that the absence of property rights contributed substantially to environmental despoliation has been linked to the propositions popularly associated with Garrett Hardin's celebrated essay, 'The Tragedy of the Commons' (1968). In his essay, Hardin argued that the 'commons' – his metaphor for those resources shared by all, such as air and water – suffer because they are freely available to all who want to use them, even if this leads inevitably to exploitation. Pollution occurs because (Hardin, 1968, p. 1245)

> it is not a question of taking something out of the commons, but of putting something in – sewage, or chemical, radioactive, and heat wastes into water; noxious and dangerous fumes into the air; and distracting and unpleasant signs into the line of sight ... The rational man finds his share of the cost of the wastes he discharges into the commons is less than the cost of purifying his wastes before releasing them. Since this is true for everyone, we are locked into a system of 'fouling our own nest', so long as we behave only as independent, rational, free enterprisers.

Hardin called for a redefinition of property rights to address, at least in part, the tragedy of the commons. Acknowledging that 'the air and waters around us cannot be fenced', Hardin accepted that property rights would not provide a universal solution. In some cases, coercive laws or taxing devices would be necessary. Indeed, Hardin accepted that assigning property rights would not always guarantee responsible stewardship of the earth's resources, observing (1968, p. 1245):

> The owner of a factory on the bank of a stream – whose property extends to the middle of the stream – often has difficulty seeing why it is not his natural right to muddy the waters flowing past his door.

The argument that environmental problems arise because property rights are not clearly defined or, if defined, are not effectively enforced, once attracted little support. But this is changing. *The Economist* (4 July 2002) reports that schemes for tradable quotas have helped revive fishing stocks in Iceland and New Zealand, while 'similar rights-based approaches have led to revivals in stocks of African elephants in southern Africa'. To Stiglitz (1997, p. 510), 'the appeal of Coase's theorem is that it assigns a minimal role for government'. However, like Hardin, Stiglitz concedes that there are serious practical limitations to property rights as a solution for environmental problems and that government must take a proactive role if the objectives of environmental protection are to be realized.

Marketable permits or trading programmes

For economists, 'the environmental pollution problem is essentially one of altering people's incentives' (Weidenbaum, 2004, p. 61). Taxes and subsidies have this effect, but so too do marketable permits or trading programmes. Once confined mainly to the United States, these have now been increasingly adopted elsewhere and are regarded by many as the most effective means of reducing greenhouse gas emissions and addressing global warming.

Rosenzweig, Varilek and Janssen (2002, p. 2) report that there are essentially two systems of marketable permits or trading programmes – 'cap and trade' systems and 'baseline and credit' systems. Under cap-and-trade systems (also known as allowance-based trading), a government authority sets the maximum level of pollution that can be released by sources. This authority also sets exactly the number of permits to produce the desired emission level. This level is the cap. All sources of pollution are required to have permits (i.e. allowances) to emit which specify exactly how much the source is allowed to emit. The permits are freely transferable and can be bought and sold. Under a baseline-and-credit system, each participant is provided a baseline against which their performance is measured. If an action is taken to reduce emissions, the difference between the baseline and the actual emissions can be credited and traded. The baseline established for crediting purposes can be fixed (based upon an absolute level of emissions) or it can be dynamic, decreasing or increasing over time. The key distinction between a cap-and-trade system and a baseline-and-credit system is that in the former each regulated source's emissions are required to achieve an emissions cap, which is a fixed quantity. Such a limit is not necessarily imposed in a baseline-and-credit system.

Marketable permits or trading programmes incorporate significant incentives for businesses to find ways and means of reducing their polluting activity. The seller in this system benefits financially from being less harmful to the environment, while the buyer (who wishes to pollute more) must bear a financial burden. Under this approach, there is a very clear incentive for business to develop ways and means of reducing pollution and thus costs. The idea of creating a market for pollution was given its first major test in the US in 1990 when the Clean Air Act Amendments imposed a cap on sulphur dioxide emissions from power plants. The level of allowable emissions was reduced in two phases. Sources could comply by installing technology, switching to fuels lower in sulphur content, purchasing allowances from other participants in the programme or engaging in other activities that would reduce sulphur dioxide emissions. Rosenzweig, Varilek and Janssen (2002, p. 3) praise the Clean Air Act Amendments legislation for achieving greater environmental benefits than required by law 'at lower cost than had been estimated prior to the program's implementation'.

Market-based environmental strategies are increasingly a 'policy of choice' for governments (Clausen, 2002, p. ii). The success of the US acid rain programme and other smaller-scale experiments has served as a catalyst for the adoption of the concept of marketable permits in continental Europe, the UK and, most notably, the Kyoto Protocol on Climate Change. Supporters of marketable permits argue that they represent a cheaper and more effective means of protecting the environment than the traditional regulatory approach. Being cheaper, there is less waste of resources and lower compliance costs make agreement on targets more achievable. The International Energy Agency, an autonomous energy forum linked to the OECD, estimates that trading will lead to cost savings of between 30 per cent and 90 per cent for countries and companies (IEA, 2001, p. 14).

The Kyoto Protocol

In 1997, the parties to the United Nations Framework Convention on Climate Change reached an historic agreement in Kyoto, Japan, in response to worldwide concern about global warming and its impact upon the ozone layer. The Kyoto Protocol sets legally binding limits on the amount of human-made greenhouse gas emissions (GHGs) permitted for nearly all of the world's developed countries which to date have overwhelmingly contributed to the build up of GHGs in the atmosphere. Under the agreement, developed countries have committed to reduce their GHG emissions by an average of 5 per cent during the 'commitment period' 2008–12. Box 9.2 shows the increases in CO_2 emissions from energy use.

Box 9.2   World carbon dioxide (CO_2) emissions from energy use

According to the OECD, global emissions of carbon dioxide have increased by 88 per cent since 1971, and are projected to rise by another 52 per cent by 2030. Although OECD nations produced 66 per cent of the total global CO_2 emissions in 1971, the rise in emissions from developing nations saw the OECD's share of total emissions fall to 49 per cent by 2004. The most significant non-OECD contributor to escalating CO_2 levels has been China, whose emissions increased by 5.5 per cent per year between 1971 and 2004. The accompanying table illustrates regional trends in carbon dioxide emissions.

World CO_2 emissions from energy use, by region, million tonnes, 1971–2004

Region	1971	1984	1994	2004
OECD total	9,357	10,328	11,450	12,911
Middle East	126	467	791	1,183
Former USSR	1,994	3,159	2,505	2,313
Non-OECD Europe	248	380	252	265
China	809	1,660	2,832	4,769
Other Asia	430	871	1,570	2,499
Latin America	366	534	678	907
Africa	266	468	575	814
Bunkers*	514	491	688	921

* Refers to emissions from 'bunker fuels', which are used for international marine transport and aviation.

Source: Data from OECD (2007). *OECD Factbook 2007*.

What is especially distinctive about the Kyoto Protocol (see Box 9.3) is the combination of ambitious GHG reduction targets, which are differentiated according to the GHG output of each country, with innovative market-based mechanisms to help countries achieve their targets at the lowest possible cost. The Protocol has four key provisions relating to emissions trading – it allows countries that cut emissions by more than they are required to to 'bank' the excess as credits for the future; it gives countries credits for reducing emissions in other countries; it allows trading in emissions credits between countries; and it offers emissions reduction units to countries financing pollution-reducing projects in another developed country (United Nations Environment Programme, 1999). While the international trading system under the Protocol is still evolving, trading markets have emerged and continue to evolve in response to new policy developments at the international, regional, national and subnational levels.

The Protocol recognizes that reducing GHGs is much more expensive in some countries than in others, and thus allows parties to use emissions trading and other flexibility mechanisms to meet their commitments at much reduced cost (Business Roundtable Environment Taskforce, 1998). Some countries have declined to ratify the Protocol on grounds of domestic economic and political considerations. The US Business Roundtable summarizes US objections in the following terms (Business Roundtable Environment Taskforce, 1998, pp. 1–3):

1. The targets and timetables require the US to make significant and immediate cuts in energy use, involving 'painful choices'. If it were to do this, the US would shoulder a disproportionate level of reduction and be at a competitive disadvantage.
2. Unless the developing countries also commit to emission reductions, the Protocol is incomplete and will not work. Many developing countries are rapidly growing their economies and will become the largest emitters of GHGs in the next 15–20 years.
3. Certain carbon 'sinks' may be used to offset emission reductions, but the Protocol does not establish how sinks will be calculated. Carbon sinks have tremendous potential as a means of reducing emissions, but too much is currently unknown to make a fair determination.
4. The Protocol contains no mechanisms for compliance and enforcement. (The Roundtable argues that it would be

inappropriate for any country to ratify a legally binding international agreement that lacks compliance guidelines and
enforcement mechanisms.)

5. The Protocol includes flexible, market-based mechanisms to
    achieve emission reductions, but it does not establish how
    these mechanisms would work and to what extent they could
    be used.

6. The Protocol leaves the door open for the imposition of
    mandatory policies and measures to meet commitments. This
    may result in the command-and-control approach favoured by
    the European Union and many developing countries being
    imposed on the US.

7. Finally, the procedures for ratification of, and amendment to,
    the Protocol make it difficult to remedy before it comes into
    force.

The US position on Kyoto has been highly contentious. In terms
of per capita emissions of carbon from fossil fuel combustion,
cement manufacturing and gas flaring, the US emits far more
GHGs per person than developing countries, or even developed
countries such as Germany, the United Kingdom and France.
Greenpeace International (2002) estimates that the US accounted
for 36.1 per cent of 1990 CO_2 emissions by industrialized countries. Certainly, the US has emitted a cumulative total many, many
times that of China (approximately 4.5 times more populous) and
India (approximately 3.5 times more populous). Most countries
affected by the emissions reductions targets have proceeded with
ratification, including EU member countries. However, without the
involvement of the world's largest economy, the future of the
Protocol remains problematic.

Problems of the market approach

Despite their current vogue, marketable permits and trading
systems have many critics. Some opposition reflects the view that it
is simply immoral to buy and sell allowances to pollute, even
though other regulatory instruments generally place no charge or
cost upon the act of pollution. One organization, Rising Tide, an
internationally active grassroots network of independent groups
and individuals, reflects this view, dismissing the market in carbon
emissions trading as 'colonialism with a modern face' (Rising Tide,

Box 9.3 The Kyoto Protocol

Who has committed to Kyoto?

The Kyoto Protocol came into force on 16 February 2005. Of the parties to the United Nations Framework Convention on Climate Change, 174 have ratified, accepted, approved or acceded to the Protocol, and are therefore expected to meet their emissions targets. The United States has not yet ratified the Protocol.

What are the targets?

The Annex I Parties to the United Nations Framework Convention on Climate Change were set the target of reducing their greenhouse gasses by a certain percentage from 1990 emission levels. The commitment period for emission limitations or reductions is 2008–12. Of the 40 Annex I parties, over half have agreed to reduce their emissions by 8 per cent from 1990 levels. Canada, Hungry, Japan and Poland will make a 6 per cent reduction. New Zealand, the Russian Federation and Great Britain have committed to maintaining their emissions at 1990 levels, while three countries – Norway, Australia and Iceland – have indicated that their emission levels will increase from 1990 levels over the commitment period.

Source: United Nations (1998). United Nations Framework Convention on Climate Change, Annex B, Kyoto Protocol to the United Nations Framework Convention on Climate Change.

2002). According to this critique, carbon-trading perpetuates and deepens unequal access to and control of resources. In this view, property rights in this new market will be allocated by those who trade fastest and those who already pollute the most. Arguments such as these reflect a fundamental distrust in the ability of markets, and capitalism, to address environmental problems.

Kopp and Toman (1998) identify additional concerns about emissions trading as an instrument of environmental protection. They argue that rich countries may simply 'buy' their way out of their commitments to reduce GHG emissions by purchasing permits from poorer countries that then have fewer allowable emissions. Richer, industrialized countries can thus avoid pressure to make long-term changes in their energy and economic systems to reduce GHG emissions. A further concern is that the effectiveness of a trading system depends on the enforceability of the cap on emissions within all countries trading permits. To the extent that countries lack the necessary institutions or the political will to enforce caps, the trading system becomes a sham.

Another potential problem with the market approach is that using allowances to offset geographically concentrated emissions could result in isolated instances of high emissions and local risks to health and the environment. Yet another concern is that emissions trading may not be transparent (Petsonk, Dudek and Goffman, 1998). However, supporters of the market approach dismiss both these concerns. They claim that GHGs mix uniformly in the atmosphere regardless of where they are emitted, rendering concerns about local concentrations baseless. As for trading regimes, supporters claim they can provide an equal or greater degree of transparency than that afforded by virtually any other regulatory instrument because emissions trading requires each source to make public its total actual emissions as well as its total allowable emissions (Petsonk *et al.*, 1998).

Advocates of emissions trading claim that properly designed markets can capitalize on the common interests of nations, emissions sources and the public to provide incentives to meet and even exceed environmental and economic goals. In the process, trading programmes have the capacity to increase environmental effectiveness, reduce compliance costs, create financial rewards for environmental performance, tap existing expertise in the search for new solutions, and create incentives for new technologies. But to do this, five key elements must be present (Petsonk *et al.*, 1998, p. 5):

1. *Measurement* – quantifying emissions, including extra allowable emissions, accurately;
2. *Transparency* – making reporting and details of programme operations publicly available;
3. *Accountability* – holding participants accountable for meeting their own goals;
4. *Fungibility* – minimizing constraints on transactions;
5. *Consistency* – applying fixed rules objectively and automatically.

In the absence of one or more of these, it is inevitable that the integrity of the process will be questioned. The challenge for governments and their agencies, and increasingly for international agencies as well, is to ensure that emissions-trading systems incorporate each of the factors listed above. The risk is that they will not, and that as a consequence the environment will suffer further.

Supporters of emissions trading acknowledge that while international emission trading is full of promise, 'difficult political and technical issues remain' (International Energy Agency, 2001, p. 15). Some question whether a market for greenhouse gases can function, given high transaction and monitoring costs, the difficulties of enforcing the market, and the uncertainty of international emission trades. Others fear that carbon taxes will introduce top-down planning of energy markets, thus potentially stifling the natural market innovation that is the source of much environmental progress. The experience of the European Emissions Trading Scheme (ETS) is perhaps instructive. Since January 2005, some 12,000 large industrial plants in the European Union have been able to buy and sell permits to release carbon dioxide into the atmosphere. Under this trading scheme, those firms that exceed their CO_2 emissions targets may buy allowances from 'greener' firms and thus help Europe to reach the targets set under the Kyoto Protocol. However, despite the scheme and the trading it fosters, *The Economist* (31 May 2007) reports that carbon emissions in Europe are not falling. Several factors may account for this – the initial generosity of the European Commission in handing out allowances to industry which subsequently forced carbon prices down; the exemption of entire sectors such as transport and building; the cheapness of certified emissions reductions, or credits, purchased from developing economies such as China; the failure of industry in Europe to move away from its historical reliance upon coal, and the failure of technological innovation to emerge as had been hoped. In short, the brief history of the European ETS suggests that it may be a while before we see any broad agreement on either the efficacy of emissions trading or how such systems are best constructed.

The role of international organizations

While the Kyoto Protocol has been the focus of considerable attention in recent years, it would be erroneous to assume that the involvement of international organizations in the environment is a relatively recent phenomenon. A number of international agencies have been active in environmental matters since the Second World War (Braithwaite and Drahos, 2000). The International Labour

Organization (ILO) is involved in matters where worker health and safety and environmental concerns overlap, the World Health Organization (WHO) where human health needs intersect with environmental protection, the Food and Agriculture Organization (FAO) with problems such as pesticides, fertilizers and soil erosion, and the United Nations Educational, Scientific and Cultural Organization (UNESCO) with the protection of cultural heritage.

As the role of government has grown in relation to the environment, so too has the influence of international bodies and instruments of international governance. The Chernobyl disaster – the world's worst nuclear accident – vividly illustrated that the consequences of one country's policies cannot be quarantined within one country's borders or to one environmental medium. The events at the Chernobyl nuclear power plant had far-reaching consequences, not only for the people of Ukraine but also for neighbouring Belarus and the countries of Northern Europe when clouds of radioactive material were blown northward, contaminating water, soil and air. Such is the nature of modern environmental disasters.

But it is not just individual disasters such as Chernobyl that prompt action at international level. One of the most pressing issues facing the planet today is due to market activities in most if not all countries around the world. Global warming is not attributable to the actions of one country or even a small number of countries. All countries contribute in some way to this phenomenon, whether their economy is developed or developing. A problem of this magnitude can only be effectively addressed by a coordinated global response in which all countries (or as many as possible) accept some responsibility for the problem and its amelioration.

With the growing consciousness of environmental issues and the increasing political influence of environmental organizations, it was inevitable that international organizations would become involved in the formulation of a global response to some of the most pressing issues. As Weidenbaum (2004, p. 77) records, 'over 200 multilateral agreements have been enacted since 1960, covering almost the entire gamut of environmental issues'. The best known of these are concerned with climate change and its effects. However, there are many international treaties dealing with environmental matters, including pollution of the oceans, dryland degradation, damage to the ozone layer, and the impending extinction of plant and animal species.

The role of the WTO

The World Trade Organization is one international organization playing an increasingly significant role in environmental matters, coinciding with the expansion of global trade and the growing prominence of the WTO as an international body. Hoekman and Kostecki (2001, p. 441) suggest that the involvement of the WTO in environmental issues was inevitable, citing:

> ... increasing recognition of the existence of cross-border environmental spillovers, perceptions that national environmental policies were inadequate, concerns that trade was bad for the environment, fears that national environmental policy would reduce the competitiveness of foreign firms, and a perception that environmental policies were increasingly being used for protectionist purposes.

Among environmentalists there is a fear that 'international trade will magnify the effects of poor environmental policies in the world [and] speed up the process of environmental degradation' (Nordstrom and Vaughan, 1999, p. 1). According to this view, the multilateral trading system, and the WTO in particular, are responsible for the lack of effective taxes and regulations necessary to protect the environment. There are two parts to this argument. The *legal* argument is that WTO rules circumscribe environmental policy-making and provide legal cover for foreign countries to challenge domestic environmental policies that interfere with their trading rights. The *political economy* argument is that competitive pressure from world markets sometimes makes it impossible to forge the necessary political support at home to upgrade environmental standards. In these circumstances, according to Nordstrom and Vaughan (1999, p. 1):

> ... the perceived costs of acting alone in terms of lost investment and jobs often take the steam out of regulatory initiatives. In a worst-case scenario, environmental regulation may even bid down in the relentless competition for market shares, investments and jobs.

There is thus some apprehension that the expansion of global trade, and the role of the WTO in enforcing this process, may be at odds with environmental regulation as expressed by treaties, conventions and laws. Linked to this is a fear that economic integration enforced by the WTO will undermine the environmental policies of member nations and regional groupings. As Hoekman and Kostecki put it, there is a perception that 'freeing trade will lead to expansion of production and thus pollution, that liberalization will facilitate relocation of firms to countries with lax regulatory environments, that greater trade implies the need for greater transport, leading to more degradation, and so forth' (2001, p. 443).

Scepticism about the WTO is rife among environmentalists, many of whom would share the view of Greenpeace International (2001, p. 6) that:

> The WTO continues to act according to an outdated economic model based on the narrow pursuit of trade liberalisation as an end in itself. WTO decisions and policies rarely take account of the broader goals of social welfare that trade is, in fact, supposed to promote. Without a social framework to guide economic activity, trade will increasingly lead the world away from sustainable development. As a result, international trade can lead to further abuse of the environment and natural resources, thereby increasing rather than alleviating poverty.

The WTO rejects these views, arguing that trade is rarely the root cause of environmental degradation (with the exception of pollution associated with the transport of goods) and that most environmental problems result from production processes, consumption and the disposal of waste products. Indeed, many of the practices the WTO is seeking to eliminate – such as subsidies to agriculture, fishing and energy – contribute materially to environmental problems. This is confirmed by Hoekman and Kostecki (2001, p. 443) who report that 'agricultural support programs have led to the use of production methods that are excessively polluting'. The WTO also argues that improved economic conditions created by trade liberalization can mitigate the causes of pollution (Nordstrom and Vaughan, 1999).

More specific concerns focus upon a perception that WTO rules, including its dispute resolution process, have led to unacceptable environmental outcomes. Braithwaite and Drahos (2000, p. 259) report that 'many green groups fear that the WTO might be used to "pull back" nations that set the highest standards on matters like recycling, packaging and green labelling, with the argument that standards are being used as non-tariff barriers to free trade'.

Several decisions are frequently cited to support this view. The first concerns the ruling by the then GATT panel in 1992 against the US Marine Mammal Protection Act which had forbidden the sale in the US of tuna caught by domestic or foreign fisheries using techniques that killed dolphins (the 'tuna/dolphins case'). The second relates to the decision by a WTO appellate panel against a US law that would have required all shrimp sold in the US to be harvested while safeguarding endangered sea turtles (the 'shrimp/turtles' case). And the third involves the ruling that the US should amend petrol cleanliness regulations under the Clean Air Act that had precluded the importation of petrol from countries including Venezuela and Brazil (the 'Venezuela gas' case).

Critics claim these and other cases demonstrate that 'the WTO has taken a stand against trade restrictions to curb the harmful effects of production, against regulations that provide greater health or environmental protection than the international status quo, and against the precautionary principle' (Wagner and Goldman, 1999, p. 19). Others argue that the decisions illustrate a 'systemic bias in the WTO rules and the WTO dispute resolution process against the rights of sovereign states to enact and effectively enforce environmental laws' which in turn undermines 'health, safety and environmental standards, human rights advocacy efforts and democratic accountability in policy making in the US and worldwide' (Public Citizen, n.d.).

The WTO asserts that it does take environmental and health and safety concerns into consideration and recognizes the right of all governments to take measures to protect the environment. But for the WTO, the key issues in free trade are non-discrimination and the prohibition of quotas. In the case of the ruling against the US Clean Air Act, the WTO argued that while the US had every right to adopt the highest possible standard to protect its air quality, it could not do so if it discriminated against foreign imports. According to the WTO, the US lost the case because its requirements for its own domestic gas producers were less stringent than those imposed on imported gasoline (in this case from Brazil and Venezuela) – it applied its gasoline standard in a discriminatory manner. A similar allegation of discrimination arose in relation to the shrimp/turtles dispute. The WTO ruled that while the US was prepared to provide some countries – mainly in the Caribbean – with technical and financial assistance and longer transition periods for their fishermen to start using turtle-excluder devices, it did not give the same advantages to four Southeast Asian countries, namely India, Malaysia, Pakistan and Thailand. In this case, the WTO argued, the US violated the 'most favoured nation principle' of treating trading partners equally.

Environmental advocates such as the Sierra Club, Greenpeace and the Earthjustice Legal Defense Fund believe the WTO's rulings would be more environmentally friendly if its structure and *modus operandi* were changed. Under WTO rules, only member countries may challenge another member country's actions. When this occurs, the 'challenges are decided by panels of three trade experts whose proceedings are shrouded in secrecy. Only the governments involved in the disputes can present arguments to the panels' (Wagner and Goldman, 1999, p. 1). The perception is that NGOs and subnational governments at state and local levels are 'locked out' of WTO dispute panels and their proceedings.

Many environmental organizations now demand fundamental change to democratize and reform the WTO. The Sierra Club and Greenpeace would like to open the WTO up to citizen participation so that environmental groups and other NGOs are integrated into WTO decision-making processes. The Earthjustice Legal Defense Fund, a non-profit public interest environmental law firm based in San Francisco, argues that the rules of the WTO should be reformed to protect (Wagner and Goldman 1999, p. 20):

- the right to restrict trade to curb harmful environmental and health effects, including such effects in the areas of logging, fishing and manufacturing;
- the right to use the precautionary principle to protect people and the environment against risks;
- the public right to access to information and to participate in proceedings that affect domestic health and environmental standards.

The gulf between the environmental NGOs and the WTO is enormous. As the street protests that now inevitably accompany each meeting of the WTO attest, the organization is increasingly regarded with suspicion, bordering upon open hostility. For its part, the WTO has attempted to address some of the concerns. As Braithwaite and Drahos (2000, p. 259) report:

When the Uruguay Round of the GATT was finalized in 1995, all signatories agreed to 'identify the relationship between trade measures and environmental measures in order to promote sustainable development' and 'to make appropriate recommendations on whether any modifications of the provisions of the multilateral trading system are required, compatible with the open, equitable and non-discriminatory nature of the system'.

But good intentions may not be sufficient. While it relies upon strictly legalistic interpretations of its rules, and while its processes seem to exclude many voices clamouring to be heard, negative perceptions of the WTO as a poor environmental citizen will continue.

Conclusion

It is difficult to overestimate the complexity and difficulty of the problems posed for both business and government by the environment. As Demmke (2001, p. 20) states:

Many environmental problems are invisible, not clearly predictable and show their effects only in the long run. New problems (such as climate change and urban environmental problems) are emerging and old problems (such as nature protection) have not yet been solved. Overall the state of the environment (despite some improvements) is still deteriorating (especially in the field of soil, waste and water policy). It is no longer sufficient to focus only on controlling pollution. We face new problems arising from non-point sources, the loss of biological diversity, the management of computer trash and the fight against global climate change which are much more difficult to monitor and to manage.

What then is the appropriate response to the environmental challenges confronting business and government? Initially, it was assumed that command-and-control mechanisms would suffice, but the approach characterized as 'mandate, regulate and litigate' no longer reigns supreme and market-based alternatives have come to the fore. Indeed, *The Economist* (31 May 2007), which reports that global investment in renewable power generation, biofuels and low carbon technologies rose from $28 billion in 2004 to $71 billion in 2006, sees 'the shift towards greenery' having positive outcomes for some companies:

New regulations requiring companies to adopt cleaner processes will mean that capital equipment is replaced more quickly ... although climate change may push up their costs, it will also provide new opportunities – new markets, new technologies, new businesses and new money to be made ... If carbon controls are tightened, the companies that will flourish are those that have positioned themselves well.

There is thus little doubt that a transformation of opinion within business and government regarding the environment and its protection has occurred. With the overwhelming imperative of global warming upon us, much of the debate about the environment has lost its ideological character and the willingness of many stakeholders to embrace the market as a means of protecting the environment seems to support this view.

Chapter 10

Globalization and Internationalization

Introduction

There is a widespread perception that we live in a period of rapid but uncertain social change through something called 'globalization'. This can be argued to be, on the whole, a positive movement, drawing together disparate parts of the world in a way not seen before. There is greater awareness of the circumstances of other countries and their citizens; greater availability of international goods and services; and arguably a reduction in international conflict, at least between the more developed nations. On the other hand, there are negative aspects too in the eyes of some. Globalization can engender feelings of powerlessness, greater concerns about competition, and fears that global culture may subsume local or national culture. Unsurprisingly, many in societies, both developed and developing, are opposed to globalization. The only consensus about globalization is 'that it is contested' (Scholte, 2005, p. 46).

Interaction has certainly increased; the world seems smaller and to run faster. Businesses are seen as increasingly international if not global; governments act together more than they once did; the international trading system underpins the economic relationship between companies and nation-states. Communication links and information flows are so much cheaper than ever before that distance by itself becomes meaningless. Capital and even labour moves around the world to find the most conducive home; governments compete with each other to attract economic activity to their borders.

Initially, it was thought that governments would be in thrall to business in an age of globalization; that multinational enterprises would so dominate the policies of sovereign nations that the latter would be unable to prevent their roles being subverted. It was also thought that national economic policy would converge in

223

accordance with the prevailing economic theory; all countries would need to follow the prescriptions of the Washington Consensus (see Chapter 3). While both effects are possible it now appears that a more subtle game is taking place. Individual businesses or even the businesses of any dominant nation are not necessarily beneficiaries of the process of globalization and have to work much harder to stay ahead of the game. To some extent, at least, firms, even global firms, are hostages to the fortunes of globalization rather than driving the process to their own advantage. A simplistic view of globalization is that it is occurring for and on behalf of business. While views differ, it is most likely that business finds globalization as difficult to cope with as do governments or individuals in societies.

One thing that does change with globalization is the relationship between government and business, even if there are various interpretations of exactly what is involved. To some extent, the locus of the government–business relationship changes away from that of the individual nation. External factors impinge on a wider range of policy areas once defined by the national government–business relationship. Governments have less control over even those businesses within their jurisdictions; businesses find it harder to obtain special deals for their benefit from government. Business and government may work together in an attempt to influence international organizations, but it is more difficult to achieve a favourable outcome than within a single nation-state. Earlier discussion on such areas as trade, regulation and environmental policy shows that while there is substantial action across countries in all of these policy areas, it is most usually organized internationally – between nations – rather than globally.

From interdependence to globalization

There are many definitions of globalization, almost as many as there are theorists. It is a new term and 'we shouldn't be surprised that the meaning of the notion isn't always clear, or that an intellectual reaction has set in against it' (Giddens, 2002, p. 7). Scholte finds four different definitions in the literature: globalization as internationalization; globalization as liberalization; globalization as universalization; globalization as Westernization; and a fifth – that he puts forward – globalization as 'the spread of transplanetary connections between people' (Scholte, 2005, pp. 54–9). Here, it was argued earlier (see Chapter 1) that there are two quite distinct meanings of 'globalization'. The first sees globalization as an *end-state* or condition, as a point where globalism as a process has reached its ultimate goal (Keohane and Nye, 2001). The second is that globalization is itself a *process* of increased interaction rather than an end-state. There is much discussion about globalization but, as yet, evidence is far from compelling. If globalization is seen as an end-state, it is quite clear that it is one that has not yet arrived. The other view of globalization as a process of greater interaction is consistent with ordinary usage, as well as Scholte's fifth definition. It is undoubted that there is increased international activity, but this could be explained just as well by the term 'internationalization'; in other words, as increased activity between nations and their governments.

Early internationalization

There has been extensive contact between different nations and peoples since prehistoric times. Herodotus, often regarded as the first historian, described interaction with other cultures. The Phoenician, Athenian and Roman empires traded with other societies. Traders crossed from Europe to Asia by land over the Great Silk Road during the medieval period, with the thirteenth-century voyage of Marco Polo being but one of many. Prior to the twelfth century, there was extensive sea trade in the northern Indian Ocean by Arab sailors.

The sea-based trading empires of Europe were arguably the real beginnings of a global marketplace, starting with the Portuguese and Spanish in the last half of the fifteenth century. As Boxer (1969, p. 2) has argued:

> It was the Portuguese pioneers and the Castilian *conquistadores* from the Western rim of Christendom who linked up, for better or worse, the widely sundered branches of the great human family. It was they who first made Humanity conscious, however dimly, of its essential unity.

And from the first, the controversy raged over whether or not bringing different parts of the world into a single system had been beneficial, especially for the poorer parts. The European empires brought prosperity of a kind as other parts of the world were colonized and the inhabitants became part of the capitalist trading system. At the same time, though, war and disease were also gifts of 'civilization' (Wright, 1992). Today, globalization is often regarded the same way. It may bring prosperity but perhaps only for some; it may bring technology but its benefits are not widely distributed. It may bring participation in a world society but only for the elite.

Depending on definition, the current phase of internationalization would be argued to be: something new; a continuation of that which started in the nineteenth century; or even the continuation of the European imperialism started by Portuguese and Spanish sailors in the fifteenth century.

Nineteenth-century globalization

The kind of trade and the underlying technology involved in pursuing it, particularly in shipping, did not change greatly from the time of Columbus through to the early nineteenth century. After that time, though, there was rapid advancement, especially in Europe, a takeoff in technology that led to far greater international integration.

By some measures the nineteenth century afforded greater economic integration than is currently the case (Hirst and Thompson, 1999; Legrain, 2002). European colonization and imperialism over most of the world, combined with the rapid communication links that came with the telegraph, telephone and reliable steamships evident from the 1880s, led to something of an integrated world economy. There were substantial linkages between nations as noted earlier, and real international institutions – over telegraph and postal exchange, for instance (see Chapter 3) – were developed at this time. The nineteenth century also experienced global trade in commodities such as: nitrates from South America; chilled beef and mutton into Europe from Argentina and Australia, and manufactures from Europe that were sent everywhere. Railway projects in the US were underwritten by investors in Britain and immigration into, especially, former European colonies was at a level not seen since. Unlike the early twenty-first century globalization there was relatively free movement of people, with the US, Latin America, Canada and Australia being destinations for people, particularly from Europe. The nineteenth century was also a time of relative peace between the developed countries as they competed for markets and colonies, rather than engaging in direct conflict. This period ended abruptly in 1914 with the outbreak of war.

Following the First World War, nations adopted policies that meant the easy commerce between them did not occur to the same extent. The Depression in the 1930s led to high tariff barriers being built by many countries, which reduced trade. Only with the end of World War II and the express intention by the leading nations at Bretton Woods that they would not continue with the failed policies of the period between the two world wars did globalism start to reappear, although many more years would elapse before trade would be as international as it had been prior to World War I. The inward-looking policies of the leading nations for some thirty years after 1914 illustrates that progress towards globalization is by no means inevitable.

What is new this time?

The globalization of the nineteenth century leads to the question as to what makes the current phase different. The nineteenth century was the apogee of imperialism, where most of the developing world became colonies of one European power or another. Now, the age of imperialism is over, indeed it is 'no longer seen as morally acceptable and its basic underlying method – territorial expansion to augment the power of the metropole – is deemed to be an unacceptable form of behaviour' (Bisley, 2007, p. 49). Colonies essentially supplied raw materials to their home country and 'had no freedom to develop modern economies' (Dollar, 2005, p. 98).

It can be argued that contemporary globalism goes faster, cheaper and deeper than its predecessors; the difference with earlier phases of globalization, such as in the nineteenth century, being in (1) increased density of networks; (2) increased 'institutional velocity', and (3) increased transnational participation (Keohane and Nye, 2001, p. 240). As they argue (p. 248):

> So what really is new in contemporary globalism? Intensive, or thick, network interconnections that have systemic effects, often unanticipated. But such 'thick globalism' is not uniform: it varies by region and locality and by issue-area. It is less a matter of communications

message velocity than of cost, which does speed up what we have called systemic and institutional velocity. Globalization shrinks distance, but distance has not become irrelevant. And the filters provided by domestic politics and political institutions play a major role in determining what effects globalization really has, and how effectively various countries adapt to it. Finally, reduced costs have enabled more actors to participate in world politics at greater distances, and this has led larger areas of world politics to approximate the ideal type of complex interdependence.

Today's computer networks are not necessarily faster than nineteenth-century communication. What is different is the sheer volume and capacity of communication and its great reduction in price. The two major drivers of economic globalization are argued to be 'reduced costs to transportation and communication in the private sector and reduced barriers to trade and investment on the part of the sector' (Frankel, 2000, p. 45). A telephone call been London and New York was a thousand times more expensive in 1927 in real terms than seventy years later (Scholte, 2005, p. 92).

There are wider perspectives. Bisley argues there are four broad differences in the current phase of globalization. First, the scale is far greater than before; second, the universality of change, that is, the extent across different societies and cultures; third, 'a broad ranging consensus on the basic ideas and ideals of economic management', and fourth, 'the speed of so many of today's globalization processes distinguishes the current period from earlier forms' (2007, pp. 52–3). This is a better set of distinctions than those that rely on economic processes alone; globalization must consider social, cultural and political change as well. The current phase of globalization is simply more intensive and extensive compared with earlier phases.

Theoretical perspectives

There are three sets of theorists about globalization (Held *et al.*, 1999): first, *hyper-globalists* who are enthusiasts and advocates; second, *sceptics* who tend to say either that globalization is not happening or has happened before; and third, *transformationalists* who argue that globalization involves a transformation of many things, some of which we cannot now foresee or, in other words, that globalization represents something altogether novel and different from the way it is defined by the hyper-globalists and the sceptics. Each of these warrants further examination. While such a stark division does not fit all theorists or views it is a good starting point in the development of arguments about globalization.

Hyper-globalists

In the early 1990s, the rapid growth in world trade and economic integration seemed to point to a decline in the power of nation-states. Perhaps the best-known hyper-globalizer is Ohmae (1990, 1995), although Micklethwait and Wooldridge (2000) could also be classified as hyper-globalist as could Thomas Friedman (1999, 2005). Giddens refers to this group as radicals (2002, pp. 8–9), a good description of the extent of their views.

Ohmae contends that governments are in decline and companies are taking their place. He argues, 'Most visibly, the nation-state itself – that artefact of the eighteenth and nineteenth centuries – has begun to crumble, battered by a pent-up storm of political resentment, ethnic prejudice, tribal hatred, and religious animosity' (1995, p. 119). This has occurred, according to Ohmae, due to three factors: first, the 'often instantaneous movement of people, ideas, information and capital across borders'; second, 'as the flow of information creates a growing awareness among consumers everywhere about how other people live, tastes and preferences begin to converge', and third, 'the nation-state which was a powerful engine of wealth creation in its mercantilist phase, has become an equally powerful engine of wealth destruction'.

By any measure these factors of decline are somewhat overstated. In the first one mentioned, there is indeed instantaneous transmission of ideas, information and capital across borders, but goods – still the major part of trade – are not transmitted instantaneously and are often subjected to barriers of some kind. Contrary to Ohmae, people are not transmitted instantaneously as there are substantial barriers to immigration and restrictions on travel or cross-border work. There are also barriers to information flow, while ideas are not necessarily adopted by countries to which they are transmitted.

As for the second point, it is in fact arguable whether tastes and preferences do converge. Even a company like McDonald's alters its products in new countries to take account of local tastes. There are certain high-end luxury goods which may be aspired to worldwide – Rolex watches, Louis Vuitton travel goods, Armani clothes and the like – but these do not represent a major part of international trade. One lesson of international business is to offer what consumers want and to alter products accordingly rather than impose generic tastes. The third point could be argued to represent Ohmae's own political frustrations, as a rather unsuccessful party leader in Japan, rather than being a serious claim.

Ohmae sees very little role for government in this borderless world. He argues that the workings of the global capital market mean that governments cannot control exchange rates or protect their currencies and that political leaders 'find themselves at the mercy of people and institutions making economic choices over which they have no control' (1995, p. 119). The role of government has been greatly reduced and the less it does the better. To him, the efficient, enterprising, innovative parts of society are companies and governments should get out the way. As he argues (1995, p. 119):

> In today's borderless economy, the workings of the 'invisible hand' have a reach and strength beyond anything Adam Smith could ever have imagined. In Smith's day, economic activity took place on a landscape largely defined – and circumscribed – by the political borders of nation-states ... Now, by contrast, economic activity is what defines the landscape on which all other institutions, including political institutions, must operate. Business and government are just beginning to live with the consequences.

Ohmae is interesting but overstated. It may be the case that international concerns have impinged on the domestic policy system in a way unknown before. The increased scope of international institutions and agreements, legal precedents and opinion in other countries does have direct influence on domestic policy. A nation's taxation or market regulations cannot be too far out of step with those of other countries or footloose industries will transfer to where there are more favourable conditions. Having a deregulated financial sector has some advantages, but also means there is a daily monitoring by global markets of domestic policy changes. In some ways governments do have less freedom to manoeuvre than they once did. Financial markets – interest rates, exchange rates, stocks and bonds – are affected by government decisions and vice versa. The scope of government is reduced to some extent as, with floating exchange rates and stock and bond markets that react very quickly to government decisions, the range of action is constrained.

The hyper-globalist view sees business as the efficient engine driving improvement in living standards. If there was more business, everyone would be better off and more globalization would mean benefits for everyone. For this to occur the power and scope of government would need to be reduced, as government is axiomatically inefficient and should give way to the efficient part of world society. It is a strangely naïve perspective in many ways. Business does not necessarily want government to get out of the way, although it does generally want regulatory certainty. It is a stretching of reality and logic to say that the world is or could become borderless. Government is not always inefficient, neither is business always efficient. In some societies, notably Japan, a highly efficient export sector exists alongside an inefficient domestic sector. In addition, the hyper-globalist perspective needs to confront the paradox of markets that 'they thrive best not under *laissez-faire* but under the watchful eye of the state' (Rodrik, 2005, p. 198). Reducing the role of government could have the effect of reducing the effectiveness of markets.

Sceptics

Sceptics are those, like Hirst and Thompson (1999), who argue that globalization has been hyped rather than being a matter of reality and that the globalization evident at the turn of the twenty-first century is no more salient – and in some respects less – than that of a hundred years earlier. They argue that globalization 'as conceived by the more extreme globalizers, is largely a myth', and that (1999, p. 2):

1. The present highly internationalized economy is not unprecedented . . . In some respects, the current international economy is less open and integrated than the regime that prevailed from 1870 to 1914.
2. Genuinely transnational companies appear to be relatively rare. Most companies are based nationally and trade internationally . . .

3. Capital mobility is not producing a massive shift of investment and employment from the advanced to the developing countries
   . . .
4. As some of the extreme advocates of globalization recognize, the world is far from being genuinely 'global'. Rather trade, investment and financial flows are concentrated in the Triad of Europe, Japan and North America and this dominance seems set to continue.
5. These major economic powers, the G3, thus have the capacity . . . to exert powerful governance pressures over financial markets and other economic tendencies. Global markets are thus by no means beyond regulation and control.

The points made by Hirst and Thompson are all useful, though not inarguable. As noted earlier, the late nineteenth century exhibited a significant degree of integration between developed countries, even if largely confined to Europe and its colonial offshoots. And, for the first time, communications links meant that buyers and sellers could be connected across the globe. There is some point to the argument that 'if the theorists of globalization mean that we have an economy in which each part of the world is linked by markets sharing close to real-time information, then that began not in the 1970s but in the 1870s' (Hirst and Thompson, 1999, p. 9). Even if the telegraph did revolutionize commerce, communications are now much cheaper. Also, the international economic integration at the end of the late nineteenth century was very much a centre–periphery relationship between Europe and its colonies. More recent economic globalization is much more about world markets. It is the case that there was freer movement of people in the earlier period but the extent of integration is much greater now.

Globalization is not dependent on the existence of genuinely transnational companies, so this can hardly be a requirement. It is the case that there is not a massive shift of investment and employment from the advanced to the developing countries, and this may reinforce the argument that globalization is hardly global if many countries are not involved. Economic linkages are indeed mostly between the already developed parts of the world, in particular Europe, Japan and North America. But the recent rapid development of China and India does disturb this equation. Both have shown that increased openness and engagement in world markets can be successful for a developing country and its people. Indeed, integration is 'basically a good thing for poor countries' and the rich countries 'could and should do more to facilitate this integration and make it freer' (Dollar, 2005, p. 97).

A general theme in sceptical thought is that markets need to be firmly under the control of governments. Hirst and Thompson argue that market economies need to be well governed 'if they are to perform effectively in meeting the substantive expectations of a wide range of economic actors' (1999, p. 193). Not only does this require the institutions of government; it also requires some consideration of the social benefits that need to be included if they are to achieve results. They argue that there are attempts to impose only one kind of capitalism, the one that is triumphant in the Anglo-Saxon countries. Other structures are not only possible but may be desirable. The extent of the dominance of Anglo-Saxon capitalism is overstated. Ideas of shareholder sovereignty, responsibilities of company directors, fiduciary and other regulations actually do vary. Rather than the US necessarily dominating the setting of such standards it is often a participant that does not get its own way, or adopts a system that is not then followed by the rest of the world, to its detriment. For instance, international accounting standards differ from those in the US, and the US failure to adopt the GSM standard for mobile telephony meant that its producers and citizens missed out on opportunities.

Sceptics believe that the state needs to be strengthened to deal with globalization and that there is no necessary and inexorable progress towards a fully globalized world. They see globalization as an ideological movement, but one that can be reversed through government action. The sceptics tend to be 'on the political left, particularly the old left' for the reason that 'if all of this is essentially a myth, governments can still control economic life and the welfare state remain intact' (Giddens, 2002, pp. 8–9). More journalistic treatments (Greider, 1997; Klein, 2000, 2002) agree with this old Left view in their arguments against globalization. Such sceptical views have found a ready audience and have been used to reinforce negative views of globalization.

Part of the sceptical perspective is to point out that globalization is neither inevitable nor unidirectional, but can be halted by the actions of governments. Prior to World War I, European countries in particular were part of an international trading system that promised prosperity and peace but was halted by war. Developed countries attempted to set in place a better international system after World War II with the Bretton Woods agreements. This delivered a greatly enhanced trading system and general prosperity for the developed countries, but there are doubts as to whether the benefits are flowing to developing countries or to the less advantaged within developed societies. The system is inherently fragile as was demonstrated by the end of the earlier phase of globalization.

It is on the issue of governmental interest and capacity that the sceptical account is unconvincing. Government is to do more but to do so without a clearly articulated theory of politics and governance. The old Left view of government still prevails here; that governments need to be wise and all-seeing and operate purely for the interest of their citizens. Government in most developed countries has become more effective and efficient in recent decades, in part, though, due to greater discrimination in taking on activities in which it can make a difference and not getting into areas where governments have failed before. Sceptics may argue for democracy and better governance but would generally not support the kinds of governmental reforms carried out since the early 1990s. The sceptical account is indeed unconvincing.

Transformationalists

Some theorists (Held *et al.*, 1999; Giddens, 2002) argue that globalization does exist but that its impacts and effects are uncertain. The movement towards globalization is, in the transformational perspective, likely to lead to substantial changes, but, importantly, in ways that cannot now be predicted. As Giddens argues, 'For better or worse, we are being propelled into a global order that no one fully understands, but which is making its effects felt upon all of us' (2002, pp. 6–7).

Giddens argues that both the radicals and sceptics, or hyper-globalists and sceptics as used here, make the mistake of concentrating on the economic aspects of globalization. He argues that globalization is 'political, technological and cultural, as well as economic' (2002, p. 10). It is undoubted that most discussion of globalization is about its economic aspects. These are the most obvious cause and effect of globalization, and can lead to political, cultural and social effects of their own. But if there is any way of separating economic from other effects, the latter should be included in globalization.

One important insight is that globalization needs to be seen more widely than being merely a process for the benefit of developed countries; it is not mere Westernization. Giddens argues that Western countries have more influence over world affairs than do the poorer states, but 'globalization is becoming increasingly decentred – not under the control of any group of nations, and still less of the large corporations' (Giddens, 2002, p. 16). Its effects are felt everywhere.

This is an important point. Once the forces of globalization are unleashed, its effects are uncertain. Companies and nations, developed and developing alike, are caught up in its effects rather than being in control; indeed, from the transformationalist perspective, no-one is in control of globalization. The transformationalist viewpoint is plausible and convincing, even though the argument that the world will be transformed in ways that are not yet known makes the question of evidence problematic.

The different views of globalization do not provide final answers. As the debate has continued the hyper-globalist perspective has tended to be dismissed as unrealistic. It is too sweeping, ascribes too much power to corporations and pays insufficient attention to the argument that companies are often vulnerable themselves rather than axiomatically being the drivers and beneficiaries of globalization. The sceptical perspective has adherents and is more attuned to the political realities within countries. It also points out, and correctly, through the nineteenth-century case, that globalization can be halted and turned back, rather than being inexorable and inevitable. But the sceptical perspective does have inconsistencies over the treatment of developing countries, in, for example, demanding that they adopt developed-world labour standards. Some developing countries may regard low wages as their comparative advantage and argue that labour-standards demands are making it hard for them to get their economies started. It is hard to simultaneously argue that globalization is hurting workers in developed countries and advocate the need to assist poorer countries to improve their living standards. Some sceptical arguments are little different from old-style economic nationalism and industry protectionism.

The transformationalists are more interesting, but thus far without real proof that there is already a great transformation in societies, the impact of which cannot be foreseen. The transformationalist perspective is also harder to substantiate given the conflicts that have arisen between cosmopolitanism and fundamentalism, notably since the terrorist attack on the World Trade Center in New York in September 2001.

Globalization or internationalization?

The precise point where the scope of economic, political and cultural activity passes from being international to being global is obviously hard to specify. The existence and actions of the WTO or the UN are, for example, used as evidence for globalization. However, both are more truly international institutions, in that it is nation-states that are members and representatives are there on behalf of their national governments. The existence of such institutions is not necessarily evidence of globalization, rather of internationalization.

There are four aspects to look at further for evidence of globalization or internationalization. These are: first, the role of the nation-state; second, opposition to globalization; third, the effect on domestic politics, and fourth, the role of business.

The role of the nation-state

The future role of the nation-state is one of the most salient points of contention in the globalization debate. As noted earlier, the hyper-globalists generally see a diminished, even vanishing role for government, where the sceptics and transformationalists see a continuing role, albeit different from the traditional one.

Government still means domestic government in most respects, as domestically it is very clear who controls the state and its instruments of enforcement. International agreements are merely that, as the parties to an agreement can renege or withdraw. International law lacks the enforcement mechanisms of domestic law in most circumstances. Even where there are enforcement mechanisms, such as within the WTO, there is always a risk that overly vigorous enforcement will cause a particular country to leave the agreement.

There has been a trend towards greater use of international mechanisms even though they rely on domestic law. The pure sovereignty specified by the Treaty of Westphalia has been in decline for some time. There has not been a sharp demarcation between a world of strictly defined nation-states, and a globalized world where states have recently given up powers to a globalized whole. Absolute jurisdiction was never quite as absolute as the model assumes. European countries often intruded into each other's affairs in the eighteenth and nineteenth centuries, as well as more recently. After 1945, the standard model of international relations became harder to justify as 'slowly, the subject, scope and very sources of the Westphalian conception of international regulation, particularly its conception of international law, were all called into question' (Held, 1993, p. 32).

The United Nations has seen fit to involve itself in disputes within the borders of countries and over matters that were domestic in nature, in, for example, the former Yugoslavia in the late 1990s. The leaders of the dictatorial regime in what became Serbia as well as other leaders in Africa and Asia have been prosecuted for war crimes carried out in domestic situations. The International Criminal Court, based in The Hague, was set up in 2002 as a permanent court to try crimes such as genocide, crimes against humanity and war crimes. All these institutions involve intrusion into events that take place within national borders. Again, though, these institutions are set up by nations and nations can withdraw.

There seems to be little dispute that the nation-state's role is changing, but the point is whether or not this is evidence of globalization. Hirst and Thompson argue that 'while the state's capacities for governance have changed and in many respects ... have weakened considerably, it remains a pivotal institution, especially in terms of creating the conditions for effective international governance' (1999, p. 256). Later they argue, 'states are less autonomous, they have less exclusive control over the economic and social processes within their territories, and they are less able to maintain national distinctiveness and cultural homogeneity' (p. 263). International regimes have been created by nations, but while national governments gain by being part of an international organization they have also given up some of their powers, most notably over economic issues. Once a nation signs up to the WTO it makes a commitment to not use some kinds of industry protection. It also agrees to comply with rulings against it by a disputes panel. This means that subsidy programmes are harder to devise in ways that are WTO-compliant; the range of possible responses is limited by virtue of international protocols. It may be more correct to say that governments have not given up any of their powers, but have rather agreed to limit their scope for action to those things allowable by the agreements entered into.

The processes of globalization may limit a nation's economic power. However, globalization also has an opposite effect. Globalization not only pulls upwards, it pushes downwards, creating new pressures for local autonomy. The nation becomes 'too small to solve the big problems, but also too large to solve the small ones' (Giddens, 2002, p. 13). Giddens also argues (p. 18):

> Everywhere we look, we see institutions that appear the same as they used to be from the outside, and carry the same names, but inside have become quite different. We continue to talk of the nation, the family, work, tradition, nature, as if they were all the same as in the past. They are not. The outer shell remains, but inside they have changed . . . Are nation-states, and hence national political leaders, still powerful, or are they becoming largely irrelevant to the forces shaping the world? Nation-states are indeed still powerful and political leaders have a large role to play in the world. Yet at the same time the nation-state is being reshaped before our eyes. National economic policy can't be as effective as it once was.

The scope for action by national governments may have been reduced in some ways, but in other ways their power has been maintained and even enhanced. Governments are not likely to evolve into one global government, neither are the attachments of individuals to their nation likely to dissipate. In non-economic matters, national governments may be stronger than ever. National feelings have probably increased since the end of the Cold War, with more nations being created and nationalist sentiments increasing among groups within existing ones. Ohmae regards the splitting up of nations such as Yugoslavia as an example of the waning of the idea of nation. It could be argued to the contrary that it reinforces the concept of nation, albeit a smaller one than before. And within the European Union, the citizens of the individual nations do not regard themselves as having given up any of the cultural, language and even political constructs that define them as a people or a nation; the Dutch or French or Germans or all the other national groups are still culturally separate, even as they might act together in a super-governmental structure.

Hirst and Thompson argue that international policies occur because 'major nation-states have agreed to create them and to confer legitimacy on them by pooling sovereignty' which is 'alienable and divisible' (1999, p. 275–6). They argue the nation-state remains powerful as 'an internationally governed economic system in which certain key policy dimensions are controlled by world agencies, trade blocs and major treaties between nation-states ensuring common policies will ... continue to give the nation-state a role' (p. 277).

The extent of decline in the power of the nation-state is possibly overrated; as it loses power in one area, it gains in another. It would be safer to argue that the nation-state has the same power as before or even 'a slight strengthening of the international position of the state' (Bisley, 2007, p. 68). Globalization does affect domestic governance, but 'it is far from making the nation-state obsolete as some prophets claim' (Keohane and Nye, 2000, p. 36). Indeed, state capability is not an anachronism; it has become 'an important advantage in international competition' (Weiss, 1998, p. 5). Elsewhere Weiss argues that states have a lot more room for manoeuvre than usually argued, particularly for social protection and wealth creation. Rather than constraining governments, globalization enables governments to 'pursue policies that would in some way compensate for the uncertainties, instability, and systemic risks that interdependence creates' (Weiss, 2003, pp. 26–7). Certainly, globalization creates risks and the strength of domestic institutions becomes decisive in responding to external pressures.

Despite the arguments about the decline in the power of the nation-state there is no sign it will disappear as an institution. States are the only non-voluntary political unit, the one that can impose order and is invested with the power to tax. Only the nation-state can meet crucial social needs that markets do not value, and as Mathews argues: 'Providing a modicum of job security, avoiding higher unemployment, preserving a liveable environment and a stable climate, and protecting consumer health and safety are but a few of the tasks that could be left dangling in a world of expanding markets and retreating states' (1997, p. 65). The nation-state does not lose power as was once thought; it rather maintains a lot of power, especially when it can act in concert with its peers. National sovereignty still exists. Perhaps globalization and internationalization can be seen as competing processes where the former is about global responses to issues and the latter a response that is essentially between nations. The nation-state will survive as no viable alternative institutional form to organize political life has yet been put forward, but its role and functions will be changed significantly.

Opposition to globalization

Globalization has attracted substantial opposition, indeed, it has become for a later generation what the Vietnam War or 1968 Paris were for an earlier one. Opposition to globalization cannot simply be dismissed as being irrational. Oddly, given the benefits that have flowed from increased living standards due to trade, there is more opposition in the developed countries. Developing countries are affected but are, in general, willing to take the risk that the benefits of greater integration will exceed the costs.

Opponents in the developed countries include the old Left, trade unionists and other anti-capitalists (Greider, 1997). Environmentalists and students are included amongst those opposing internationalization and globalization in an 'unlikely alliance of media-savvy pressure groups and old-fashioned protectionists' (Legrain, 2002, p. 17). There are also those, notably from NGOs, who speak for and on behalf of developing countries in arguing, for instance, that the present system is unfair to commodity producers and others who are bypassed or even made poorer.

Interestingly, there are those on the far Right and some religious groups who have found common cause with the old Left. Gilpin argues, 'the tendency to blame globalization for many vexing problems of modern life is due in part to nationalistic and xenophobic attitudes on the political right and an anti-capitalist mentality on the political left' (2001, p. 368). And it is 'worrying that opposition to globalization is spreading inward from the political extremes' (Micklethwait and Wooldridge, 2000, p. 283). The old Left and far Right may well be more nationalistic than the centre; they certainly appear to be less cosmopolitan, indeed share their opposition to any kind of cosmopolitan project.

At the same time as there is more discussion about globalization and a seemingly inexorable increase in its scope and power there has been increased opposition. The WTO ministerial meeting in Seattle in 1999 marks a significant point of departure along with the similar protests against other meetings that followed in other countries. The Seattle protest came as 'a surprise to the advocates of open markets' (Stiglitz, 2007, p. 7), signalled the beginning of a series of protests, seemingly wherever economic ministers gather, and pointed to some dissatisfaction with the direction that national leaders were heading in. The public mind has tended to be innately protectionist; even as individuals may prefer cheaper goods they still appear to wish to look after their own national industries. But opposition to globalization appears rather to reflect stronger dissatisfaction in developed countries, both as reflecting the need to look after domestic industry, but also, somewhat illogically, in wanting developing countries to gain a better deal. Developing countries have real complaints about the fairness of the trading system, but generally want it to be improved and to thereby gain more of the benefits of greater globalization rather than less. As Bhagwati argues, 'anti-globalization sentiments are more prevalent in the rich countries of the North, while pluralities of the policy-makers and public in the poor countries of the South see globalization as a positive force' (2003, p. 26).

It is undoubted that there is an unequal distribution of the benefits of globalization. As Box 10.1 shows, there is a great disparity not only in access to the internet, but also in something far more basic, access to a good water supply. But reducing access to global markets may well make developing countries even worse off. Perhaps a more inclusive globalization can be conceived.

Quite why the protests occur or exactly what the opponents of globalization want is not altogether clear but even if hyper-globalists regard such opposition as irrational, it still has its political impacts. In even the most developed of countries there are interest groups coalescing around opposition to globalization, mainly looking at domestic impacts, even though, as we have seen, there is an inconsistency between increased protectionism in developed countries to ameliorate the impacts of globalization and the wish to assist developing countries. The best way of assisting developing countries would be to allow more access rather than less.

Globalization as an end-point is by no means inevitable. The end of the earlier phase with World War I could happen again; if governments wanted to, 'they could put globalization into reverse again' (Legrain, 2002, p. 7). There is some reason to believe that the high-point of globalization might have been reached in the current phase, and some barriers may start to rise. It is argued that 'the institutional foundations of globalization – such as the rules that oblige governments to keep their markets open and the

Box 10.1   Globalization – who benefits?

While increasing numbers of people enjoy unprecedented access to information and communication technologies that enable greater social participation, many still struggle to access the most basic resources and services, as the accompanying tables show.

People with access to the internet (per 1,000)

Country	As at 2003
Sweden	756
United States	630
United Kingdom	628
Japan	587
France	414
Hungary	267
Brazil	120
Russian Federation	111
India	32
Pakistan	13
Rwanda	4
Sierra Leone	2
Tajikistan	1

Sources: Adapted from United Nations (2006) *Human Development Report, 2006.* New York: UNDP; World Bank (2006) *World Development Indicators 2006.* CD-ROM. Washington, DC: World Bank.

Population without sustainable access to an improved water source[1] (%)

Country	As at 2004
United States	0
United Kingdom	0
Hungary	1
Pakistan	9
Brazil	10
India	14
Morocco	19
Rwanda	26
Tanzania	38
Sierra Leone	43
Chad	58
Papua New Guinea	61
Ethiopia	78

Note:
1. 'Reasonable access' is defined as the availability of at least 20 litres of water a person per day from a source within 1 kilometre of the user's dwelling.

Source: Adapted from United Nations (2006) *Human Development Report, 2006.* New York: UNDP.

domestic and international politics that allow policymakers to liberalize their economies – have weakened considerably in the past few years', and there is increased nervousness about 'letting capital, goods, and people move freely across their borders' (Abdelal and Segal, 2007, p. 104).

The lack of support for globalization has been most noticeable from large players who have done very well from the system in the past. Rugman argues, 'NGO activities, the possible withdrawal of the United States from the WTO, its lack of commitment to free trade, and the dissolution of the post-war consensus about the virtues of free trade will lead to the end of globalization' (2001, p. 21). And if this occurs, the driving force will be domestic politics within large countries.

Domestic political constraints

While it might be tempting to see globalization as meaning that national governments have only a limited role to play, there is still substantial room for domestic politics and policy. And it is largely at the domestic political level that anti-global feelings have some impact. In turn this leads to quite fundamental questions about the adequacy of domestic institutional settings and the political system itself. Nations may no longer be in direct military competition, or even direct economic competition, but they may well be in competition over the adaptability of their political institutions and the competence of their leaders. The problem here is that attachment to international norms and facilitating competition with other nations through changes to domestic institutions and policies can attract political and electoral cost at home.

Governmental reforms at the domestic level to allow greater international integration have not been popular; indeed, they have often been very unpopular. As Kapstein argues (1996, p. 16):

> It is hardly sensationalist to claim that in the absence of broad-based policies and programs designed to help working people, the political debate in the United States and many other countries will soon turn sour. Populists and demagogues of various stripes will find 'solutions' to contemporary economic problems in protectionism and xenophobia. Indeed, in every industrialized nation, such figures are widely seen as the flip side of globalization. That perception must be changed if Western leaders wish to maintain the international system their predecessors created. After all, the fate of the global economy ultimately rests on domestic politics in its constituent states.

Kapstein also argues that the global economy 'is leaving millions of disaffected workers in its train', with subsequent 'inequality, unemployment and endemic poverty' (1996, p. 16). Disaffected people have a voice and use it to effect; for instance, the anti-globalization protest in 1999 at a McDonald's in France by farmer José Bové made headlines around the world.

Rodrik too argues that the most serious challenge for the world economy lies in 'ensuring that international economic integration does not contribute to domestic social disintegration' (1997, p. 2). He argues there are three sources of tension. The first is that those workers whose skills can readily cross borders become advantaged compared to the less skilled. Second, globalization 'engenders conflicts within and between nations over domestic norms and the social institutions that embody them' (p. 5). Standards and processes that may be highly valued within a society come under pressure from international competition. Third, Rodrik argues that globalization 'has made it exceedingly difficult for governments to provide social insurance' (p. 6). A nation may not be able to afford higher levels of social welfare than its competitors. The first of these has become largely correct; there is a global war for talent and those with particular skills that are transferable – in finance, high-level computing or engineering, high-level management – are in great demand and command high salaries. The other points, though, have not been borne out. Particularly with regard to social protection and social insurance, governments have not been as constrained by the forces of globalization as was once thought would occur. Certainly there are challenges for domestic institutions but there is no sign of a race to the bottom.

Governments do not have many domestic options in dealing with globalization. There can be economic measures such as imposing trade barriers or capital controls, or using export subsidies to gain an advantageous market position. Some of these are not real options. Four possible strategies are: autarchy; harmonization with other countries; direct intervention in the domestic economy, and multilateral solutions.

Retreating to autarchy is a possible solution but as discussed earlier (see Chapter 7) leads to lower living standards. Countries that have been autarchies – former communist countries, such as China, the Soviet Union, and Cuba and North Korea still – suffered as autarchies. A form of autarchy is argued by some of those opposing the international trade system for various reasons such as reducing environmental damage, but it would lead to reduced living standards.

Harmonization with other countries – following the same policy prescriptions – is a viable option, provided it does not result in lowering standards. Corporate tax rates are becoming harmonized as countries do not want to appear out of step with their national competitors and companies can relocate. But such competition needs to result in harmonization rather than going too far and leading to a race to the bottom. Friedman refers to the policy prescriptions of open markets and trade, combined with cutting government domestically, as the 'Golden Straitjacket' (1999, pp. 83–92). He argues that 'as your country puts on the Golden Straitjacket, two things happen: your economy grows and your politics shrinks' (p. 87). This is a good summary; there are benefits but political choices become constrained.

Governments may try direct intervention, using economic measures such as tariff and non-tariff barriers, capital controls, competition policy, or subsidies for certain kinds of production deemed important. They may also target specific sectors such as education where increased spending 'appears to be the only policy intervention that meets with universal approval across the political spectrum' (Kapstein, 1996, p. 33). Infrastructure spending, including on education, has benefits, but more direct assistance to industries is, for a start, likely to be inconsistent with WTO obligations and, second, has to be paid for by the community as a whole (see Chapter 8).

The only other alternative is to try multilateral solutions. If many countries act together, policy can be developed that benefits all of them. They can also use the fact of a multilateral agreement to overcome domestic opposition. There is increased action in institutions such as the WTO, with countries acting together more often to solve common problems. The problem here is that multilateral solutions appear less popular than in the past, as countries engage in games to try to skew the rules to their benefit, as well as responding to what is often a lack of domestic political support.

Altogether, however, these solutions do not gain traction unless there is political support within countries. The domestic political battle undoubtedly affects the extent of internationalization.

Internationalization not globalization

The debate over internationalization and globalization is a debate over ideas, but also over evidence. There are real questions as to where policy is or should be made. Should policy become global through international institutions? Do national governments make policy or are there a variety of actors, governmental and non-governmental? If the world is becoming globalized, should the making of policy be globalized as well (Reinicke, 1998)?

Agreements between states are, by their very nature, international – between nations, literally – with each nation using its powers over its own jurisdiction to make agreements with other nations using their powers in the same way. There is no sign of genuine global governance appearing in the near future. The nearest analogue may be the European Union, but that institution has found it difficult to implement any kind of EU-wide policy, such as foreign policy, that is not dependent for implementation on the individual states that are members. International organizations such as the UN are not universally supported; the WTO is the object of widespread protest whenever it meets. The WTO is often cited as an institution of globalization. However, its members are nation-states and decisions reached are by consensus among the nations present. Accordingly, the WTO could be argued to be an institution of internationalization, rather than globalization.

Stiglitz argues that globalization 'can be reshaped to realize its potential for good' and that international institutions can be reshaped in order to bring this about (2002, p. 215). And as Giddens argues (2002, p. 19):

> Many of us feel in the grip of forces over which we have no control. Can we re-impose our will upon them? I believe we can. The powerlessness we experience is not a sign of personal failings, but reflects the incapacities of our institutions. We need to reconstruct those we have, or create new ones.

In reality, there is some distance to go in setting up an institutional architecture that will work. The world remains a set of nations. These nations may agree with each other, they may disagree and there is still substantial international conflict. Nations still have jurisdiction over matters inside their territory, at least within the limits that their membership of international bodies allows.

It follows that the best term now and for at least the near future is 'internationalization'. There is substantial integration occurring.

Nations are in collaboration as never before, but neither the scope of this in terms of the issues it addresses, nor its geographical extent, is anywhere near being global. As Weiss argues (1998, p. 212):

> 'Globalization' is a big idea resting on slim foundations. Its main basis would seem to be the financial deregulation of the post-Bretton Woods era. But big ideas excite. This may partly explain why enthusiasm has transcended the evidence. There are now sufficient grounds to suggest that globalization tendencies have been exaggerated, and that we need to employ the language of internationalization to understand better the changes taking place in the world economy. In this kind of economy, the nation-state retains its importance as a political and economic actor. So rather than a uniformity of national responses producing convergence on a single neoliberal model, we can expect to find a firming up of the different varieties of capitalism with their correspondingly varied state capacities for domestic adjustment.

If globalization is regarded as an end-state, there is no likelihood of that end appearing soon. If it is regarded as a process, it will clearly be one that is ongoing. The difference in views about globalization includes the *extent* of change rather than whether or not change is occurring; in other words whether the undoubted change is best described as *globalization* or *internationalization*. The creation of a series of international institutions may reduce national power to some extent and this could be considered evidence of globalization. However, depending on the scope of the institution, its membership and the rules it operates under, it could also be evidence of internationalization.

Government and business in a globalizing world

It could be argued that business is the winner from internationalization in that business can move to more conducive locations if necessary. Business can influence government policy by making demands to set up within a jurisdiction and can make threats to leave if the local government will not do what it wants. Kapstein argues that workers find it difficult to have their wishes recognized and met by multilateral organizations, and 'contrast this with the case of mobile capital, which can state with great clarity its demand for macroeconomic stability, balanced budgets, free-trade policies, and so forth' (Kapstein, 2001, pp. 373–4).

Governments can seem to be in thrall to multinational companies, who appear to have the power where domestic governments are relatively powerless. Large companies can have revenues larger than the entire GDP of countries with which they deal, although the comparison, even if often made, is not a meaningful one. But the power relationship is not necessarily one-sided. Of course, some companies are arrogant in their dealings with governments, particularly in the developing world, but the incidence of such behaviour is often overstated. As Giddens argues, the power of the big companies can easily be exaggerated – and 'is greatly exaggerated by those who say that corporations "run the world"' (2002, p. xxiv). Governments have powers that companies do not. Companies need to obey national laws and even the smallest country can exert great power over companies that are located within its borders. If nations act together they have far more power than any corporation. As globalization advances, 'it actually becomes more difficult for the big companies to act irresponsibly, rather than the other way around' (Giddens, 2002, pp. xxiv–xxv). Corporations have reputational interests as well as the more direct interests of shareholders or management in maximizing profits; being known for corporate social responsibility is a decided asset for a company. A short-term profit in one country that has adverse reputational consequences elsewhere is not likely to be a good strategic option.

Corporations have more limited power than is often thought, but arguments about rapacious international firms can readily lead to ill-conceived restrictions. As Wolf argues (2004, pp. 318–19):

> Transnational companies do not rule the world. Neither the WTO nor the IMF can force countries to do what they would prefer not to do. Crises do not afflict sound financial systems. Global economic integration does not render states helpless. Nor has it created unprecedented poverty and inequality. The critics represent the latest – and least intellectually impressive – of a long series of assaults on the market economy. Yet, however unimpressive their arguments, these critics are dangerous, because they can give protectionist interests legitimacy.

In a hyper-globalist international economy, governments would have little power and companies would dominate. This world is not yet here and is unlikely to arrive in the near future. Governments remain powerful.

Some theorists maintain that it is the West or Western companies that benefit from globalization; yet in reality they are not in control, and are caught up in the positives and negatives themselves. Competition and resulting consumer benefit may even be greatly enhanced by globalization, indeed, 'if you are worried about corporate power, you should support globalization' (Legrain, 2002, p. 142). National champions and domestic monopolies, natural or otherwise, become unsustainable if companies have to face international competition in what were once their own domestic markets. On the other hand, consumers benefit from competition and most care little where the goods they buy are sourced from.

There is now greater consensus between nations as to those things that governments or businesses should do and substantial cooperation between nations about matters involving business. Regulation and economic policy-making have become largely international rather than purely domestic. Business, too, is increasingly internationalized. Even if it operates completely within a domestic market, some awareness and understanding of international challenges remains essential. The smallest domestic firm can be affected by trade agreements run from Geneva; international standards affect product design everywhere. Some firms are so international that their home base is often obscured or irrelevant. International firms can decide to locate in one country or another depending on their perception of political risk.

There are a number of policy areas where the business–government relationship is itself internationalized. Governments may still be able to make trade policy, but only within limits that are set by their membership of the WTO. Competition or antitrust policy is still made by national governments but with explicit or implicit agreement to similar rules in other countries. There are international environmental agreements such as the Montreal Protocol over chlorofluorocarbons and the Kyoto Protocol over greenhouse gases. In these and other areas there is greater policy harmonization than before. While international cooperation is increasing, national governments remain firmly in charge of their nation-states. They do, however, cooperate, make binding agreements, and engage in diplomatic and other political behaviours that increasingly impinge on domestic policy. An 'Ohmae world' where companies dominate is not in sight either, indeed, one of the main internationalizing features has been enhanced regulation of companies.

A new pragmatism has emerged in more recent years as the highly ideological debate over the role of government – particularly the economic role – has become more muted. Governments were not very good at running their own businesses – enterprises – but markets had limitations too, notably in areas of high social costs, or in the provision of welfare. Government as an idea did not disappear, but it was recognized that government operations needed to be efficient and effective and to concentrate on those activities that they were most capable of dealing with. There is a greater degree of consensus as to those kinds of things governments should or should not do. There may be arguments at the edges or arguments about levels – social spending is too high or too low, for instance – but these are at the margins.

As Rodrik argues, 'the broader challenge for the 21st century is to engineer a new balance between market and society, one that will continue to unleash the creative energies of private entrepreneurship without eroding the social basis of cooperation' (1997, p. 85). Business and government do need to work together. Markets have been shown to provide goods and services more efficiently than alternatives and living standards have risen as a result. And yet business needs regulation in order to be efficient, but also to maintain support for the market system amongst the population at large.

Conclusion

As we have seen, if globalization is viewed as an end-state, it is quite clearly one that has not yet arrived. If, however, globalization is seen as a process, it is under way and with substantial effects on all countries in the world. As Giddens argues, 'globalization is not incidental to our lives today. It is a shift in our very life circumstances. It is the way we now live' (2002, p. 19).

For present purposes, it is similarly clear that the relationship between government and business is altered fundamentally by the process of globalization. Individual businesses, large or small, are affected by international markets and the presence or potential presence of international competitors and competition. Governments, too, find their interactions with business complicated by international pressures of various kinds: an international company may depart if the regulatory system is not conducive; a domestic company employing locals may complain about international competition; taxation and other revenue-setting needs to have consideration of norms elsewhere. It was so much easier when the relationship between business and government could be seen as purely domestic.

Globalization has two main problems. The first is that its benefits have not been distributed widely enough, notably to developing countries. Stiglitz argues that globalization has 'the potential to bring enormous benefits to those in both the developing and the developed world'; however, the evidence is 'overwhelming that it has failed to live up to this potential' (2007, p. 4). This is largely correct, particularly with regard to developing countries which have found that the detailed rules and procedures of, for example, the WTO, favour developed societies. On the other hand, once there are international institutions such as the WTO in place they have the possibility of being reformed. Debates over the Doha Round of trade talks have centred on improving the position of developing countries. Rather than less globalization or less engagement, most developing countries wish to follow China and India into greater engagement, greater participation in the world economy, but wish the rules to be fairer.

The second main problem concerns political action within developed countries. Globalization is not popular for a host of reasons. It is argued to lead to: loss of jobs; reductions in wage rates; homogenization of cultures; loss of social protection; incapacity in national governments; disillusionment with politics and politicians, and, in some places, has led to protest and increased xenophobia. Most of these points are arguable or exaggerations, but the point is that all have become more salient within domestic political debates and have become allied with the ever-present demand for industry protection. It is no longer inconceivable, for instance, that the US – the postwar leader in open markets – could become heavily protectionist.

The second problem has a greater probability of leading to a collapse in the system than does the first. The interests of developing countries could be incorporated into existing structures and systems relatively easily and at quite modest cost, given that developing countries – China and India excepted – are not big players in world markets. Western countries would need to make concessions, but they are ones that need to be made anyway. However, if protectionist sentiments do return on a large scale there would be great damage to the international system altogether; security as well as markets would be adversely affected.

In all of this there is a real question as to the competence of governments. Markets work better when they are well regulated and the theories and practices of good government and good regulation are better than they once were. If business and government can cooperate over issues of globalization and set about developing new institutions to deal with its effects, the prosperity that comes from greater engagement can be pursued with a fair likelihood of success, as well as leading to a reduction in international tension. Whether it is termed internationalization or globalization matters less than trying to make it work.

References

Abdelal, Rawi and Segal, Adam (2007) 'Has Globalization Passed Its Peak?', *Foreign Affairs*, 86(1).

Adams, Walter and Brock, James W. (1989) 'Government and Competitive Free Enterprise', in Warren J. Samuels (ed.) *Fundamentals of the Economic Role of Government* (New York: Greenwood).

Adams, Walter and Brock, James W. (1994) 'The Sherman Act and the Economic Power Problem', in Theodore P. Kovaleff (ed.) *The Antitrust Impulse, Vol. I* (New York: M. E. Sharpe).

Adler, Jonathan (1996) 'Rent Seeking Behind the Green Curtain', *Regulation*, 19(4).

Amsden, Alice (1996) 'Competitiveness and Industrial Policy: East and West', *JPRI Critique* [online], 3(8).

Armentano, D. T. (1994). 'Time to Repeal Antitrust Regulation?', in Theodore P. Kovaleff (ed.) *The Antitrust Impulse, Volume II* (New York: M. E. Sharpe).

Audretsch, David B. and Bonser, Charles F. (2002) 'Introduction', in David B. Audretsch and Charles F. Bonser (eds) *Globalization and Regionalization: Challenges for Public Policy* (Dordrecht: Kluwer).

Australia, Independent Committee of Inquiry into Competition Policy in Australia (1993) *National Competition Policy* (Canberra: Australian Government Publishing Service).

Ayres, Ian, and Braithwaite, John (1992) *Responsive Regulation: Transcending the Deregulation Debate* (Oxford and New York: Oxford University Press).

Bhagwati, Jagdish (1988) *Protectionism* (Cambridge, MA: MIT Press).

Bhagwati, Jagdish (1997) *The Feuds over Free Trade* (Singapore: Institute of South East Asian Studies).

Bhagwati, Jagdish (2003) 'Coping with Anti-Globalization', in Horst Siebert (ed.) *Global Governance: An Architecture for the World Economy* (Berlin: Springer).

Bisley, Nick (2007) *Rethinking Globalization* (Basingstoke and New York: Palgrave Macmillan).

Bollard, Alan and Vautier, Kerrin M. (1998) 'The Convergence of Competition Law within APEC and the CER Agreement', in Rong-I Wu and Yun-Peng Chu (eds) *Business, Markets and Government in the Asia Pacific* (London: Routledge).

Boltho, Andrea (1996) 'The Assessment: International Competitiveness', *Oxford Review of Economic Policy*, 12(3).

Bonnafous-Boucher, Maria and Pesqueux, Yvon (eds) (2005) *Stakeholder Theory: A European Perspective* (Basingstoke and New York: Palgrave Macmillan).

Botticelli, Peter (1997) 'British Capitalism and the Three Industrial Revolutions', in Thomas K. McCraw (ed.) *Creating Modern Capitalism* (Cambridge, MA: Harvard University Press).

Boxer, C. R. (1969) *The Dutch Seaborne Empire* (Harmondsworth: Penguin).

Braithwaite, John (1993) 'Responsive Regulation for Australia', in Peter Grabowsky and John Braithwaite (eds) *Business Regulation and Australia's Future* (Canberra: Australian Institute of Criminology).

Braithwaite, John (2006) 'Responsive Regulation and World Economies', *World Development*, 34(5).

Braithwaite. John and Drahos, Peter (2000) *Global Business Regulation* (Cambridge: Cambridge University Press).

Brown, Bob and Singer, Peter (1996) *The Greens* (Melbourne: Text Publishing).

Business Roundtable Environment Taskforce (1998) *The Kyoto Protocol: A Gap Analysis* (Washington, DC: Business Roundtable).

Cameron, Rondo and Neal, Larry (2003) *A Concise Economic History of the World: From Paleolithic Times to the Present*, 4th edition (Oxford and New York: Oxford University Press).

Canada, Consumer and Corporate Affairs Canada, Director of Investigation and Research (1992) *Annual Report* (Ottawa: Supply and Services Canada).

Carson, Rachel (1962, reprinted 2002) *Silent Spring* (Boston, MA: Houghton Mifflin).

Causa, Orsetta and Cohen, Daniel (2006) *The Ladder of Competitiveness: How to Climb It*. OECD Development Centre Studies (Paris: OECD).

Chandler, Alfred D. (1977) *The Visible Hand: The Managerial Revolution in American Business* (Cambridge, MA: Harvard University Press).

Clark, Philip and Corones, Stephen (1999) *Competition Law and Policy: Cases and Materials* (Melbourne: Oxford University Press).

Clausen, Eileen (2002) 'Foreword', in Richard Rosenzweig, Mathew Varilek and Josef Janssen (eds) *The Emerging International Greenhouse Gas Market* (Arlington, VA: Pew Center on Global Climate Change).

Clinton, Bill and Gore, Al (1995) 'State of the Union Address: Reinventing Environmental Regulation', 25 January 1995.

Coase, R. H. (1960) 'The Problem of Social Cost', *Journal of Law and Economics*, 3, October.

Coase, R. H. (1988) *The Firm, the Market and the Law* (Chicago: University of Chicago Press).

Cohen, Stephen (1994) 'Speaking Freely', *Foreign Affairs*, 73(4).

Cohen, Stephen D., Paul, Joel R. and Blecker, Robert R. (1996) *Fundamentals of US Foreign Trade Policy* (Boulder, CO: Westview).

Council on Competitiveness (1998) *Going Global: The New Shape of American Innovation* (Washington, DC: Council on Competitiveness).

Crews, Clyde Wayne (2006) *Ten Thousand Commandments: An Annual Snapshot of the Federal Regulatory State* (Washington, DC: Competitive Enterprise Institute).

DeHart-Davis, Leisha and Bozeman, Barry (2001) 'Regulatory Compliance and Air Quality Permitting: Why Do Firms Over Comply?', *Journal of Public Administration Research and Theory*, 11(4).

Demmke, Christoph (2001) *Towards Effective Environmental Regulation: Innovative Approaches in Implementing and Enforcing European Environmental Law and Policy*. Jean Monnet Working Paper 5/01 (New York: New York University Law School).

Doern, G. Bruce (1995) *Fairer Play: Canadian Competition Policy Institutions in a Global Market* (Toronto: C. D. Howe Institute).

Dollar, David (2005) 'Globalization, Poverty, and Inequality', in Michael M. Weinstein (ed.) *Globalization: What's New?* (New York: Columbia University Press).

Downs, Anthony (1957) *An Economic Theory of Democracy* (New York: Harper and Row).

Eisner, Marc (1991) *Antitrust and the Triumph of Economics* (Chapel Hill, NC: University of North Carolina Press).

Eisner, Marc, Worsham, J. and Ringquist, E. J. (2000) *Contemporary Regulatory Policy* (Boulder, CO: Lynne Rienner).

Ernst, J. (1994) *Whose Utility? The Social Impact of Public Utility Privatization and Regulation in Britain* (Buckingham: Open University Press).

European Commission (2000) *Competition Policy in Europe and the Citizen* (Luxembourg: Office for Official Publications of the European Communities).

European Commission (2001) *XXXth Report on Competition Policy: 2000* (Brussels: Commission of the European Communities).

Fear, Jeffrey R. (1997a) 'Constructing Big Business: The Cultural Concept of the Firm', in Alfred D. Chandler, Franco Amatori and Takashi Hikino (eds) *Big Business and the Wealth of Nations* (Cambridge: Cambridge University Press).

Fear, Jeffrey R. (1997b) 'German Capitalism', in Thomas K. McCraw (ed.) *Creating Modern Capitalism* (Cambridge, MA: Harvard University Press).

Fieldhouse, D. K. (1999) *The West and the Third World: Trade, Colonialism, Dependence and Development* (Oxford: Blackwell).

Frankel, Jeffrey (2000) 'Globalization of the Economy', in Joseph S. Nye and John D. Donahue (eds) *Governance in a Globalizing World* (Washington, DC: Brookings Institution).

Friedman, Milton (1962) *Capitalism and Freedom* (Chicago: University of Chicago Press).

Friedman, Milton (1983) *Bright Promises, Dismal Performance: An Economist's Protest* (San Diego, CA: Harcourt Brace Jovanovich).

Friedman, Milton and Friedman, Rose (1980) *Free to Choose* (Harmondsworth: Penguin).

Friedman, Milton and Friedman, Rose (1984) *Tyranny of the Status Quo* (London: Secker and Warburg).

Friedman, Thomas L. (1999) *The Lexus and the Olive Tree* (New York: Farrar, Straus and Giroux).

Friedman, Thomas L. (2005) *The World Is Flat: A Brief History of the Twenty-First Century* (New York: Farrar, Straus and Giroux).

Fukuyama, Francis (1992) *The End of History and the Last Man* (New York: Free Press).

Giddens, Anthony (2002) *Runaway World: How Globalisation Is Reshaping Our Lives*, 2nd edition (London: Profile).

Gilpin, Robert (2001) *Global Political Economy: Understanding the International Economic Order* (Princeton, NJ: Princeton University Press).

Goldman, Calvin S., Bodrug, John D. and Warner, Mark A. (1997) 'Canada', in Edward M. Graham and J. David Richardson (eds) *Global Competition Policy* (Washington, DC: Institute for International Economics).

Gore, Al (1994) 'Introduction', in Rachel Carson, *Silent Spring* (first published 1962) (Boston, MA: Houghton Mifflin).

Gow, D. J. and Maher, A. (1994) 'Regulation in Theory and Practice', in Randal G. Stewart (ed.) *Government and Business Regulation in Australia* (St Leonards, NSW: Allen and Unwin).

Graham, Edward M. and Richardson, J. David (1997) 'Issue Overview', in Edward M. Graham and J. David Richardson (eds) *Global Competition Policy* (Washington, DC: Institute for International Economics).

Greenpeace International (2001) *Safe Trade in the 21st Century* (Amsterdam: Greenpeace International).

Greenpeace International (2002) 'EU Ratifies the Kyoto Protocol – Back to Its Leadership Role?', press release, 31 May.

Greider, William (1997) *One World, Ready or Not: The Manic Logic of Global Capitalism* (London: Allen Lane).

Grindle, Merilee S. (2000) 'Ready or Not: The Developing World and Globalization', in Joseph S. Nye and John D Donahue (eds) *Governance in a Globalizing World* (Washington, DC: Brookings Institution).

Hall, Peter (1986) *Governing the Economy* (Cambridge: Polity).

Hamilton, Earl (1934) *American Treasure and the Price Revolution in Spain, 1501–1650* (Cambridge, MA: Harvard University Press).

Hardin, Garrett (1968) 'The Tragedy of the Commons', *Science*, 162(3859).

Healy, Judith and Braithwaite, John (2006) 'Designing Safer Health Care Through Responsive Regulation', *Medical Journal of Australia*, 184(10).

Hecksher, Eli F. (1935) *Mercantilism* (London: Allen and Unwin).

Hecksher, Eli F. (1969) 'Mercantilism', in D. C. Coleman (ed.) *Revisions in Mercantilism* (London: Methuen).

Held, David (1993) 'Democracy: From City-states to a Cosmopolitan Order?', in David Held (ed.) *Prospects for Democracy: North, South, East, West* (Cambridge: Polity).

Held, David, McGrew, Anthony, Goldblatt, David and Perraton, Jonathon (1999) *Global Transformations: Politics, Economics and Culture* (Oxford: Polity).

Hicks, U. K. (1958) *Public Finance* (London: Shepheard Walwyn).

Hirst, Paul and Thompson, Grahame (1999) *Globalization in Question*, 2nd edition (Cambridge: Polity).

Hoekman, Bernard M. and Kostecki, Michel M. (2001) *The Political Economy of the World Trading System: The WTO and Beyond*, 2nd edition (Oxford: Oxford University Press).

Hoerner, J. Andrew and Muller, Frank (1996) 'Carbon Taxes for Climate Protection in a Competitive World', paper prepared for the Swiss Federal Office for Foreign Economic Affairs by the Environmental Tax Program of the Centre for Global Change, University of Maryland, College Park.

Holmes, M. and Shand, D. (1995) 'Management Reform: Some Practitioner Perspectives on the Past Ten Years', *Governance*, 8(5).

Hughes, Owen E. (1998) *Australian Politics*, 3rd edition (Melbourne: Macmillan).

Hughes, Owen E. (2003) *Public Management and Administration*, 3rd edition (Basingstoke: Palgrave Macmillan).

Huntington, Samuel P. (1996) *The Clash of Civilizations and the Remaking of World Order* (New York: Simon and Schuster).

International Energy Agency (2001) *International Emission Trading: From Concept to Reality* (Paris: OECD).

International Institute for Management Development (2000) *World Competitiveness Yearbook* (Lausanne: IMD).

International Institute for Management Development (2006) *World Competitiveness Yearbook* (Lausanne: IMD).

Invest Australia (2006) *Australia: Your Competitive Edge*, 2006–07 edition (Canberra: Commonwealth of Australia).

Invest Australia (2007) *Ten Good Reasons to Invest in Australia* (Canberra: Commonwealth of Australia).

Irwin, Douglas (2002) *Free Trade Under Fire* (Princeton NJ: Princeton University Press).

Kakar, Sudhir (1970) *Frederick Taylor: A Study in Personality and Innovation* (Cambridge, MA: MIT Press).

Kanigel, Robert (1997) *The One Best Way: Frederick Winslow Taylor and the Enigma of Efficiency* (New York: Viking).

Kapstein, Ethan B. (1996) 'Workers and the World Economy', *Foreign Affairs*, 75(3).

Kapstein, Ethan B. (2001) 'The Third Way and the International Order', in Anthony Giddens (ed.) *The Global Third Way Debate* (Cambridge: Polity).

Kay, J. and Vickers, J. (1990) 'Regulatory Reform: An Appraisal', in G. Majone (ed.) *Deregulation or Reregulation? Regulatory Reform in Europe and the United States* (London: Pinter).

Kennedy, Paul (1983) *The Rise and Fall of British Naval Mastery* (London: Macmillan (now Palgrave Macmillan)).

Keohane, Robert O. and Nye, Joseph S. (1998) 'Power and Interdependence in the Information Age', *Foreign Affairs*, 77(5).

Keohane, Robert O. and Nye, Joseph S. (2000) 'Introduction', in Joseph S. Nye and John D. Donahue (eds) *Governance in a Globalizing World* (Washington, DC: Brookings Institution).

Klein, Naomi (2000) *No Logo: No Space, No Choice, No Jobs: Taking Aim at the Brand Bullies* (London: Flamingo).

Klein, Naomi (2002) *Fences and Windows: Dispatches from the Front Lines of the Globalization Debate* (London: Flamingo).

Kopp, Raymond and Toman, Michael (1998) 'International Emissions Trading and "Joint Implementation": A Primer', in Raymond Kopp, Michel Toman and Marina Cazorla, *International Emissions Trading and the Clean Development Mechanism.* Resources for the Future (RFF) Climate Issue Brief 13, October.

Krauss, Melvyn (1997) *How Nations Grow Rich: The Case for Free Trade* (Oxford and New York: Oxford University Press).

Krueger, Anne O. (1974) 'The Political Economy of the Rent-Seeking Society', *American Economic Review*, 64(3).

Krugman, Paul (1987) 'Is Free Trade Passé?', *Economic Perspectives*, 1(2).

Krugman, Paul (1994a) *The Age of Diminished Expectations* (Cambridge, MA: MIT Press).

Krugman, Paul (1994b) 'Competitiveness: A Dangerous Obsession', *Foreign Affairs*, 73(2).

Kuhn, Kai-Uwe (1997) 'Germany', in Edward M. Graham and J. David Richardson (eds) *Global Competition Policy* (Washington, DC: Institute for International Economics).

Lall, Sanjaya (2001) 'Competitiveness Indices and Developing Countries: An Economic Evaluation of the Global Competitiveness Report', *World Development*, 29(9).

Lawrence, Ann T., Weber, James and Post, James E. (2005) *Business and Society: Stakeholders, Ethics, Public Policy*, 11th edition (Boston, MA: McGraw-Hill Irwin).

Legrain, Philippe (2002) *Open World: The Truth about Globalisation* (London:Abacus).

Levy, David and Prakash, Aseem (2003) 'Bargains Old and New: Multinational Corporations in Global Governance', *Business and Politics*, 5(2).

Lipton, P. and Herzberg, A. (2001) *Understanding Company Law*, 10th edition (Pyrmont, NSW: Law Book Company).

List, Friedrich (1885 [1841]) *The National System of Political Economy.* Reprints of Economic Classics (New York: Augustus Kelley).

Liu, L. S. (1995) 'Efficiency, Fairness, Adversary and Moral Suasion: A Tale of Two Chinese Competition Laws', in C. K. Wang, C. J. Cheng and L.S. Liu (eds) *International Harmonisation of Competition Laws* (Dordrecht: Martinus Nijhoff).

Lodge, George C. (1990) *Comparative Business–Government Relations* (Englewood Cliffs, NJ: Prentice-Hall).

McCraw, Thomas K. (1997a) 'American Capitalism', in Thomas K. McCraw (ed.) *Creating Modern Capitalism* (Cambridge, MA: Harvard University Press).

McCraw, Thomas K. (1997b) 'Retrospect and Prospect', in Thomas K. McCraw (ed.) *Creating Modern Capitalism* (Cambridge, MA: Harvard University Press).

McCraw, Thomas K. (1997c) 'Government, Big Business, and the Wealth of Nations', in Alfred D. Chandler, Franco Amatori and Takashi Hikino (eds) *Big Business and the Wealth of Nations* (Cambridge: Cambridge University Press).

Mahoney, D., Trigg, M., Griffin, R. and Pusley, M. (1998) *International Business: A Managerial Perspective* (Melbourne: Addison-Wesley Longman).

Majone, G. (1990) 'Introduction', in G. Majone (ed.) *Deregulation or Reregulation? Regulatory Reform in Europe and the United States* (London: Pinter).

Majone, G. (1996) *Regulating Europe* (London: Routledge).

Mathews, Jessica (1997) 'Power Shift', *Foreign Affairs*, 76(1).

May, Ernest R. (1997) 'The Evolving Scope of Government', in Joseph S. Nye, Philip D. Zelikow and David C. King (eds) *Why People Don't Trust Government* (Cambridge, MA: Harvard University Press).

Means, Howard (2001) *Money and Power: The History of Business* (New York: Wiley).

Micklethwait, John and Wooldridge, Adrian (1996) *The Witch Doctors: What the Management Gurus Are Saying, Why It Matters and How to Make Sense of It* (London: Heinemann).

Micklethwait, John and Wooldridge, Adrian (2000) *A Future Perfect: The Challenge and Hidden Promise of Globalisation* (London: Heinemann).

Mickelthwait, John and Wooldridge, Adrian (2003) *The Company: A Short History of a Revolutionary Idea* (London: Weidenfeld and Nicholson).

Mintzberg, Henry (1996) 'Managing Government: Governing Management', *Harvard Business Review*, 74(3).

Moore, Karl and Lewis, David (1999) *Birth of the Multinational* (Copenhagen: Copenhagen Business School Press).

Moran, Michael and Wright, Maurice (1991) 'Conclusion: The Interdependence of Markets and States', in Michael Moran and Maurice Wright (eds) *The Market and the State: Studies in Interdependence* (New York: St. Martin's).

Nader, Ralph (1965) Unsafe at Any Speed (New York: Grossman).

Nader, Ralph (1993) 'Introduction: Free Trade and the Decline of Democracy', in Ralph Nader (ed.) *The Case Against Free Trade: GATT, NAFTA and the Globalization of Corporate Power* (San Francisco: Earth Island).

Niskanen, William A. (1968) 'The Peculiar Economics of Bureaucracy', *American Economic Review*, 58(2).

Niskanen, William A. (1999) 'Regulatory Reform No Silver Bullet', in E. H. Crane and D. Boaz (eds) *Cato Handbook for Congress: Policy Recommendations for the 106th Congress* (Washington, DC: Cato Institute).

Nordstrom, Hakan and Vaughn, Scott (1999) *Trade and Environment.* WTO Special Studies, 4 (Geneva: World Trade Organization).

Norris, Pippa (2000) 'Global Governance and Cosmopolitan Citizens', in Joseph S. Nye and John D. Donahue (eds) (2000) *Governance in a Globalizing World* (Washington, DC: Brookings Institution).

North, Douglass C. (1990) *Institutions, Institutional Change and Economic Performance* (Cambridge and New York: Cambridge University Press).

Nye, Joseph S. and Donahue, John D. (eds) (2000) *Governance in a Globalizing World* (Washington, DC: Brookings Institution).

OECD (1992) *Technology and the Economy: The Key Relationship* (Paris: OECD).

OECD (1998) *Open Markets Matter: The Benefits of Trade and Investment Liberalisation* (Paris: OECD).

OECD (2000) *Reducing the Risk of Policy Failure: Challenges for Regulatory Compliance* (Paris: OECD).

Ohmae, Kenichi (1990) *The Borderless World* (New York: HarperCollins).

Ohmae, Kenichi (1995) *The End of the Nation State* (New York: HarperCollins).

Olson, Mancur (1965) *The Logic of Collective Action* (Cambridge, MA: Harvard University Press).

Olson, Mancur (1982) *The Rise and Decline of Nations* (New Haven, CT: Yale University Press).

Organization of Petroleum Exporting Countries (OPEC) (2007) *What is OPEC?* (Vienna: OPEC).

Ostrom, Vincent (1989) *The Intellectual Crisis in American Public Administration*, 2nd edition (Tuscaloosa, AL: University of Alabama Press).

Overbeek, Johannes (1999) *Free Trade versus Protectionism* (Cheltenham: Edward Elgar).

Padfield, Peter (2000) *Maritime Supremacy and the Opening of the Western Mind* (London: Pimlico).

Papadakis, Elim and Rainbow, Stephen (1996) 'Labour and Green Politics: Contrasting Strategies for Environmental Reform', in Francis Castles, Rolf Gerritsen and Jack Vowles (eds) *The Great Experiment: Labour Parties and Public Policy Transformation in Australia and New Zealand* (St Leonards, NSW: Allen and Unwin).

Petsonk, Annie, Dudek, Daniel and Goffman, Joseph (1998) *Market Mechanisms and Global Climate Change*. Trans-Atlantic Dialogues on Market Mechanisms, Bonn, 23 October 1998 and Paris, 27 October 1998 (Environmental Defense Fund in cooperation with the Pew Center on Global Climate Change).

Porter, Michael E. (1990) *The Competitive Advantage of Nations* (New York: Free Press).

Porter, Michael E. (1998) *On Competition* (Cambridge, MA: Harvard Business School Press).

Porter, Michael E. (2001) 'Enhancing the Microeconomic Foundations of Prosperity: The Current Competitiveness Index', in World Economic Forum (ed.) *Global Competitiveness Report* (Geneva: World Economic Forum).

Post, James E. and Crittenden, Frederick William (1996) *Business and Society: Corporate Strategy, Public Policy, Ethics* (New York: McGraw-Hill).

Prestowitz, Clyde V. Jr (1994) 'Playing to Win', *Foreign Affairs*, 73(2).

Public Citizen (n.d.) *WTO and Environment, Health and Safety*, www.citizen.org/trade/wto/ENVIRONMENT, accessed 25 June 2002.

Putnam, Robert (1993) *Making Democracy Work: Civic Tradition in Modern Italy* (Princeton, NJ: Princeton University Press).

Quiggin, J. (1996) *Great Expectations: Microeconomic Reform in Australia* (St Leonards, NSW: Allen and Unwin).

Reagan, Ronald (1983) 'Statement on Establishment of the President's Commission on Industrial Effectiveness', 4 August 1983. The American Presidency Project, University of California at Santa Barbara.

Reinicke, Wolfgang H. (1998) *Global Public Policy: Governing without Government?* (Washington, DC: Brookings Institution).

Report on the President's Commission on Industrial Competitiveness (1985) (Washington, DC: US Government Printing Office).

Rising Tide (2002) 'The Rising Tide Coalition for Climate Justice Political Statement', http://risingtide.org.uk/about/political, accessed 18 June 2002.

Rodrik, Dani (1997) *Has Globalization Gone too Far?* (Washington, DC: Institute of International Economics).

Rodrik, Dani (2005) 'Feasible Globalizations', in Michael M. Weinstein (ed.) *Globalization: What's New?* (New York: Columbia University Press).

Rosenzweig, Richard, Varilek, Matthew and Janssen, Josef (2002) *The Emerging International Greenhouse Gas Market* (Arlington, VA: Pew Center on Global Climate Change).

Rugman, Alan M. (2001) 'The World Trade Organization and the International Political Economy', in Alan M. Rugman and Gavin Boyd (eds) *The World Trade Organization in the New Global Economy* (Cheltenham: Edward Elgar).

Scherer, F. M. (1994) *Competition Policies for an Integrated World Economy* (Washington, DC: Brookings Institution).

Scholte, Jan Aart (2005) *Globalization: A Critical Introduction*, 2nd edition (Basingstoke: Palgrave Macmillan).

Self, Peter (1993) *Government by the Market? The Politics of Public Choice* (London: Macmillan (now Palgrave Macmillan)).

Slaughter, Anne-Marie (1997) 'The Real New World Order', *Foreign Affairs*, 76(5).

Smith, Adam (1976 [1776]) *The Wealth of Nations, Vol. I and Vol. II*, ed. Edwin Cannan (Chicago: University of Chicago Press).

Sparrow, Malcolm (2000) *The Regulatory Craft* (Washington, DC: Brookings Institution).

Stigler, George (1972) 'The Process of Economic Regulation', Antitrust Bulletin, 17(1).

Stigler, George (1975) *The Citizen and the State: Essays on Regulation* (Chicago: University of Chicago Press).

Stigler, George (1988) *Memoirs of an Unregulated Economist* (New York: Basic Books).

Stiglitz, Joseph E. (1989) *The Economic Role of the State* (Oxford and Malden, MA: Blackwell).

Stiglitz, Joseph E. (1997) *Economics*, 2nd edition (New York: W.W. Norton).

Stiglitz, Joseph E. (2000) *Economics of the Public Sector*, 3rd edition (New York: W.W. Norton).

262 *References*

Stiglitz, Joseph E. (2001) 'An Agenda for Development for the Twenty-First Century', in Anthony Giddens (ed.) *The Global Third Way Debate* (Cambridge: Polity).

Stiglitz, Joseph E. (2002) *Globalization and its Discontents* (New York: W.W. Norton).

Stiglitz, Joseph E. (2007) *Making Globalization Work* (New York: W.W. Norton)

Stretton, Hugh and Orchard, Lionel (1994) *Public Goods, Public Enterprise, Public Choice: Theoretical Foundations of the Contemporary Attack on Government* (Basingstoke: Macmillan (now Palgrave Macmillan); New York: St. Martin's).

Strange, Susan (1988) *States and Markets* (London: Pinter).

Taylor, Frederick Winslow (1911) *Principles and Methods of Scientific Management* (New York: Harper).

Thurow, Lester (1992) *Head to Head: The Coming Economic Battle Among Japan, Europe and America* (Sydney: Allen and Unwin).

Thurow, Lester (1994) 'Microchips, Not Potato Chips', *Foreign Affairs*, 73(4).

Trebilcock, Michael J. (1998) 'The Evolution of Competition Policy: Lessons from Comparative Experience', in Rong-I Wu and Yun-Peng Chu (eds) *Business, Markets and Government in the Asia Pacific* (London: Routledge).

United Nations Conference on Environment and Development (1992) *Agenda 21: Programme of Action for Sustainable Development: Rio Declaration on Environment and Development; Statement of Forest Principles: the Final Text of Agreements Negotiated by Governments at the United Nations Conference on Environment and Development (UNCED), 3–14 June, 1992, Rio de Janeiro, Brazil* (New York: United Nations Department of Public Information).

United Nations Environment Programme (UNEP) (1999) *Understanding Climate Change: A Beginner's Guide to the UN Framework Convention and its Kyoto Protocol* (Geneva: UNEP/UNFCCC).

Vickers, John and Yarrow, George (1988) *Privatization: An Economic Analysis* (Cambridge, MA: MIT Press).

Vogel, S. K. (1996) *Freer Markets, More Rules* (Ithaca, NY: Cornell University Press).

Weizsäcker, Ernst Ulrich von (1990) 'Regulatory Reform and the Environment: The Case for Environmental Taxes', in D. Majone (ed.) *Deregulation or Re-regulation? Regulatory Reform in Europe and the United States* (London: Pinter).

Wade, Robert (1990) *Governing the Market; Economic Theory and the Role of Government in East Asian Industrialization* (Princeton, NJ: Princeton University Press).

Wade, Robert (2004) *Governing the Market; Economic Theory and the Role of Government in East Asian Industrialization*, 2nd paperback edition (Princeton, NJ: Princeton University Press).

Wagner, Martin and Goldman, Patti (1999) *The Case for Rethinking the WTO* (San Francisco: Earthjustice Legal Defense Fund).

Walker, James L. (2002) *Policy Implications of Sri Lanka's Competitiveness Rankings* (Washington, DC: USAID / The Competitiveness Program).
Weaver, R. K. and Rockman, B. A. (1993) *Do Institutions Matter?* (Washington, DC: Brookings Institution).
Weidenbaum, Murray L. (1995) *Business and Government in the Global Marketplace*, 5th edition (Englewood Cliffs, NJ: Prentice-Hall).
Weidenbaum, Murray L. (2004) *Business and Government in the Global Marketplace*, 7th edition (Upper Saddle River, NJ: Pearson/Prentice-Hall).
Weiss, Linda (1998) *The Myth of the Powerless State: Governing the Economy in a Global Era* (Cambridge: Polity).
Weiss, Linda (2003) 'Introduction: Bringing Domestic Institutions Back In', in Linda Weiss (ed.) *States in the Global Economy: Bringing Domestic Institutions Back In* (Cambridge: Cambridge University Press)
Wilks, Stephen (1999) *In the Public Interest: Competition Policy and the Monopolies and Mergers Commission* (Manchester: Manchester University Press).
Williamson, Oliver E. (1985) *The Economic Institutions of Capitalism* (New York: Free Press).
Wilson, Graham K. (1990) *Business and Politics* (Basingstoke: Macmillan (now Palgrave Macmillan).
Wilson, Graham K. (2002) *Business and Politics*, 3rd edition (Basingstoke: Palgrave Macmillan).
Wolf, Charles (1994) *Markets or Governments: Choosing between Imperfect Alternatives* (Cambridge, MA: MIT Press).
Wolf, Martin (2004) *Why Globalization Works* (New Haven, CT and London: Yale University Press).
World Bank (1993) *The East Asian Miracle: Economic Growth and Public Policy* (Oxford and New York: Oxford University Press).
World Bank (1997) *World Development Report 1997* (Washington, DC: World Bank).
World Economic Forum (2006) *Global Competitiveness Report: Creating an Improved Business Environment* (Geneva: World Economic Forum).
World Trade Organization (WTO) (1998) *Australia – Measures Affecting Importation of Salmon, Dispute Settlement: Dispute DS18*. WTO Appellate Body Report (Geneva: WTO).
Wright, Ronald (1992) *Stolen Continents: The Indian Story* (London: John Murray).
Yeager, Timothy J. (1999) *Institutions, Transition Economies, and Economic Development* (Boulder, CO: Westview).
Yergin, Daniel and Stanislaw, Joseph (1998) *The Commanding Heights: The Battle Between Government and the Marketplace That Is Remaking the Modern World* (New York: Simon and Schuster).

Index

United Nations (UN), 59–60, 237
United Nations Conference on
Environment and Development
(UNCED, 1992), 199
United Nations Educational,
Scientific and Cultural
Organization (UNESCO), 216
United Nations Environment
Programme (UNEP), 211
United States, 10, 11–12, 99–101,
106–9
and Foreign Corrupt Practices Act,
29
Uruguay Round, 59, 151, 221
utility regulation, 74–5

Vereenigde Oost-Indiche Compagnie
(VOC), *see* Dutch East India
Company, 21
Vickers, J. and Yarrow, G., 30, 31
Vogel, S. K., 65, 83
voluntary export restraints, 69, 150

Wade, R., 11, 181, 182
Wagner, M. and Goldman, P., 219,
220
Walker, J. L., 125, 126

Washington Consensus, 61, 224
Weaver, R. K. and Rockman, B. A., 50
Weidenbaum, M. L., 10, 65, 74, 80,
112, 197, 204, 208, 216
Weiss, L., 239, 247
Weizsäcker, E. U. von, 203
welfare state, 43–4, 46
Westphalia, 40–1, 61
Wilks, S., 10, 103, 112
Williamson, O., 25
Wilson, G., 11, 15, 35
Wolf, C., 17
Wolf, M., 248
workforce regulation, 70–1
World Bank, 50, 51, 61, 181
world competitiveness, 121–7
World Economic Forum, 116, 119
World Health Organization (WHO),
216
World Trade Center, 62
World Trade Organization (WTO), 15,
59, 61, 134–5,144–52, 156–67,
172, 176, 192, 217–21, 246
Wright, R., 226

Yeager, T. J., 51, 54, 55
Yergin, D. and Stanislaw, J., 36, 44